_____

By

_____

On the Occasion of

_____

Date

_____

Daily
IN HIS STEPS

*366 Daily Readings
with Scripture Included*

CHARLES M. SHELDON'S
CLASSIC NOVEL THAT ASKS
"WHAT WOULD JESUS DO?"

BARBOUR
PUBLISHING

Daily
In His Steps

Our mission is to publish and distribute inspirational products offering exceptional value and biblical encouragement to the masses.

ECPA Member of the
Evangelical Christian
Publishers Association

Printed in the United States of America.
5 4 3 2 1

Introduction

Charles M. Sheldon's novel *In His Steps* owns a well-deserved status as a classic of Christian literature. Since 1896, the book has challenged millions upon millions of Christians to consider "What would Jesus do?" as they live out their daily lives.

Now, this book—*Daily In His Steps*—provides a full year's worth of inspiration from Sheldon's masterwork. The brief, daily readings, 366 in all, will take you through *In His Steps* in twelve months. A relevant, thought-provoking scripture accompanies each day's reading. Together, they'll challenge you to consider "What would Jesus do?" as you see exactly what God says in His Word.

Few books have had the long-standing impact of Charles M. Sheldon's classic novel. We hope you'll find this edition, *Daily In His Steps,* to be one of the most challenging books you've ever read.

Chapter One

"For hereunto were ye called; because Christ also suffered for you, leaving you an example, that ye should follow in his steps."

It was Friday morning and the Rev. Henry Maxwell was trying to finish his Sunday morning sermon. He had been interrupted several times and was growing nervous as the morning wore away, and the sermon grew very slowly toward a satisfactory finish.

"Mary," he called to his wife, as he went upstairs after the last interruption, "if any one comes after this, I wish you would say I am very busy and cannot come down unless it is something very important."

"Yes, Henry. But I am going over to visit the kindergarten and you will have the house all to yourself."

The minister went up into his study and shut the door. In a few minutes he heard his wife go out, and then everything was quiet. He settled himself at his desk with a sigh of relief and began to write. His text was from 1 Peter 2:21: "For even hereunto were ye called: because Christ also suffered for us, leaving an example, that ye should follow his steps."

Daily In His Word
This suffering is all part of what God has called you to.
Christ, who suffered for you, is your example. Follow in his steps.
1 Peter 2:21 nlt

He had emphasized in the first part of the sermon the Atonement as a personal sacrifice, calling attention to the fact of Jesus' suffering in various ways, in His life as well as in His death. He had then gone on to emphasize the Atonement from the side of example, giving illustrations from the life and teachings of Jesus to show how faith in the Christ helped to save men because of the pattern or character He displayed for their imitation. He was now on the third and last point, the necessity of following Jesus in His sacrifice and example.

He had put down "Three Steps. What are they?" and was about to enumerate them in logical order when the bell rang sharply. It was one of those clock-work bells, and always went off as a clock might go if it tried to strike twelve all at once.

Henry Maxwell sat at his desk and frowned a little. He made no movement to answer the bell. Very soon it rang again; then he rose and walked over to one of his windows which commanded the view of the front door. A man was standing on the steps. He was a young man, very shabbily dressed.

"Looks like a tramp," said the minister. "I suppose I'll have to go down and—"

Daily In His Word

Do not forget to entertain strangers, for by so doing some people have entertained angels without knowing it.

Hebrews 13:2 NIV

He did not finish his sentence but he went downstairs and opened the front door. There was a moment's pause as the two men stood facing each other, then the shabby-looking young man said:

"I'm out of a job, sir, and thought maybe you might put me in the way of getting something."

"I don't know of anything. Jobs are scarce—" replied the minister, beginning to shut the door slowly.

"I didn't know but you might perhaps be able to give me a line to the city railway or the superintendent of the shops, or something," continued the young man, shifting his faded hat from one hand to the other nervously.

"It would be of no use. You will have to excuse me. I am very busy this morning. I hope you will find something. Sorry I can't give you something to do here. But I keep only a horse and a cow and do the work myself."

The Rev. Henry Maxwell closed the door and heard the man walk down the steps. As he went up into his study he saw from his hall window that the man was going slowly down the street, still holding his hat between his hands. There was something in the figure so dejected, homeless and forsaken that the minister hesitated a moment as he stood looking at it. Then he turned to his desk and with a sigh began the writing where he had left off.

Daily In His Word

"And if you give even a cup of cold water to one of the least of my followers, you will surely be rewarded."

MATTHEW 10:42 NLT

He had no more interruptions, and when his wife came in two hours later the sermon was finished, the loose leaves gathered up and neatly tied together, and laid on his Bible all ready for the Sunday morning service.

"A queer thing happened at the kindergarten this morning, Henry," said his wife while they were eating dinner. "You know I went over with Mrs. Brown to visit the school, and just after the games, while the children were at the tables, the door opened and a young man came in holding a dirty hat in both hands. He sat down near the door and never said a word; only looked at the children. He was evidently a tramp, and Miss Wren and her assistant Miss Kyle were a little frightened at first, but he sat there very quietly and after a few minutes he went out."

"Perhaps he was tired and wanted to rest somewhere. The same man called here, I think. Did you say he looked like a tramp?"

"Yes, very dusty, shabby and generally tramp-like. Not more than thirty or thirty-three years old, I should say."

"The same man," said the Rev. Henry Maxwell thoughtfully.

Daily In His Word
"Do not oppress an alien; you yourselves know how it feels to be aliens, because you were aliens in Egypt."

Exodus 23:9 NIV

Did you finish your sermon, Henry?" his wife asked after a pause.

"Yes, all done. It has been a very busy week with me. The two sermons have cost me a good deal of labor."

"They will be appreciated by a large audience, Sunday, I hope," replied his wife smiling. "What are you going to preach about in the morning?"

"Following Christ. I take up the Atonement under the head of sacrifice and example, and then show the steps needed to follow His sacrifice and example."

"I am sure it is a good sermon. I hope it won't rain Sunday. We have had so many stormy Sundays lately."

"Yes, the audiences have been quite small for some time. People will not come out to church in a storm." The Rev. Henry Maxwell sighed as he said it. He was thinking of the careful, laborious effort he had made in preparing sermons for large audiences that failed to appear.

But Sunday morning dawned on the town of Raymond one of the perfect days that sometimes come after long periods of wind and mud and rain. The air was clear and bracing, the sky was free from all threatening signs, and everyone in Mr. Maxwell's parish prepared to go to church. When the service opened at eleven o'clock, the large building was filled with an audience of the best-dressed, most comfortable looking people of Raymond.

Daily In His Word

Let us not give up meeting together, as some are in the habit of doing, but let us encourage one another— and all the more as you see the Day approaching.

HEBREWS 10:25 NIV

The First Church of Raymond believed in having the best music that money could buy, and its quartet choir this morning was a source of great pleasure to the congregation. The anthem was inspiring. All the music was in keeping with the subject of the sermon. And the anthem was an elaborate adaptation to the most modern music of the hymn,

> *"Jesus, I my cross have taken,*
> *All to leave and follow Thee."*

Just before the sermon, the soprano sang a solo, the well-known hymn,

> *"Where He leads me I will follow,*
> *I'll go with Him, with Him, all the way."*

Rachel Winslow looked very beautiful that morning as she stood up behind the screen of carved oak which was significantly marked with the emblems of the cross and the crown. Her voice was even more beautiful than her face, and that meant a great deal. There was a general rustle of expectation over the audience as she rose. Mr. Maxwell settled himself contentedly behind the pulpit. Rachel Winslow's singing always helped him. He generally arranged for a song before the sermon. It made possible a certain inspiration of feeling that made his delivery more impressive.

Daily In His Word
And he said to them all, If any man will come after me, let him deny himself, and take up his cross daily, and follow me.

Luke 9:23 KJV

People said to themselves they had never heard such singing even in the First Church. It is certain that if it had not been a church service, her solo would have been vigorously applauded. It even seemed to the minister when she sat down that something like an attempted clapping of hands or a striking of feet on the floor swept through the church. He was startled by it. As he rose, however, and laid his sermon on the Bible, he said to himself he had been deceived. Of course it could not occur. In a few moments he was absorbed in his sermon and everything else was forgotten in the pleasure of his delivery.

No one had ever accused Henry Maxwell of being a dull preacher. On the contrary, he had often been charged with being sensational; not in what he had said so much as in his way of saying it. But the First Church people liked that. It gave their preacher and their parish a pleasant distinction that was agreeable.

It was also true that the pastor of the First Church loved to preach. He seldom exchanged. He was eager to be in his own pulpit when Sunday came. There was an exhilarating half hour for him as he faced a church full of people and knew that he had a hearing.

Daily In His Word

How then shall they call on him in whom they have not believed? and how shall they believe in him of whom they have not heard? and how shall they hear without a preacher?

Romans 10:14 KJV

He was peculiarly sensitive to variations in the attendance. He never preached well before a small audience. The weather also affected him decidedly. He was at his best before just such an audience as faced him now, on just such a morning. He felt a glow of satisfaction as he went on. The church was the first in the city. It had the best choir. It had a membership composed of the leading people, representatives of the wealth, society and intelligence of Raymond. He was going abroad on a three months vacation in the summer, and the circumstances of his pastorate, his influence and his position as pastor of the First Church in the city—

It is not certain that the Rev. Henry Maxwell knew just how he could carry on that thought in connection with his sermon, but as he drew near the end of it he knew that he had at some point in his delivery had all those feelings. They had entered into the very substance of his thought; it might have been all in a few seconds of time, but he had been conscious of defining his position and his emotions as well as if he had held a soliloquy, and his delivery partook of the thrill of deep personal satisfaction.

Daily In His Word

Pride goes before destruction, a haughty spirit before a fall.

PROVERBS 16:18 NIV

The sermon was interesting. It was full of striking sentences. They would have commanded attention printed. Spoken with the passion of a dramatic utterance that had the good taste never to offend with a suspicion of ranting or declamation, they were very effective. If the Rev. Henry Maxwell that morning felt satisfied with the conditions of his pastorate, the First Church also had a similar feeling as it congratulated itself on the presence in the pulpit of this scholarly, refined, somewhat striking face and figure, preaching with such animation and freedom from all vulgar, noisy or disagreeable mannerism.

Suddenly, into the midst of this perfect accord and concord between preacher and audience, there came a very remarkable interruption. It would be difficult to indicate the extent of the shock which this interruption measured. It was so unexpected, so entirely contrary to any thought of any person present that it offered no room for argument or, for the time being, of resistance.

The sermon had come to a close. Mr. Maxwell had just turned the half of the big Bible over upon his manuscript and was about to sit down as the quartet prepared to arise to sing the closing selection,

> *"All for Jesus, all for Jesus,*
> *All my being's ransomed powers. . ."*

when the entire congregation was startled by the sound of a man's voice.

Daily In His Word

"I know your deeds; you have a reputation of being alive, but you are dead. Wake up! Strengthen what remains and is about to die, for I have not found your deeds complete in the sight of my God."
REVELATION 3:1–2 NIV

It came from the rear of the church, from one of the seats under the gallery. The next moment the figure of a man came out of the shadow there and walked down the middle aisle.

Before the startled congregation fairly realized what was going on the man had reached the open space in front of the pulpit and had turned about facing the people.

"I've been wondering since I came in here"—they were the words he used under the gallery, and he repeated them— "if it would be just the thing to say a word at the close of the service. I'm not drunk and I'm not crazy, and I am perfectly harmless, but if I die, as there is every likelihood I shall in a few days, I want the satisfaction of thinking that I said my say in a place like this, and before this sort of a crowd."

Henry Maxwell had not taken his seat, and he now remained standing, leaning on his pulpit, looking down at the stranger. It was the man who had come to his house the Friday before, the same dusty, worn, shabby-looking young man.

Daily In His Word

But God hath chosen the foolish things of the world to confound the wise; and God hath chosen the weak things of the world to confound the things which are mighty.

1 CORINTHIANS 1:27 KJV

He held his faded hat in his two hands. It seemed to be a favorite gesture. He had not been shaved and his hair was rough and tangled. It is doubtful if any one like this had ever confronted the First Church within the sanctuary. It was tolerably familiar with this sort of humanity out on the street, around the railroad shops, wandering up and down the avenue, but it had never dreamed of such an incident as this so near.

There was nothing offensive in the man's manner or tone. He was not excited and he spoke in a low but distinct voice. Mr. Maxwell was conscious, even as he stood there smitten into dumb astonishment at the event, that somehow the man's action reminded him of a person he had once seen walking and talking in his sleep.

No one in the house made any motion to stop the stranger or in any way interrupt him. Perhaps the first shock of his sudden appearance deepened into a genuine perplexity concerning what was best to do. However that may be, he went on as if he had no thought of interruption and no thought of the unusual element which he had introduced into the decorum of the First Church service.

Daily In His Word

Suppose a man comes into your meeting wearing a gold ring and fine clothes, and a poor man in shabby clothes also comes in. If you show special attention to the man wearing fine clothes and say, "Here's a good seat for you," but say to the poor man, "You stand there" or "Sit on the floor by my feet," have you not discriminated among yourselves and become judges with evil thoughts?

James 2:2–4 NIV

Aﾠnd all the while he was speaking, the minister leaned over the pulpit, his face growing more white and sad every moment. But he made no movement to stop him, and the people sat smitten into breathless silence. One other face, that of Rachel Winslow from the choir, stared white and intent down at the shabby figure with the faded hat. Her face was striking at any time. Under the pressure of the present unheard-of incident it was as personally distinct as if it had been framed in fire.

"I'm not an ordinary tramp, though I don't know of any teaching of Jesus that makes one kind of a tramp less worth saving than another. Do you?" He put the question as naturally as if the whole congregation had been a small Bible class. He paused just a moment and coughed painfully. Then he went on.

"I lost my job ten months ago. I am a printer by trade. The new linotype machines are beautiful specimens of invention, but I know six men who have killed themselves inside of the year just on account of those machines. Of course I don't blame the newspapers for getting the machines. Meanwhile, what can a man do? I know I never learned but the one trade, and that's all I can do."

Daily In His Word

"Foxes have dens to live in, and birds have nests,
but I, the Son of Man, have no home of my own,
not even a place to lay my head."

LUKE 9:58 NLT

I've tramped all over the country trying to find something. There are a good many others like me. I'm not complaining, am I? Just stating facts. But I was wondering as I sat there under the gallery, if what you call following Jesus is the same thing as what He taught. What did He mean when He said: 'Follow Me!'? The minister said,"—here he turned about and looked up at the pulpit—"that it is necessary for the disciple of Jesus to follow His steps, and he said the steps are 'obedience, faith, love and imitation.' But I did not hear him tell you just what he meant that to mean, especially the last step. What do you Christians mean by following the steps of Jesus?

"I've tramped through this city for three days trying to find a job; and in all that time I've not had a word of sympathy or comfort except from your minister here, who said he was sorry for me and hoped I would find a job somewhere. I suppose it is because you get so imposed on by the professional tramp that you have lost your interest in any other sort. I'm not blaming anybody, am I? Just stating facts."

Daily In His Word

"Come, follow me," Jesus said, "and I will make you fishers of men." At once they left their nets and followed him.

MATTHEW 4:19–20 NIV

Of course, I understand you can't all go out of your way to hunt up jobs for other people like me. I'm not asking you to; but what I feel puzzled about is, what is meant by following Jesus. What do you mean when you sing 'I'll go with Him, with Him, all the way?' Do you mean that you are suffering and denying yourselves and trying to save lost, suffering humanity just as I understand Jesus did? What do you mean by it? I see the ragged edge of things a good deal. I understand there are more than five hundred men in this city in my case. Most of them have families. My wife died four months ago. I'm glad she is out of trouble. My little girl is staying with a printer's family until I find a job. Somehow I get puzzled when I see so many Christians living in luxury and singing 'Jesus, I my cross have taken, all to leave and follow Thee,' and remember how my wife died in a tenement in New York City, gasping for air and asking God to take the little girl too. Of course I don't expect you people can prevent every one from dying of starvation, lack of proper nourishment and tenement air, but what does following Jesus mean?"

Daily In His Word

"Then the King will say to those on his right, 'Come, you who are blessed by my Father; take your inheritance, the kingdom prepared for you since the creation of the world. For I was hungry and you gave me something to eat, I was thirsty and you gave me something to drink, I was a stranger and you invited me in, I needed clothes and you clothed me, I was sick and you looked after me, I was in prison and you came to visit me. . . . I tell you the truth, whatever you did for one of the least of these brothers of mine, you did for me.' "

MATTHEW 25:34–36, 40 NIV

I understand that Christian people own a good many of the tenements. A member of a church was the owner of the one where my wife died, and I have wondered if following Jesus all the way was true in his case. I heard some people singing at a church prayer meeting the other night,

> *'All for Jesus, all for Jesus,*
> *All my being's ransomed powers,*
> *All my thoughts, and all my doings,*
> *All my days, and all my hours.'*

and I kept wondering as I sat on the steps outside just what they meant by it. It seems to me there's an awful lot of trouble in the world that somehow wouldn't exist if all the people who sing such songs went and lived them out. I suppose I don't understand. But what would Jesus do? Is that what you mean by following His steps?"

Daily In His Word
He died for all, so that they who live might no longer live for themselves, but for Him who died and rose again on their behalf.
2 Corinthians 5:15 nasb

It seems to me sometimes as if the people in the big churches had good clothes and nice houses to live in, and money to spend for luxuries, and could go away on summer vacations and all that, while the people outside the churches, thousands of them, I mean, die in tenements, and walk the streets for jobs, and never have a piano or a picture in the house, and grow up in misery and drunkenness and sin."

The man suddenly gave a queer lurch over in the direction of the communion table and laid one grimy hand on it. His hat fell upon the carpet at his feet. A stir went through the congregation. Dr. West half rose from his pew, but as yet the silence was unbroken by any voice or movement worth mentioning in the audience. The man passed his other hand across his eyes, and then, without any warning, fell heavily forward on his face, full length up the aisle. Henry Maxwell spoke:

"We will consider the service closed."

Daily In His Word

Do not be hard-hearted or tight-fisted toward your needy neighbor. You should rather open your hand, willingly lending enough to meet the need.

DEUTERONOMY 15:7–8 NRSV

Chapter Two

Henry Maxwell and a group of his church members remained some time in the study. The man lay on the couch there and breathed heavily. When the question of what to do with him came up, the minister insisted on taking the man to his own house; he lived near by and had an extra room. Rachel Winslow said:

"Mother has no company at present. I am sure we would be glad to give him a place with us."

She looked strongly agitated. No one noticed it particularly. They were all excited over the strange event, the strangest that First Church people could remember. But the minister insisted on taking charge of the man, and when a carriage came, the unconscious but living form was carried to his house; and with the entrance of that humanity into the minister's spare room a new chapter in Henry Maxwell's life began, and yet no one, himself least of all, dreamed of the remarkable change it was destined to make in all his after definition of the Christian discipleship.

The event created a great sensation in the First Church parish. People talked of nothing else for a week. It was the general impression that the man had wandered into the church in a condition of mental disturbance caused by his troubles, and that all the time he was talking he was in a strange delirium of fever and really ignorant of his surroundings. That was the most charitable construction to put upon his action.

Daily In His Word

"So which of these three do you think was neighbor to him who fell among the thieves?" And he said, "He who showed mercy on him." Then Jesus said to him, "Go and do likewise."

Luke 10:36–37 nkjv

It was the general agreement also that there was a singular absence of anything bitter or complaining in what the man had said. He had, throughout, spoken in a mild, apologetic tone, almost as if he were one of the congregation seeking for light on a very difficult subject.

The third day after his removal to the minister's house there was a marked change in his condition. The doctor spoke of it but offered no hope. Saturday morning he still lingered, although he had rapidly failed as the week drew near its close. Sunday morning, just before the clock struck one, he rallied and asked if his child had come. The minister had sent for her at once as soon as he had been able to secure her address from some letters found in the man's pocket. He had been conscious and able to talk coherently only a few moments since his attack.

"The child is coming. She will be here," Mr. Maxwell said as he sat there, his face showing marks of the strain of the week's vigil; for he had insisted on sitting up nearly every night.

"I shall never see her in this world," the man whispered. Then he uttered with great difficulty the words, "You have been good to me. Somehow I feel as if it was what Jesus would do."

Daily In His Word

Let heaven fill your thoughts. Do not think only about things down here on earth. For you died when Christ died, and your real life is hidden with Christ in God.

Colossians 3:2–3 NLT

After a few minutes he turned his head slightly, and before Mr. Maxwell could realize the fact, the doctor said quietly, "He is gone."

The Sunday morning that dawned on the city of Raymond was exactly like the Sunday of a week before. Mr. Maxwell entered his pulpit to face one of the largest congregations that had ever crowded the First Church. He was haggard and looked as if he had just risen from a long illness. His wife was at home with the little girl, who had come on the morning train an hour after her father had died. He lay in that spare room, his troubles over, and the minister could see the face as he opened the Bible and arranged his different notices on the side of the desk as he had been in the habit of doing for ten years.

The service that morning contained a new element. No one could remember when Henry Maxwell had preached in the morning without notes. As a matter of fact he had done so occasionally when he first entered the ministry, but for a long time he had carefully written every word of his morning sermon, and nearly always his evening discourses as well. It cannot be said that his sermon this morning was striking or impressive. He talked with considerable hesitation.

Daily In His Word

The last enemy that shall be destroyed is death.

1 Corinthians 15:26 kjv

It was evident that some great idea struggled in his thought for utterance, but it was not expressed in the theme he had chosen for his preaching. It was near the close of his sermon that he began to gather a certain strength that had been painfully lacking at the beginning.

He closed the Bible and, stepping out at the side of the desk, faced his people and began to talk to them about the remarkable scene of the week before.

"Our brother," somehow the words sounded a little strange coming from his lips, "passed away this morning. I have not yet had time to learn all his history. He had one sister living in Chicago. I have written her and have not yet received an answer. His little girl is with us and will remain for the time."

He paused and looked over the house. He thought he had never seen so many earnest faces during his entire pastorate. He was not able yet to tell his people his experiences, the crisis through which he was even now moving. But something of his feeling passed from him to them, and it did not seem to him that he was acting under a careless impulse at all to go on and break to them this morning something of the message he bore in his heart.

Daily In His Word

"Blessed are those who mourn, for they shall be comforted."
Matthew 5:4 nkjv

So he went on: "The appearance and words of this stranger in the church last Sunday made a very powerful impression on me. I am not able to conceal from you or myself the fact that what he said, followed as it has been by his death in my house, has compelled me to ask as I never asked before 'What does following Jesus mean?' I am not in a position yet to utter any condemnation of this people or, to a certain extent, of myself, either in our Christlike relations to this man or the numbers that he represents in the world. But all that does not prevent me from feeling that much that the man said was so vitally true that we must face it in an attempt to answer it or else stand condemned as Christian disciples. A good deal that was said here last Sunday was in the nature of a challenge to Christianity as it is seen and felt in our churches. I have felt this with increasing emphasis every day since.

"And I do not know that any time is more appropriate than the present for me to propose a plan, or a purpose, which has been forming in my mind as a satisfactory reply to much that was said here last Sunday."

Daily In His Word

*"And anyone who does not carry his cross
and follow me cannot be my disciple."*

Luke 14:27 NIV

Again Henry Maxwell paused and looked into the faces of his people. There were some strong, earnest men and women in the First Church.

He could see Edward Norman, editor of the Raymond *Daily News*. He had been a member of the First Church for ten years. No man was more honored in the community. There was Alexander Powers, superintendent of the great railroad shops in Raymond, a typical railroad man, one who had been born into the business. There sat Donald Marsh, president of Lincoln College, situated in the suburbs of Raymond. There was Milton Wright, one of the great merchants of Raymond, having in his employ at least one hundred men in various shops. There was Dr. West who, although still comparatively young, was quoted as authority in special surgical cases. There was young Jasper Chase, the author, who had written one successful book and was said to be at work on a new novel. There was Miss Virginia Page, the heiress, who through the recent death of her father had inherited a million at least—and was gifted with unusual attractions of person and intellect. And not least of all, Rachel Winslow, from her seat in the choir, glowed with her peculiar beauty of light this morning because she was so intensely interested in the whole scene.

Daily In His Word

". . .guiding them along an unfamiliar way. I will make the darkness bright before them and smooth out the road ahead of them. Yes, I will indeed do these things; I will not forsake them."
ISAIAH 42:16 NLT

There was some reason, perhaps, in view of such material in the First Church, for Henry Maxwell's feeling of satisfaction whenever he considered his parish as he had the previous Sunday. There was an unusually large number of strong, individual characters who claimed membership there. But as he noted their faces this morning, he was simply wondering how many of them would respond to the strange proposition he was about to make. He continued slowly, taking time to choose his words carefully and giving the people an impression they had never felt before, even when he was at his best with his most dramatic delivery.

"What I am going to propose now is something which ought not to appear unusual or at all impossible of execution. Yet I am aware that it will be so regarded by a large number, perhaps, of the members of this church. But in order that we may have a thorough understanding of what we are considering, I will put my proposition very plainly, perhaps bluntly. I want volunteers from the First Church who will pledge themselves, earnestly and honestly for an entire year, not to do anything without first asking the question, 'What would Jesus do?' And after asking that question, each one will follow Jesus as exactly as he knows how, no matter what the result may be."

Daily In His Word
For they are spiritually undefiled, pure as virgins,
following the Lamb wherever he goes.

Revelation 14:4 nlt

I will, of course, include myself in this company of volunteers and shall take for granted that my church here will not be surprised at my future conduct, as based upon this standard of action, and will not oppose whatever is done if they think Christ would do it. Have I made my meaning clear? At the close of the service I want all those members who are willing to join such a company to remain and we will talk over the details of the plan. Our motto will be, 'What would Jesus do?' Our aim will be to act just as He would if He was in our places, regardless of immediate results. In other words, we propose to follow Jesus' steps as closely and as literally as we believe He taught His disciples to do. And those who volunteer to do this will pledge themselves for an entire year, beginning with today, so to act."

Henry Maxwell paused again and looked out over his people. It is not easy to describe the sensation that such a simple proposition apparently made. Men glanced at one another in astonishment. It was not like Henry Maxwell to define Christian discipleship in this way. There was evident confusion of thought over his proposition. It was understood well enough, but there was, apparently, a great difference of opinion as to the application of Jesus' teaching and example.

Daily In His Word

"If anyone comes to Me, and does not hate his own father and mother and wife and children and brothers and sisters, yes, and even his own life, he cannot be My disciple."

Luke 14:26 NASB

He calmly closed the service with a brief prayer. The organist began his postlude immediately after the benediction, and the people began to go out. There was a great deal of conversation. Animated groups stood all over the church discussing the minister's proposition. It was evidently provoking great discussion. After several minutes he asked all who expected to remain to pass into the lecture-room which joined the large room on the side. He was himself detained at the front of the church talking with several persons there, and when he finally turned around, the church was empty. He walked over to the lecture-room entrance and went in. He was almost startled to see the people who were there. He had not made up his mind about any of his members, but he had hardly expected that so many were ready to enter into such a literal testing of their Christian discipleship as now awaited him. There were perhaps fifty present, among them Rachel Winslow and Virginia Page, Mr. Norman, President Marsh, Alexander Powers the railroad superintendent, Milton Wright, Dr. West, and Jasper Chase.

He closed the door of the lecture-room and went and stood before the little group. His face was pale and his lips trembled with genuine emotion. It was to him a genuine crisis in his own life and that of his parish.

Daily In His Word

"A disciple is not above his teacher, nor a servant above his master. It is enough for a disciple that he be like his teacher, and a servant like his master."

Matthew 10:24–25 nkjv

Noman can tell until he is moved by the Divine Spirit what he may do, or how he may change the current of a lifetime of fixed habits of thought and speech and action. Henry Maxwell did not, as we have said, yet know himself all that he was passing through, but he was conscious of a great upheaval in his definition of Christian discipleship, and he was moved with a depth of feeling he could not measure as he looked into the faces of those men and women on this occasion.

It seemed to him that the most fitting word to be spoken first was that of prayer. He asked them all to pray with him. And almost with the first syllable he uttered there was a distinct presence of the Spirit felt by them all. As the prayer went on, this presence grew in power. They all felt it. The room was filled with it as plainly as if it had been visible. When the prayer closed there was a silence that lasted several moments. All the heads were bowed. Henry Maxwell's face was wet with tears. If an audible voice from heaven had sanctioned their pledge to follow the Master's steps, not one person present could have felt more certain of the divine blessing. And so the most serious movement ever started in the First Church of Raymond was begun.

Daily In His Word

"If you then, though you are evil, know how to give good gifts to your children, how much more will your Father in heaven give the Holy Spirit to those who ask him!"

LUKE 11:13 NIV

W e all understand," said he, speaking very quietly, "what we have undertaken to do. We pledge ourselves to do everything in our daily lives after asking the question, 'What would Jesus do?' regardless of what may be the result to us. Some time I shall be able to tell you what a marvelous change has come over my life within a week's time. I cannot now. But the experience I have been through since last Sunday has left me so dissatisfied with my previous definition of Christian discipleship that I have been compelled to take this action. I did not dare begin it alone. I know that I am being led by the hand of divine love in all this. The same divine impulse must have led you also.

"Do we understand fully what we have undertaken?"

"I want to ask a question," said Rachel Winslow. Every one turned towards her. Her face glowed with a beauty that no physical loveliness could ever create.

"I am a little in doubt as to the source of our knowledge concerning what Jesus would do. Who is to decide for me just what He would do in my case? It is a different age. There are many perplexing questions in our civilization that are not mentioned in the teachings of Jesus. How am I going to tell what He would do?"

Daily In His Word

And the LORD shall guide thee continually, and satisfy thy soul in drought, and make fat thy bones: and thou shalt be like a watered garden, and like a spring of water, whose waters fail not.
ISAIAH 58:11 KJV

T here is no way that I know of," replied the pastor, "except as we study Jesus through the medium of the Holy Spirit. You remember what Christ said speaking to His disciples about the Holy Spirit: "Howbeit when he, the Spirit of truth, is come, he shall guide you into all the truth: for he shall not speak from himself; but what things soever he shall hear, these shall he speak: and he shall declare unto you the things that are to come. He shall glorify me; for he shall take of mine, and shall declare it unto you. All things whatsoever the Father hath are mine: therefore said I, that he taketh of mine, and shall declare it unto you.' There is no other test that I know of. We shall all have to decide what Jesus would do after going to that source of knowledge."

"What if others say of us, when we do certain things, that Jesus would not do so?" asked the superintendent of railroads.

"We cannot prevent that. But we must be absolutely honest with ourselves. The standard of Christian action cannot vary in most of our acts."

Daily In His Word

And whatever you do or say, let it be as a
representative of the Lord Jesus, all the while
giving thanks through him to God the Father.
COLOSSIANS 3:17 NLT

And yet what one church member thinks Jesus would do, another refuses to accept as His probable course of action. What is to render our conduct uniformly Christlike? Will it be possible to reach the same conclusions always in all cases?" asked President Marsh.

Mr. Maxwell was silent some time. Then he answered, "No; I don't know that we can expect that. But when it comes to a genuine, honest, enlightened following of Jesus' steps, I cannot believe there will be any confusion either in our own minds or in the judgment of others. We must be free from fanaticism on one hand and too much caution on the other. If Jesus' example is the example for the world to follow, it certainly must be feasible to follow it. But we need to remember this great fact. After we have asked the Spirit to tell us what Jesus would do and have received an answer to it, we are to act regardless of the results to ourselves. Is that understood?"

All the faces in the room were raised towards the minister in solemn assent. There was no misunderstanding that proposition. Henry Maxwell's face quivered again as he noted the president of the Endeavor Society with several members seated back of the older men and women.

Daily In His Word

But be doers of the word, and not hearers only, deceiving yourselves.

JAMES 1:22 NKJV

CHAPTER THREE

Edward Norman, editor of the Raymond *Daily News,* sat in his office room Monday morning and faced a new world of action. He had made his pledge in good faith to do everything after asking "What would Jesus do?" and, as he supposed, with his eyes open to all the possible results. But as the regular life of the paper started on another week's rush and whirl of activity, he confronted it with a degree of hesitation and a feeling nearly akin to fear.

He had come down to the office very early and for a few minutes was by himself. He sat at his desk in a growing thoughtfulness that finally became a desire which he knew was as great as it was unusual. He had yet to learn, with all the others in that little company pledged to do the Christlike thing, that the Spirit of Life was moving in power through his own life as never before. He rose and shut his door and then did what he had not done for years. He knelt down by his desk and prayed for the Divine Presence and wisdom to direct him.

Daily In His Word

He that saith he abideth in him ought
himself also so to walk, even as he walked.

1 JOHN 2:6 KJV

H e rose with the day before him, and his promise distinct and clear in his mind. "Now for action," he seemed to say. But he would be led by events as fast as they came on.

He opened his door and began the routine of the office work. The managing editor had just come in and was at his desk in the adjoining room. One of the reporters there was pounding out something on a typewriter. Edward Norman began to write an editorial. The *Daily News* was an evening paper, and Norman usually completed his leading editorial before nine o'clock.

He had been writing for fifteen minutes when the managing editor called out: "Here's this press report of yesterday's prize fight at the Resort. It will make up three columns and a half. I suppose it all goes in?"

Norman was one of those newspaper men who keep an eye on every detail of the paper. The managing editor always consulted his chief in matters of both small and large importance. Sometimes, as in this case, it was merely a nominal inquiry.

"Yes—No. Let me see it."

He took the typewritten matter just as it came from the telegraph editor and ran over it carefully. Then he laid the sheets down on his desk and did some very hard thinking.

Daily In His Word
And the world passeth away, and the lust thereof: but he that doeth the will of God abideth for ever.

1 JOHN 2:17 KJV

W e won't run this today," he said finally.

The managing editor was standing in the doorway between the two rooms. He was astounded at his chief's remark, and thought he had perhaps misunderstood him.

"What did you say?"

"Leave it out. We won't use it."

"But—" The managing editor was simply dumbfounded. He stared at Norman as if the man was out of his mind.

"I don't think, Clark, that it ought to be printed, and that's the end of it," said Norman, looking up from his desk.

Clark seldom had any words with the chief. His word had always been law in the office and he had seldom been known to change his mind. The circumstances now, however, seemed to be so extraordinary that Clark could not help expressing himself.

"Do you mean that the paper is to go to press without a word of the prize fight in it?"

"Yes. That's what I mean."

"But it's unheard of. All the other papers will print it. What will our subscribers say? Why, it is simply—" Clark paused, unable to find words to say what he thought.

Daily In His Word

"For my thoughts are not your thoughts,
neither are your ways my ways," declares the LORD.

ISAIAH 55:8 NIV

Norman looked at Clark thoughtfully. The managing editor was a member of a church of a different denomination from that of Norman's. The two men had never talked together on religious matters although they had been associated on the paper for several years.

"Come in here a minute, Clark, and shut the door," said Norman.

Clark came in and the two men faced each other alone. Norman did not speak for a minute. Then he said abruptly: "Clark, if Christ was editor of a daily paper, do you honestly think He would print three columns and a half of prize fight in it?"

"No, I don't suppose He would."

"Well, that's my only reason for shutting this account out of the *News*. I have decided not to do a thing in connection with the paper for a whole year that I honestly believe Jesus would not do."

Clark could not have looked more amazed if the chief had suddenly gone crazy. In fact, he did think something was wrong, though Mr. Norman was one of the last men in the world, in his judgment, to lose his mind.

"What effect will that have on the paper?" he finally managed to ask in a faint voice.

"What do you think?" asked Norman with a keen glance.

"I think it will simply ruin the paper," replied Clark promptly.

Daily In His Word

Follow God's example in everything you do,
because you are his dear children.

Ephesians 5:1 NLT

He was gathering up his bewildered senses, and began to remonstrate, "Why, it isn't feasible to run a paper nowadays on any such basis. It's too ideal. The world isn't ready for it. You can't make it pay. Just as sure as you live, if you shut out this prize fight report you will lose hundreds of subscribers. It doesn't take a prophet to see that. The very best people in town are eager to read it. They know it has taken place, and when they get the paper this evening they will expect half a page at least. Surely, you can't afford to disregard the wishes of the public to such an extent. It will be a great mistake if you do, in my opinion."

Norman sat silent a minute. Then he spoke gently but firmly.

"Clark, what in your honest opinion is the right standard for determining conduct? Is the only right standard for every one the probable action of Jesus Christ? Would you say that the highest, best law for a man to live by was contained in asking the question, 'What would Jesus do?' And then doing it regardless of results? In other words, do you think men everywhere ought to follow Jesus' example as closely as they can in their daily lives?"

Daily In His Word

And the things that you have heard from me
among many witnesses, commit these to faithful
men who will be able to teach others also.

2 TIMOTHY 2:2 NKJV

Clark turned red, and moved uneasily in his chair before he answered the editor's question.

"Why—yes—I suppose if you put it on the ground of what men ought to do there is no other standard of conduct. But the question is, What is feasible? Is it possible to make it pay? To succeed in the newspaper business we have got to conform to custom and the recognized methods of society. We can't do as we would in an ideal world."

"Do you mean that we can't run the paper strictly on Christian principles and make it succeed?"

"Yes, that's just what I mean. It can't be done. We'll go bankrupt in thirty days."

Norman did not reply at once. He was very thoughtful.

"We shall have occasion to talk this over again, Clark. Meanwhile I think we ought to understand each other frankly. I have pledged myself for a year to do everything connected with the paper after answering the question, 'What would Jesus do?' as honestly as possible. I shall continue to do this in the belief that not only can we succeed but that we can succeed better than we ever did."

Clark rose. "The report does not go in?"

"It does not. There is plenty of good material to take its place, and you know what it is."

Daily In His Word
Wisdom is supreme; therefore get wisdom.
Though it cost all you have, get understanding.

PROVERBS 4:7 NIV

Clark hesitated. "Are you going to say anything about the absence of the report?"

"No, let the paper go to press as if there had been no such thing as a prize fight yesterday."

Clark walked out of the room to his own desk feeling as if the bottom had dropped out of everything. He was astonished, bewildered, excited, and considerably angered. His great respect for Norman checked his rising indignation and disgust, but with it all was a feeling of growing wonder at the sudden change of motive which had entered the office of the *Daily News* and threatened, as he firmly believed, to destroy it.

Before noon every reporter, pressman and employee on the *Daily News* was informed of the remarkable fact that the paper was going to press without a word in it about the famous prize fight of Sunday. The reporters were simply astonished beyond measure at the announcement of the fact. Every one in the stereotyping and composing rooms had something to say about the unheard-of omission. Two or three times during the day when Mr. Norman had occasion to visit the composing rooms the men stopped their work or glanced around their cases looking at him curiously. He knew that he was being observed, but said nothing and did not appear to note it.

Daily In His Word
What if some did not have faith? Will their lack of faith nullify God's faithfulness? Not at all!

Romans 3:3–4 niv

There had been several minor changes in the paper, suggested by the editor, but nothing marked. He was waiting and thinking deeply.

He felt as if he needed time and considerable opportunity for the exercise of his best judgment in several matters before he answered his ever-present question in the right way. It was not because there were not a great many things in the life of the paper that were contrary to the spirit of Christ that he did not act at once, but because he was yet honestly in doubt concerning what action Jesus would take.

When the *Daily News* came out that evening it carried to its subscribers a distinct sensation.

The presence of the report of the prize fight could not have produced anything equal to the effect of its omission. Hundreds of men in the hotels and stores down town, as well as regular subscribers, eagerly opened the paper and searched it through for the account of the great fight; not finding it, they rushed to the *News* stands and bought other papers. Even the newsboys had not understood the fact of omission. One of them was calling out *"Daily News!* Full 'count great prize fight 't Resort. *News,* sir?"

Daily In His Word

If iniquity were in your hand, and you put it far away,
and would not let wickedness dwell in your tents;
then surely you could lift up your face without spot;
Yes, you could be steadfast, and not fear.

Job 11:14–15 NKJV

A man on the corner of the avenue close by the *News* office bought the paper, looked over its front page hurriedly and then angrily called the boy back.

"Here, boy! What's the matter with your paper? There's no prize fight here! What do you mean by selling old papers?"

"Old papers nuthin'!" replied the boy indignantly. "Dat's today's paper. What's de matter wid you?"

"But there is no account of the prize fight here! Look!"

The man handed back the paper and the boy glanced at it hurriedly. Then he whistled, while a bewildered look crept over his face. Seeing another boy running by with papers he called out "Say, Sam, le'me see your pile." A hasty examination revealed the remarkable fact that all the copies of the *News* were silent on the subject of the prize fight.

"Here, give me another paper!" shouted the customer, "one with the prize fight account."

He received it and walked off, while the two boys remained comparing notes and lost in wonder at the result. "Sump'n slipped a cog in the Newsy, sure," said the first boy. But he couldn't tell why and ran over to the *News* office to find out.

Daily In His Word

The man without the Spirit does not accept the things that come from the Spirit of God, for they are foolishness to him, and he cannot understand them, because they are spiritually discerned.

1 Corinthians 2:14 NIV

There were several other boys at the delivery room, and they were all excited and disgusted. The amount of slangy remonstrance hurled at the clerk back of the long counter would have driven anyone else to despair.

He was used to more or less of it all the time and consequently hardened to it. Mr. Norman was just coming downstairs on his way home, and he paused as he went by the door of the delivery room and looked in.

"What's the matter here, George?" he asked the clerk as he noted the unusual confusion.

"The boys say they can't sell any copies of the *News* tonight because the prize fight isn't in it," replied George, looking curiously at the editor as so many of the employees had done during the day. Mr. Norman hesitated a moment, then walked into the room and confronted the boys.

"How many papers are there here? Boys, count them out, and I'll buy them tonight."

There was a combined stare and a wild counting of papers on the part of the boys.

Daily In His Word

Do not repay anyone evil for evil. Be careful to
do what is right in the eyes of everybody.

ROMANS 12:17 NIV

Give them their money, George, and if any of the other boys come in with the same complaint buy their unsold copies. Is that fair?" he asked the boys who were smitten into unusual silence by the unheard-of action on the part of the editor.

"Fair! Well, I should—But will you keep this up? Will this be a continual performance for the benefit of de fraternity?"

Mr. Norman smiled slightly but he did not think it was necessary to answer the question.

He walked out of the office and went home. On the way he could not avoid that constant query, "Would Jesus have done it?" It was not so much with reference to this last transaction as to the entire motive that had urged him on since he had made the promise.

The newsboys were necessarily sufferers through the action he had taken. Why should they lose money by it? They were not to blame. He was a rich man and could afford to put a little brightness into their lives if he chose to do it. He believed, as he went on his way home, that Jesus would have done either what he did or something similar in order to be free from any possible feeling of injustice.

Daily In His Word
Let me be weighed in a just balance,
and let God know my integrity!

JOB 31:6 NRSV

Chapter Four

During the week he was in receipt of numerous letters commenting on the absence from the *News* of the account of the prize fight. Two or three of these letters may be of interest.

> *Editor of the News:*
>
> *Dear Sir—I have been thinking for some time of changing my paper. I want a journal that is up to the times, progressive and enterprising, supplying the public demand at all points. The recent freak of your paper in refusing to print the account of the famous contest at the Resort has decided me finally to change my paper.*
>
> *Please discontinue it.*
>
> *Very truly yours,———*

Here followed the name of a businessman who had been a subscriber for many years.

> *Edward Norman,*
>
> *Editor of the* Daily News, *Raymond:*
>
> *Dear Ed.—What is this sensation you have given the people of your burg? What new policy have you taken up? Hope you don't intend to try the "Reform Business" through the avenue of the press. It's dangerous to experiment much along that line. Take my advice and stick to the enterprising modern methods you have made so successful for the News. The public wants prize fights and such. Give it what it wants, and let someone else do the reforming business.*
>
> *Yours,———*

Daily In His Word

Do you not know that friendship with the world is enmity with God?

JAMES 4:4 NRSV

Here followed the name of one of Norman's old friends, the editor of a daily in an adjoining town.

> *My Dear Mr. Norman:*
>
> *I hasten to write you a note of appreciation for the evident carrying out of your promise. It is a splendid beginning and no one feels the value of it more than I do. I know something of what it will cost you, but not all. Your pastor,*
>
> *Henry Maxwell*

One other letter which he opened immediately after reading this from Maxwell revealed to him something of the loss to his business that possibly awaited him.

> *Mr. Edward Norman,*
>
> *Editor of the Daily News:*
>
> *Dear Sir—At the expiration of my advertising limit, you will do me the favor not to continue it as you have done heretofore. I enclose check for payment in full and shall consider my account with your paper closed after date.*
>
> *Very truly yours,———*

Here followed the name of one of the largest dealers in tobacco in the city. He had been in the habit of inserting a column of conspicuous advertising and paying for it a very large price.

Daily In His Word

I count all things to be loss in view of the surpassing value of knowing Christ Jesus my Lord, for whom I have suffered the loss of all things, and count them but rubbish so that I may gain Christ.

PHILIPPIANS 3:8 NASB

Norman laid this letter down thoughtfully, and then after a moment he took up a copy of his paper and looked through the advertising columns. There was no connection implied in the tobacco merchant's letter between the omission of the prize fight and the withdrawal of the advertisement, but he could not avoid putting the two together. In point of fact, he afterward learned that the tobacco dealer withdrew his advertisement because he had heard that the editor of the *News* was about to enter upon some queer reform policy that would be certain to reduce its subscription list.

But the letter directed Norman's attention to the advertising phase of his paper. He had not considered this before.

As he glanced over the columns he could not escape the conviction that his Master could not permit some of them in his paper.

What would He do with that other long advertisement of choice liquors and cigars? As a member of a church and a respected citizen, he had incurred no special censure because the saloon men advertised in his columns. No one thought anything about it. It was all legitimate business. Why not? Raymond enjoyed a system of high license, and the saloon and the billiard hall and the beer garden were a part of the city's Christian civilization.

Daily In His Word

He who walks righteously and speaks with sincerity, He who rejects unjust gain and shakes his hands so that they hold no bribe. . .He will dwell on the heights, His refuge will be the impregnable rock; His bread will be given him, His water will be sure.

Isaiah 33:15–16 nasb

He was simply doing what every other businessman in Raymond did. And it was one of the best paying sources of revenue. What would the paper do if it cut these out? Could it live? That was the question. But was that the question after all? "What would Jesus do?" That was the question he was answering, or trying to answer, this week. Would Jesus advertise whiskey and tobacco in his paper?

Edward Norman asked it honestly, and after a prayer for help and wisdom he asked Clark to come into the office.

Clark came in, feeling that the paper was at a crisis, and prepared for almost anything after his Monday morning experience. This was Thursday.

"Clark," said Norman, speaking slowly and carefully, "I have been looking at our advertising columns and have decided to dispense with some of the matter as soon as the contracts run out. I wish you would notify the advertising agent not to solicit or renew the ads that I have marked here."

He handed the paper with the marked places over to Clark, who took it and looked over the columns with a very serious air.

"This will mean a great loss to the *News*. How long do you think you can keep this sort of thing up?" Clark was astounded at the editor's action and could not understand it.

Daily In His Word

"This is the will of the Father who sent Me, that of all He has given Me I should lose nothing, but should raise it up at the last day."
John 6:39 NKJV

Clark, do you think if Jesus was the editor and proprietor of a daily paper in Raymond He would permit advertisements of whiskey and tobacco in it?"

"Well no—I—don't suppose He would. But what has that to do with us? We can't do as He would. Newspapers can't be run on any such basis."

"Why not?" asked Norman quietly.

"Why not? Because they will lose more money than they will make, that's all!" Clark spoke out with an irritation that he really felt. "We shall certainly bankrupt the paper with this sort of business policy."

"Do you think so?" Norman asked the question not as if he expected an answer, but simply as if he were talking with himself. After a pause he said:

"You may direct Marks to do as I have said. I believe it is what Christ would do, and as I told you, Clark, that is what I have promised to try to do for a year, regardless of what the results may be to me. I cannot believe that by any kind of reasoning we could reach a conclusion justifying our Lord in the advertisement, in this age, of whiskey and tobacco in a newspaper. There are some other advertisements of a doubtful character I shall study into. Meanwhile, I feel a conviction in regard to these that cannot be silenced."

Daily In His Word

"And he who receives a righteous man in the name of a righteous man shall receive a righteous man's reward."

MATTHEW 10:41 NKJV

Clark went back to his desk feeling as if he had been in the presence of a very peculiar person. He could not grasp the meaning of it all. He felt enraged and alarmed. He was sure any such policy would ruin the paper as soon as it became generally known that the editor was trying to do everything by such an absurd moral standard.

What would become of business if this standard was adopted? It would upset every custom and introduce endless confusion. It was simply foolishness. It was downright idiocy. So Clark said to himself, and when Marks was informed of the action he seconded the managing editor with some very forcible ejaculations. What was the matter with the chief? Was he insane? Was he going to bankrupt the whole business?

But Edward Norman had not yet faced his most serious problem. When he came down to the office Friday morning he was confronted with the usual program for the Sunday morning edition.

Daily In His Word

A righteous man who walks in his
integrity—how blessed are his sons after him.

PROVERBS 20:7 NASB

The *News* was one of the few evening papers in Raymond to issue a Sunday edition, and it had always been remarkably successful financially. There was an average of one page of literary and religious items to thirty or forty pages of sport, theatre, gossip, fashion, society and political material. This made a very interesting magazine of all sorts of reading matter and had always been welcomed by all the subscribers, church members and all, as a Sunday morning necessity. Edward Norman now faced this fact and put to himself the question: "What would Jesus do?" If He was editor of a paper, would he deliberately plan to put into the homes of all the church people and Christians of Raymond such a collection of reading matter on the one day in the week which ought to be given up to something better holier? He was of course familiar with the regular arguments of the Sunday paper, that the public needed something of the sort; and the working-man especially, who would not go to church any way, ought to have something entertaining and instructive on Sunday, his only day of rest. But suppose the Sunday morning paper did not pay? Suppose there was no money in it? How eager would the editor or publisher be then to supply this crying need of the poor workman? Edward Norman communed honestly with himself over the subject.

Daily In His Word

Ill-gotten gains do not profit,
but righteousness delivers from death.

Proverbs 10:2 NASB

Taking everything into account, would Jesus probably edit a Sunday morning paper? No matter whether it paid. That was not the question. As a matter of fact, the Sunday *News* paid so well that it would be a direct loss of thousands of dollars to discontinue it. Besides, the regular subscribers had paid for a seven-day paper. Had he any right now to give them less than they supposed they had paid for?

He was honestly perplexed by the question. So much was involved in the discontinuance of the Sunday edition that for the first time he almost decided to refuse to be guided by the standard of Jesus' probable action. He was sole proprietor of the paper; it was his to shape as he chose. He had no board of directors to consult as to policy. But as he sat there surrounded by the usual quantity of material for the Sunday edition he reached some definite conclusions. And among them was a determination to call in the force of the paper and frankly state his motive and purpose.

Daily In His Word

The LORD will not let the godly starve to death,
but he refuses to satisfy the craving of the wicked.

PROVERBS 10:3 NLT

He sent word for Clark and the other men in the office, including the few reporters who were in the building and the foreman, with what men were in the composing room (it was early in the morning and they were not all in) to come into the mailing room. This was a large room, and the men came in curiously and perched around on the tables and counters. It was a very unusual proceeding, but they all agreed that the paper was being run on new principles anyhow, and they all watched Mr. Norman carefully as he spoke.

"I called you in here to let you know my further plans for the *News*. I propose certain changes which I believe are necessary. I understand very well that some things I have already done are regarded by the men as very strange. I wish to state my motive in doing what I have done."

Here he told the men what he had already told Clark, and they stared as Clark had done and looked as painfully conscious.

"Now, in acting on this standard of conduct I have reached a conclusion which will, no doubt, cause some surprise.

"I have decided that the Sunday morning edition of the *News* shall be discontinued after next Sunday's issue."

Daily In His Word

"For the LORD is a God of knowledge,
and with him actions are weighed."

I SAMUEL 2:3 NASB

I shall state in that issue my reasons for discontinuing. In order to make up to the subscribers the amount of reading matter they may suppose themselves entitled to, we can issue a double number on Saturday, as is done by many evening papers that make no attempt at a Sunday edition. I am convinced that from a Christian point of view more harm than good has been done by our Sunday morning paper. I do not believe that Jesus would be responsible for it if He were in my place today. It will occasion some trouble to arrange the details caused by this change with the advertisers and subscribers. That is for me to look after. The change itself is one that will take place. So far as I can see, the loss will fall on myself. Neither the reporters nor the pressmen need make any particular changes in their plans."

He looked around the room and no one spoke. He was struck for the first time in his life with the fact that in all the years of his newspaper life he had never had the force of the paper together in this way. Would Jesus do that? That is, would He probably run a newspaper on some loving family plan, where editors, reporters, pressmen and all meet to discuss and devise and plan for the making of a paper that should have in view—

Daily In His Word

There is an appointed time for everything. And there is a time for every event under heaven. . . . A time to keep and a time to throw away. A time to tear apart and a time to sew together.

Ecclesiastes 3:1, 6–7 NASB

He caught himself drawing almost away from the facts of typographical unions and office rules and reporters' enterprise and all the cold, businesslike methods that make a great daily successful. But still the vague picture that came up in the mailing room would not fade away when he had gone into his office and the men had gone back to their places with wonder in their looks and questions of all sorts on their tongues as they talked over the editor's remarkable actions.

Clark came in and had a long, serious talk with his chief. He was thoroughly roused, and his protest almost reached the point of resigning his place. Norman guarded himself carefully. Every minute of the interview was painful to him, but he felt more than ever the necessity of doing the Christlike thing. Clark was a very valuable man. It would be difficult to fill his place. But he was not able to give any reasons for continuing the Sunday paper that answered the question, "What would Jesus do?" by letting Jesus print that edition.

Daily In His Word

"Whoever serves me must follow me, and where I am, there will my servant be also. Whoever serves me, the Father will honor."
JOHN 12:26 NRSV

It comes to this, then," said Clark frankly, "you will bankrupt the paper in thirty days. We might as well face that future fact."

"I don't think we shall. Will you stay by the *News* until it is bankrupt?" asked Norman with a strange smile.

"Mr. Norman, I don't understand you. You are not the same man this week that I always knew before."

"I don't know myself either, Clark. Something remarkable has caught me up and borne me on. But I was never more convinced of final success and power for the paper. You have not answered my question. Will you stay with me?"

Daily In His Word

The fear of the LORD is the beginning of wisdom;
all who follow his precepts have good understanding.
To him belongs eternal praise.

PSALM 111:10 NIV

CHAPTER FIVE

Sunday morning dawned again on Raymond, and Henry Maxwell's church was again crowded. Before the service began Edward Norman attracted great attention. He sat quietly in his usual place about three seats from the pulpit. The Sunday morning issue of the *News* containing the statement of its discontinuance had been expressed in such remarkable language that every reader was struck by it. No such series of distinct sensations had ever disturbed the usual business custom of Raymond. The events connected with the *News* were not all. People were eagerly talking about strange things done during the week by Alexander Powers at the railroad shops and Milton Wright in his stores on the avenue. The service progressed upon a distinct wave of excitement in the pews. Henry Maxwell faced it all with a calmness which indicated a strength and purpose more than usual. His prayers were very helpful. His sermon was not so easy to describe.

How would a minister be apt to preach to his people if he came before them after an entire week of eager asking, "How would Jesus preach? What would He probably say?" It is very certain that he did not preach as he had done two Sundays before. Tuesday of the past week he had stood by the grave of the dead stranger and said the words, "Earth to earth, ashes to ashes, dust to dust," and still he was moved by the spirit of a deeper impulse than he could measure as he thought of his people and yearned for the Christ message when he should be in his pulpit again.

Daily In His Word

But how can they call on him to save them unless they believe in him? And how can they believe in him if they have never heard about him? And how can they hear about him unless someone tells them?

ROMANS 10:14 NLT

Now that Sunday had come and the people were there to hear, what would the Master tell them? He agonized over his preparation for them, and yet he knew he had not been able to fit his message into his ideal of the Christ. Nevertheless no one in the First Church could remember ever hearing such a sermon before. There was in it rebuke for sin, especially hypocrisy, there was definite rebuke of the greed of wealth and the selfishness of fashion, two things that First Church never heard rebuked this way before, and there was a love of his people that gathered new force as the sermon went on. When it was finished there were those who were saying in their hearts, "The Spirit moved that sermon." And they were right.

Then Rachel Winslow rose to sing, this time after the sermon, by Mr. Maxwell's request. Rachel's singing did not provoke applause this time. What deeper feeling carried the people's hearts into a reverent silence and tenderness of thought? Rachel was beautiful. But her consciousness of her remarkable loveliness had always marred her singing with those who had the deepest spiritual feeling. It had also marred her rendering of certain kinds of music with herself. Today this was all gone. There was no lack of power in her grand voice. But there was an actual added element of humility and purity which the audience distinctly felt and bowed to.

Daily In His Word

"The Holy Spirit will teach you
at that time what you should say."

Luke 12:12 NIV

Before service closed Mr. Maxwell asked those who had remained the week before to stay again for a few moments of consultation, and any others who were willing to make the pledge taken at that time. When he was at liberty he went into the lecture-room. To his astonishment it was almost filled. This time a large proportion of young people had come, but among them were a few businessmen and officers of the church.

As before, he, Maxwell, asked them to pray with him. And, as before, a distinct answer came from the presence of the divine Spirit. There was no doubt in the minds of any present that what they purposed to do was so clearly in line with the divine will, that a blessing rested upon it in a very special manner.

They remained some time to ask questions and consult together. There was a feeling of fellowship such as they had never known in their church membership. Mr. Norman's action was well understood by them all, and he answered several questions.

"What will be the probable result of your discontinuance of the Sunday paper?" asked Alexander Powers, who sat next to him.

"I don't know yet. I presume it will result in the falling off of subscriptions and advertisements. I anticipate that."

Daily In His Word
*Behold, how good and how pleasant it is
for brethren to dwell together in unity!*
Psalm 133:1 KJV

Do you have any doubts about your action? I mean, do you regret it, or fear it is not what Jesus would do?" asked Mr. Maxwell.

"Not in the least. But I would like to ask, for my own satisfaction, if any of you here think Jesus would issue a Sunday morning paper?"

No one spoke for a minute. Then Jasper Chase said, "We seem to think alike on that, but I have been puzzled several times during the week to know just what He would do. It is not always an easy question to answer."

"I find that trouble," said Virginia Page. She sat by Rachel Winslow. Every one who knew Virginia Page was wondering how she would succeed in keeping her promise. "I think perhaps I find it specially difficult to answer that question on account of my money. Our Lord never owned any property, and there is nothing in His example to guide me in the use of mine. I am studying and praying. I think I see clearly a part of what He would do, but not all. *What would He do with a million dollars?* is my question really. I confess I am not yet able to answer it to my satisfaction."

Daily In His Word

"If you want to be perfect, go, sell what you have and give to the poor, and you will have treasure in heaven; and come, follow Me."
MATTHEW 19:21 NKJV

I could tell you what you could do with a part of it," said Rachel, turning her face toward Virginia.

"That does not trouble me," replied Virginia with a slight smile. "What I am trying to discover is a principle that will enable me to come to the nearest possible to His action as it ought to influence the entire course of my life so far as my wealth and its use are concerned."

"That will take time," said the minister slowly. All the rest of the room were thinking hard of the same thing. Milton Wright told something of his experience. He was gradually working out a plan for his business relations with his employees, and it was opening up a new world to him and to them. A few of the young men told of special attempts to answer the question. There was almost general consent over the fact that the application of the Christ spirit and practice to the everyday life was the serious thing. It required a knowledge of Him and an insight into His motives that most of them did not yet possess.

When they finally adjourned after a silent prayer that marked with growing power the Divine Presence, they went away discussing earnestly their difficulties and seeking light from one another.

Daily In His Word

Jesus told them, "I'm not teaching my own ideas, but those of God who sent me. Anyone who wants to do the will of God will know whether my teaching is from God or is merely my own."
JOHN 7:16–17 NLT

Rachel Winslow and Virginia Page went out together. Edward Norman and Milton Wright became so interested in their mutual conference that they walked on past Norman's house and came back together. Jasper Chase and the president of the Endeavor Society stood talking earnestly in one corner of the room. Alexander Powers and Henry Maxwell remained, even after the others had gone.

"I want you to come down to the shops tomorrow and see my plan and talk to the men. Somehow I feel as if you could get nearer to them than any one else just now."

"I don't know about that, but I will come," replied Mr. Maxwell a little sadly. How was he fitted to stand before two or three hundred workingmen and give them a message? Yet in the moment of his weakness, as he asked the question, he rebuked himself for it. What would Jesus do? That was an end to the discussion.

Daily In His Word

Servants, be obedient to them that are your masters. . .not with eyeservice, as menpleasers; but as the servants of Christ, doing the will of God from the heart; with good will doing service, as to the Lord, and not to men.

EPHESIANS 6:5–7 KJV

He went down the next day and found Mr. Powers in his office. It lacked a few minutes of twelve and the superintendent said, "Come upstairs, and I'll show you what I've been trying to do."

They went through the machine shop, climbed a long flight of stairs, and entered a very large, empty room. It had once been used by the company for a store room.

"Since making that promise a week ago I have had a good many things to think of," said the superintendent, "and among them is this: The company gives me the use of this room, and I am going to fit it up with tables and a coffee plant in the corner there where those steam pipes are. My plan is to provide a good place where the men can come up and eat their noon lunch, and give them, two or three times a week, the privilege of a fifteen minutes' talk on some subject that will be a real help to them in their lives."

Maxwell looked surprised and asked if the men would come for any such purpose.

"Yes, they'll come. After all, I know the men pretty well. They are among the most intelligent workingmen in the country today. But they are, as a whole, entirely removed from church influence."

Daily In His Word

Serve wholeheartedly, as if you were serving the Lord, not men, because you know that the Lord will reward everyone for whatever good he does, whether he is slave or free.
Ephesians 6:7–8 niv

I asked, 'What would Jesus do?' and among other things it seemed to me He would begin to act in some way to add to the lives of these men more physical and spiritual comfort. It is a very little thing, this room and what it represents, but I acted on the first impulse, to do the first thing that appealed to my good sense, and I want to work out this idea. I want you to speak to the men when they come up at noon. I have asked them to come up and see the place and I'll tell them something about it."

Maxwell was ashamed to say how uneasy he felt at being asked to speak a few words to a company of workingmen. How could he speak without notes, or to such a crowd? He was honestly in a condition of genuine fright over the prospect. He actually felt afraid of facing those men. He shrank from the ordeal of confronting such a crowd, so different from the Sunday audiences he was familiar with.

There were a dozen rude benches and tables in the room, and when the noon whistle sounded the men poured upstairs from the machine shops below and, seating themselves at the tables, began to eat their lunch. There were present about three hundred of them. They had read the superintendent's notice which he had posted up in various places and came largely out of curiosity.

Daily In His Word

"Not even a sparrow, worth only half a penny, can fall to the ground without your Father knowing it."

MATTHEW 10:29 NLT

They were favorably impressed. The room was large and airy, free from smoke and dust, and well warmed from the steam pipes. At about twenty minutes to one Mr. Powers told the men what he had in mind. He spoke very simply, like one who understands thoroughly the character of his audience, and then introduced the Rev. Henry Maxwell of the First Church, his pastor, who had consented to speak a few minutes.

Maxwell will never forget the feeling with which for the first time he stood before the grimy-faced audience of workingmen. Like hundreds of other ministers, he had never spoken to any gatherings except those made up of people of his own class in the sense that they were familiar in their dress and education and habits. This was a new world to him, and nothing but his new rule of conduct could have made possible his message and its effect. He spoke on the subject of satisfaction with life; what caused it, what its real sources were. He had the great good sense on this his first appearance not to recognize the men as a class distinct from himself. He did not use the term *workingman* and did not say a word to suggest any difference between their lives and his own.

Daily In His Word

"Come, all you who are thirsty, come to the waters; and you who have no money, come, buy and eat! Come, buy wine and milk without money and without cost."

ISAIAH 55:1 NIV

The men were pleased. A good many of them shook hands with him before going down to their work, and the minister telling it all to his wife when he reached home, said that never in all his life had he known the delight he then felt in having the handshake from a man of physical labor. The day marked an important one in his Christian experience, more important than he knew. It was the beginning of a fellowship between him and the working world. It was the first plank laid down to help bridge the chasm between the church and labor in Raymond.

Alexander Powers went back to his desk that afternoon much pleased with his plan and seeing much help in it for the men. He knew where he could get some good tables from an abandoned eating house at one of the stations down the road, and he saw how the coffee arrangement could be made a very attractive feature. The men had responded even better than he anticipated, and the whole thing could not help being a great benefit to them.

He took up the routine of his work with a glow of satisfaction. After all, he wanted to do as Jesus would, he said to himself.

Daily In His Word
We have confidence in the Lord concerning you, that you are doing and will continue to do what we command.

2 Thessalonians 3:4 NASB

It was nearly four o'clock when he opened one of the company's long envelopes which he supposed contained orders for the purchasing of stores. He ran over the first page of typewritten matter in his usual quick, businesslike manner, before he saw that what he was reading was not intended for his office but for the superintendent of the freight department.

He turned over a page mechanically, not meaning to read what was not addressed to him, but before he knew it, he was in possession of evidence which conclusively proved that the company was engaged in a systematic violation of the Interstate Commerce Laws of the United States. It was as distinct and unequivocal a breaking of law as if a private citizen should enter a house and rob the inmates. The discrimination shown in rebates was in total contempt of all the statutes. Under the laws of the state it was also a distinct violation of certain provisions recently passed by the legislature to prevent railroad trusts. There was no question that he had in his hands evidence sufficient to convict the company of willful, intelligent violation of the law of the commission and the law of the state also.

He dropped the papers on his desk as if they were poison, and instantly the question flashed across his mind, "What would Jesus do?"

Daily In His Word

"Do not follow the crowd in doing wrong."

EXODUS 23:2 NIV

He tried to shut the question out. He tried to reason with himself by saying it was none of his business. He had known in a more or less definite way, as did nearly all the officers of the company, that this had been going on right along on nearly all the roads. He was not in a position, owing to his place in the shops, to prove anything direct, and he had regarded it as a matter which did not concern him at all. The papers now before him revealed the entire affair. They had through some carelessness been addressed to him. What business of his was it? If he saw a man entering his neighbor's house to steal, would it not be his duty to inform the officers of the law? Was a railroad company such a different thing? Was it under a different rule of conduct, so that it could rob the public and defy law and be undisturbed because it was such a great organization? What would Jesus do? Then there was his family. Of course, if he took any steps to inform the commission it would mean the loss of his position. His wife and daughter had always enjoyed luxury and a good place in society. If he came out against this lawlessness as a witness it would drag him into courts, his motives would be misunderstood, and the whole thing would end in his disgrace and the loss of his position. Surely it was none of his business. He could easily get the papers back to the freight department and no one be the wiser. Let the iniquity go on. Let the law be defied. What was it to him?

Daily In His Word

Anyone, then, who knows the good he ought to do and doesn't do it, sins.

JAMES 4:17 NIV

He would work out his plans for bettering the condition just before him. What more could a man do in this railroad business when there was so much going on anyway that made it impossible to live by the Christian standard? But what would Jesus do if He knew the facts? That was the question that confronted Alexander Powers as the day wore into evening.

The lights in the office had been turned on. The whirr of the great engine and the clash of the planers in the big shop continued until six o'clock. Then the whistle blew, the engine slowed up, the men dropped their tools and ran for the block house.

Powers heard the familiar *click, click* of the clocks as the men filed past the window of the blockhouse just outside. He said to his clerks, "I'm not going just yet. I have something extra tonight." He waited until he heard the last man deposit his block. The men behind the block case went out. The engineer and his assistants had work for half an hour but they went out by another door.

Daily In His Word

Love is not irritable, and it keeps no record of when it has been wronged. It is never glad about injustice but rejoices whenever the truth wins out.

1 CORINTHIANS 13:5–6 NLT

CHAPTER SIX

"If any man cometh unto me and hateth not his own father and mother and wife and children and brethren and sisters, yea, and his own life also, he cannot be my disciple."

"And whosoever forsaketh not all that he hath, he cannot be my disciple."

When Rachel Winslow and Virginia Page separated after the meeting at the First Church on Sunday they agreed to continue their conversation the next day. Virginia asked Rachel to come and lunch with her at noon, and Rachel accordingly rang the bell at the Page mansion about half-past eleven. Virginia herself met her and the two were soon talking earnestly.

"The fact is," Rachel was saying, after they had been talking a few moments, "I cannot reconcile it with my judgment of what Christ would do. I cannot tell another person what to do, but I feel that I ought not to accept this offer."

"What will you do then?" asked Virginia with great interest.

"I don't know yet, but I have decided to refuse this offer."

Daily In His Word
For our gospel came not unto you in word only, but also in power, and in the Holy Ghost.

1 THESSALONIANS 1:5 KJV

Rachel picked up a letter that had been lying in her lap and ran over its contents again. It was a letter from the manager of a comic opera offering her a place with a large traveling company of the season. The salary was a very large figure, and the prospect held out by the manager was flattering. He had heard Rachel sing that Sunday morning when the stranger had interrupted the service. He had been much impressed. There was money in that voice and it ought to be used in comic opera, so said the letter, and the manager wanted a reply as soon as possible.

"There's no great virtue in saying 'No' to this offer when I have the other one," Rachel went on thoughtfully. "That's harder to decide. But I've about made up my mind. To tell the, truth, Virginia, I'm completely convinced in the first case that Jesus would never use any talent like a good voice just to make money. But now, take this concert offer. Here is a reputable company, to travel with an impersonator and a violinist and a male quartet, all people of good reputation. I'm asked to go as one of the company and sing leading soprano. The salary—I mentioned it, didn't I?—is guaranteed to be $200 a month for the season. But I don't feel satisfied that Jesus would go. What do you think?"

Daily In His Word

Choose you this day whom ye will serve.

Joshua 24:15 kjv

Y ou mustn't ask me to decide for you," replied Virginia with a sad smile. "I believe Mr. Maxwell was right when he said we must each one of us decide according to the judgment we feel for ourselves to be Christlike. I am having a harder time than you are, dear, to decide what He would do."

"Are you?" Rachel asked. She rose and walked over to the window and looked out. Virginia came and stood by her. The street was crowded with life and the two young women looked at it silently for a moment. Suddenly Virginia broke out as Rachel had never heard her before:

"Rachel, what does all this contrast in conditions mean to you as you ask this question of what Jesus would do? It maddens me to think that the society in which I have been brought up, the same to which we are both said to belong, is satisfied year after year to go on dressing and eating and having a good time, giving and receiving entertainments, spending its money on houses and luxuries and, occasionally, to ease its conscience, donating, without any personal sacrifice, a little money to charity."

Daily In His Word

"This poor widow has given more than all the others have given. For they gave a tiny part of their surplus, but she, poor as she is, has given everything she has."

MARK 12:43–44 NLT

I have been educated, as you have, in one of the most expensive schools in America; launched into society as an heiress; supposed to be in a very enviable position. I'm perfectly well; I can travel or stay at home. I can do as I please. I can gratify almost any want or desire; and yet when I honestly try to imagine Jesus living the life I have lived and am expected to live, and doing for the rest of my life what thousands of other rich people do, I am under condemnation for being one of the most wicked, selfish, useless creatures in all the world. I have not looked out of this window for weeks without a feeling of horror toward myself as I see the humanity that passes by this house."

Virginia turned away and walked up and down the room. Rachel watched her and could not repress the rising tide of her own growing definition of discipleship. Of what Christian use was her own talent of song? Was the best she could do to sell her talent for so much a month, go on a concert company's tour, dress beautifully, enjoy the excitement of public applause and gain a reputation as a great singer? Was that what Jesus would do?

Daily In His Word

"To those who use well what they are given, even more will be given, and they will have an abundance. But from those who are unfaithful, even what little they have will be taken away."
Matthew 25:29 NLT

She was not morbid. She was in sound health, was conscious of her great powers as a singer, and knew that if she went out into public life she could make a great deal of money and become well known. It is doubtful if she overestimated her ability to accomplish all she thought herself capable of. And Virginia—what she had just said smote Rachel with great force because of the similar position in which the two friends found themselves.

Lunch was announced and they went out and were joined by Virginia's grandmother, Madam Page, a handsome, stately woman of sixty-five, and Virginia's brother Rollin, a young man who spent most of his time at one of the clubs and had no ambition for anything but a growing admiration for Rachel Winslow, and whenever she dined or lunched at the Page's, if he knew of it he always planned to be at home.

These three made up the Page family. Virginia's father had been a banker and grain speculator. Her mother had died ten years before, her father within the past year. The grandmother, a Southern woman in birth and training, had all the traditions and feelings that accompany the possession of wealth and social standing that have never been disturbed.

Daily In His Word

"But you shall remember the LORD your God, for it is He who is giving you power to make wealth."

DEUTERONOMY 8:18 NASB

She was a shrewd, careful businesswoman of more than average ability. The family property and wealth were invested, in large measure, under her personal care. Virginia's portion was, without any restriction, her own. She had been trained by her father to understand the ways of the business world, and even the grandmother had been compelled to acknowledge the girl's capacity for taking care of her own money.

Perhaps two persons could not be found anywhere less capable of understanding a girl like Virginia than Madam Page and Rollin. Rachel, who had known the family since she was a girl playmate of Virginia's, could not help thinking of what confronted Virginia in her own home when she once decided on the course which she honestly believed Jesus would take. Today at lunch, as she recalled Virginia's outbreak in the front room, she tried to picture the scene that would at some time occur between Madam Page and her granddaughter.

"I understand that you are going on the stage, Miss Winslow. We shall all be delighted, I'm sure," said Rollin during the conversation, which had not been very animated.

Rachel colored and felt annoyed. "Who told you?" she asked, while Virginia, who had been very silent and reserved, suddenly roused herself and appeared ready to join in the talk.

Daily In His Word

Who can find a virtuous wife? For her worth is far above rubies. The heart of her husband safely trusts her; so he will have no lack of gain.

PROVERBS 31:10–11 NKJV

Oh! We hear a thing or two on the street. Besides, every one saw Crandall the manager at church two weeks ago. He doesn't go to church to hear the preaching. In fact, I know other people who don't either, not when there's something better to hear."

Rachel did not color this time, but she answered quietly, "You're mistaken. I'm not going on the stage."

"It's a great pity. You'd make a hit. Everybody is talking about your singing."

This time Rachel flushed with genuine anger. Before she could say anything, Virginia broke in: "Whom do you mean by 'everybody'?"

"Whom? I mean all the people who hear Miss Winslow on Sundays. What other time do they hear her? It's a great pity, I say, that the general public outside of Raymond cannot hear her voice."

"Let us talk about something else," said Rachel a little sharply. Madam Page glanced at her and spoke with a gentle courtesy.

"My dear, Rollin never could pay an indirect compliment. He is like his father in that. But we are all curious to know something of your plans. We claim the right from old acquaintance, you know; and Virginia has already told us of your concert company offer."

Daily In His Word

Do you see a man skilled in his work? He will serve before kings; he will not serve before obscure men.

Proverbs 22:29 niv

I supposed of course that was public property," said Virginia, smiling across the table. "I was in the *News* office day before yesterday."

"Yes, yes," replied Rachel hastily. "I understand that, Madam Page. Well, Virginia and I have been talking about it. I have decided not to accept, and that is as far as I have gone at present."

Rachel was conscious of the fact that the conversation had, up to this point, been narrowing her hesitation concerning the concert company's offer down to a decision that would absolutely satisfy her own judgment of Jesus' probable action. It had been the last thing in the world, however, that she had desired, to have her decision made in any way so public as this. Somehow what Rollin Page had said and his manner in saying it had hastened her decision in the matter.

"Would you mind telling us, Rachel, your reasons for refusing the offer? It looks like a great opportunity for a young girl like you. Don't you think the general public ought to hear you? I feel like Rollin about that. A voice like yours belongs to a larger audience than Raymond and the First Church."

Daily In His Word

"'Do not go about spreading slander among your people.' "
LEVITICUS 19:16 NIV

Rachel Winslow was naturally a girl of great reserve. She shrank from making her plans or her thoughts public. But with all her repression there was possible in her an occasional sudden breaking out that was simply an impulsive, thoroughly frank, truthful expression of her most inner personal feeling. She spoke now in reply to Madam Page in one of those rare moments of unreserve that added to the attractiveness of her whole character.

"I have no other reason than a conviction that Jesus Christ would do the same thing," she said, looking into Madam Page's eyes with a clear, earnest gaze.

Madam Page turned red and Rollin stared. Before her grandmother could say anything, Virginia spoke. Her rising color showed how she was stirred. Virginia's pale, clear complexion was that of health, but it was generally in marked contrast with Rachel's tropical type of beauty.

"Grandmother, you know we promised to make that the standard of our conduct for a year. Mr. Maxwell's proposition was plain to all who heard it. We have not been able to arrive at our decisions very rapidly. The difficulty in knowing what Jesus would do has perplexed Rachel and me a good deal."

Daily In His Word
What business is it of mine to judge those outside the church? Are you not to judge those inside?

1 CORINTHIANS 5:12 NIV

Madam Page looked sharply at Virginia before she said anything.

"Of course I understand Mr. Maxwell's statement. It is perfectly impracticable to put it into practice. I felt confident at the time that those who promised would find it out after a trial and abandon it as visionary and absurd. I have nothing to say about Miss Winslow's affairs, but," she paused and continued with a sharpness that was new to Rachel, "I hope you have no foolish notions in this matter, Virginia."

"I have a great many notions," replied Virginia quietly. "Whether they are foolish or not depends upon my right understanding of what He would do. As soon as I find out I shall do it."

"Excuse me, ladies," said Rollin, rising from the table. "The conversation is getting beyond my depth. I shall retire to the library for a cigar."

He went out of the dining room and there was silence for a moment. Madam Page waited until the servant had brought in something and then asked her to go out. She was angry and her anger was formidable, although checked in some measure by the presence of Rachel.

Daily In His Word

Do not love the world or the things in the world. If anyone loves the world, the love of the Father is not in him.

1 John 2:15 nkjv

I am older by several years than you, young ladies," she said, and her traditional type of bearing seemed to Rachel to rise up like a great frozen wall between her and every conception of Jesus as a sacrifice. "What you have promised, in a spirit of false emotion I presume, is impossible of performance."

"Do you mean, grandmother, that we cannot possibly act as our Lord would? Or do you mean that, if we try to, we shall offend the customs and prejudices of society?" asked Virginia.

"It is not required! It is not necessary! Besides how can you act with any—" Madam Page paused, broke off her sentence, and then turned to Rachel. "What will your mother say to your decision? My dear, is it not foolish? What do you expect to do with your voice anyway?"

"I don't know what Mother will say yet," Rachel answered, with a great shrinking from trying to give her mother's probable answer. If there was a woman in all Raymond with great ambitions for her daughter's success as a singer, Mrs. Winslow was that woman.

"Oh! You will see it in a different light after wiser thought of it. My dear," continued Madam Page rising from the table, "you will live to regret it if you do not accept the concert company's offer or something like it."

Daily In His Word

But may the God of all grace, who called us to His eternal glory by Christ Jesus, after you have suffered a while, perfect, establish, strengthen, and settle you.

1 PETER 5:10 NKJV

CHAPTER SEVEN

Rachel was glad to escape and be by herself. A plan was slowly forming in her mind, and she wanted to be alone and think it out carefully. But before she had walked two blocks she was annoyed to find Rollin Page walking beside her.

"Sorry to disturb your thoughts, Miss Winslow, but I happened to be going your way and had an idea you might not object. In fact, I've been walking here for a whole block and you haven't objected."

"I did not see you," said Rachel briefly.

"I wouldn't mind that if you only thought of me once in a while," said Rollin suddenly. He took one last nervous puff on his cigar, tossed it into the street and walked along with a pale look on his face.

Rachel was surprised, but not startled. She had known Rollin as a boy, and there had been a time when they had used each other's first name familiarly. Lately, however, something in Rachel's manner had put an end to that. She was used to his direct attempts at compliments and was sometimes amused by them. Today she honestly wished him anywhere else.

Daily In His Word
We are from God; he who knows God listens to us; he who is not from God does not listen to us.

1 JOHN 4:6 NASB

Do you ever think of me, Miss Winslow?" asked Rollin after a pause.

"Oh, yes, quite often!" said Rachel with a smile.

"Are you thinking of me now?"

"Yes. That is—yes—I am."

"What?"

"Do you want me to be absolutely truthful?"

"Of course."

"Then I was thinking that I wished you were not here."

Rollin bit his lip and looked gloomy. "Now look here, Rachel—oh, I know that's forbidden, but I've got to speak sometime!—you know how I feel. What makes you treat me so? You used to like me a little, you know."

"Did I? Of course we used to get on very well as boy and girl. But we are older now."

Rachel still spoke in the light, easy way she had used since her first annoyance at seeing him. She was still somewhat preoccupied with her plan which had been disturbed by Rollin's sudden appearance.

Daily In His Word

"Show me your intentions so I will understand you more fully and do exactly what you want me to do."

EXODUS 33:13 NLT

T hey walked along in silence a little way. The avenue was full of people. Among the persons passing was Jasper Chase. He saw Rachel and Rollin and bowed as they went by. Rollin was watching Rachel closely.

"I wish I was Jasper Chase. Maybe I would stand some chance then," he said moodily.

Rachel colored in spite of herself. She did not say anything and quickened her pace a little. Rollin seemed determined to say something, and Rachel seemed helpless to prevent him. After all, she thought, he might as well know the truth one time as another.

"You know well enough, Rachel, how I feel toward you. Isn't there any hope? I could make you happy. I've loved you a good many years—"

"Why, how old do you think I am?" broke in Rachel with a nervous laugh. She was shaken out of her usual poise of manner.

"You know what I mean," went on Rollin doggedly. "And you have no right to laugh at me just because I want you to marry me."

"I'm not! But it is useless for you to speak, Rollin," said Rachel after a little hesitation, and then using his name in such a frank, simple way that he could attach no meaning to it beyond the familiarity of the old family acquaintance. "It is impossible." She was still a little agitated by the fact of receiving a proposal of marriage on the avenue. But the noise on the street and sidewalk made the conversation as private as if they were in the house.

Daily In His Word

Be completely humble and gentle; be patient, bearing with one another in love.

EPHESIANS 4:2 NIV

Would, that is—do you think—if you gave me time I would?"

"No!" said Rachel. She spoke firmly; perhaps, she thought afterward, although she did not mean to, she spoke harshly.

They walked on for some time without a word. They were nearing Rachel's home and she was anxious to end the scene.

As they turned off the avenue into one of the quieter streets Rollin spoke suddenly and with more manliness than he had yet shown. There was a distinct note of dignity in his voice that was new to Rachel.

"Miss Winslow, I ask you to be my wife. Is there any hope for me that you will ever consent?"

"None in the least." Rachel spoke decidedly.

"Will you tell me why?" He asked the question as if he had a right to a truthful answer.

"Because I do not feel toward you as a woman ought to feel toward the man she marries."

"In other words, you do not love me?"

"I do not and I cannot."

Daily In His Word

Speaking the truth in love, we will in all things grow up into him who is the Head, that is, Christ.

EPHESIANS 4:15 NIV

W hy?" That was another question, and Rachel was a little surprised that he should ask it.

"Because—" she hesitated for fear she might say too much in an attempt to speak the exact truth.

"Tell me just why. You can't hurt me more than you have already."

"Well, I do not and I cannot love you because you have no purpose in life. What do you ever do to make the world better? You spend your time in club life, in amusements, in travel, in luxury. What is there in such a life to attract a woman?"

"Not much, I guess," said Rollin with a bitter laugh. "Still, I don't know that I'm any worse than the rest of the men around me. I'm not so bad as some. I'm glad to know your reasons."

He suddenly stopped, took off his hat, bowed gravely and turned back. Rachel went on home and hurried into her room, disturbed in many ways by the event which had so unexpectedly thrust itself into her experience.

When she had time to think it all over she found herself condemned by the very judgment she had passed on Rollin Page. What purpose had she in life?

Daily In His Word

Be ye not unequally yoked together with unbelievers: for what fellowship hath righteousness with unrighteousness? and what communion hath light with darkness?

2 CORINTHIANS 6:14 KJV

She had been abroad and studied music with one of the famous teachers of Europe. She had come home to Raymond and had been singing in the First Church choir now for a year. She was well paid. Up to that Sunday two weeks ago she had been quite satisfied with herself and with her position. She had shared her mother's ambition and anticipated growing triumphs in the musical world. What possible career was before her except the regular career of every singer?

She asked the question again and, in the light of her recent reply to Rollin, asked again, if she had any very great purpose in life herself. What would Jesus do? There was a fortune in her voice. She knew it, not necessarily as a matter of personal pride or professional egotism, but simply as a fact. And she was obliged to acknowledge that until two weeks ago she had purposed to use her voice to make money and win admiration and applause. Was that a much higher purpose, after all, than Rollin Page lived for?

She sat in her room a long time and finally went downstairs, resolved to have a frank talk with her mother about the concert company's offer and the new plan which was gradually shaping in her mind. She had already had one talk with her mother and knew that she expected Rachel to accept the offer and enter on a successful career as a public singer.

Daily In His Word

*" 'You shall worship the Lord your God,
and Him only you shall serve.' "*

Matthew 4:10 nkjv

M other," Rachel said, coming at once to the point, much as she dreaded the interview, "I have decided not to go out with the company. I have a good reason for it."

Mrs. Winslow was a large, handsome woman, fond of much company, ambitious for distinction in society and devoted, according to her definitions of success, to the success of her children. Her youngest boy, Louis, two years younger than Rachel, was ready to graduate from a military academy in the summer. Meanwhile she and Rachel were at home together. Rachel's father, like Virginia's, had died while the family was abroad. Like Virginia she found herself, under her present rule of conduct, in complete antagonism with her own immediate home circle. Mrs. Winslow waited for Rachel to go on.

"You know the promise I made two weeks ago, Mother?"

"Mr. Maxwell's promise?"

"No, mine. You know what it was, do you not, Mother?"

"I suppose I do. Of course all the church members mean to imitate Christ and follow Him, as far as is consistent with our present day surroundings. But what has that to do with your decision in the concert company matter?"

"It has everything to do with it."

Daily In His Word

For as many as are the promises of God, in Him they are yes; therefore also through Him is our Amen to the glory of God through us.

2 Corinthians 1:20 nasb

After asking, 'What would Jesus do?' and going to the source of authority for wisdom, I have been obliged to say that I do not believe He would, in my case, make that use of my voice."

"Why? Is there anything wrong about such a career?"

"No, I don't know that I can say there is."

"Do you presume to sit in judgment on other people who go out to sing in this way? Do you presume to say they are doing what Christ would not do?"

"Mother, I wish you to understand me. I judge no one else; I condemn no other professional singer. I simply decide my own course. As I look at it, I have a conviction that Jesus would do something else."

"What else?" Mrs. Winslow had not yet lost her temper. She did not understand the situation nor Rachel in the midst of it, but she was anxious that her daughter's course should be as distinguished as her natural gifts promised. And she felt confident that when the present unusual religious excitement in the First Church had passed away Rachel would go on with her public life according to the wishes of the family. She was totally unprepared for Rachel's next remark.

"What? Something that will serve mankind where it most needs the service of song."

Daily In His Word

I have good advice and sound wisdom; I have insight,
I have strength.

PROVERBS 8:14 NRSV

Mother, I have made up my mind to use my voice in some way so as to satisfy my own soul that I am doing something better than pleasing fashionable audiences, or making money, or even gratifying my own love of singing. I am going to do something that will satisfy me when I ask: 'What would Jesus do?' I am not satisfied, and cannot be, when I think of myself as singing myself into the career of a concert company performer."

Rachel spoke with a vigor and earnestness that surprised her mother. But Mrs. Winslow was angry now; and she never tried to conceal her feelings.

"It is simply absurd! Rachel, you are a fanatic! What can you do?"

"The world has been served by men and women who have given it other things that were gifts. Why should I, because I am blessed with a natural gift, at once proceed to put a market price on it and make all the money I can out of it? You know, Mother, that you have taught me to think of a musical career always in the light of financial and social success. I have been unable, since I made my promise two weeks ago, to imagine Jesus joining a concert company to do what I should do and live the life I should have to live if I joined it."

Daily In His Word

Every good gift and every perfect gift is from above, and comes down from the Father of lights.

JAMES 1:17 NKJV

Mrs. Winslow rose and then sat down again. With a great effort she composed herself.

"What do you intend to do then? You have not answered my question."

"I shall continue to sing for the time being in the church. I am pledged to sing there through the spring. During the week I am going to sing at the White Cross meetings, down in the Rectangle."

"What! Rachel Winslow! Do you know what you are saying? Do you know what sort of people those are down there?"

Rachel almost quailed before her mother. For a moment she shrank back and was silent. Then she spoke firmly: "I know very well. That is the reason I am going. Mr. and Mrs. Gray have been working there for several weeks. I learned only this morning that they want singers from the churches to help them in their meetings. They use a tent. It is in a part of the city where Christian work is most needed. I shall offer them my help. Mother!" Rachel cried out with the first passionate utterance she had yet used, "I want to do something that will cost me something in the way of sacrifice. I know you will not understand me. But I am hungry to suffer for something. What have we done all our lives for the suffering, sinning side of Raymond?"

Daily In His Word

For it is commendable if a man bears up under the pain of unjust suffering because he is conscious of God.

1 PETER 2:19 NIV

How much have we denied ourselves or given of our personal ease and pleasure to bless the place in which we live or imitate the life of the Savior of the world? Are we always to go on doing as society selfishly dictates, moving on its little narrow round of pleasures and entertainments, and never knowing the pain of things that cost?"

"Are you preaching at me?" asked Mrs. Winslow slowly. Rachel rose and understood her mother's words.

"No. I am preaching at myself," she replied gently. She paused a moment as if she thought her mother would say something more, and then went out of the room. When she reached her own room she felt that so far as her own mother was concerned she could expect no sympathy, nor even a fair understanding from her.

She kneeled. It is safe to say that within the two weeks since Henry Maxwell's church had faced that shabby figure with the faded hat more members of his parish had been driven to their knees in prayer than during all the previous term of his pastorate.

She rose, and her face was wet with tears. She sat thoughtfully a little while and then wrote a note to Virginia Page. She sent it to her by a messenger and then went downstairs and told her mother that she and Virginia were going down to the Rectangle that evening to see Mr. and Mrs. Gray, the evangelists.

Daily In His Word

You also, like living stones, are being built into a spiritual house to be a holy priesthood, offering spiritual sacrifices acceptable to God through Jesus Christ.

1 PETER 2:5 NIV

Virginia's uncle, Dr. West, will go with us, if she goes. I have asked her to call him up by telephone and go with us. The Doctor is a friend of the Grays, and attended some of their meetings last winter."

Mrs. Winslow did not say anything. Her manner showed her complete disapproval of Rachel's course, and Rachel felt her unspoken bitterness.

About seven o'clock the Doctor and Virginia appeared, and together the three started for the scene of the White Cross meetings.

The Rectangle was the most notorious district in Raymond. It was on the territory close by the railroad shops and the packing houses. The great slum and tenement district of Raymond congested its worst and most wretched elements about the Rectangle. This was a barren field used in the summer by circus companies and wandering showmen. It was shut in by rows of saloons, gambling hells and cheap, dirty boarding and lodging houses.

The First Church of Raymond had never touched the Rectangle problem. It was too dirty, too coarse, too sinful, too awful for close contact. Let us be honest. There had been an attempt to cleanse this sore spot by sending down an occasional committee of singers or Sunday school teachers or gospel visitors from various churches. But the First Church of Raymond, as an institution, had never really done anything to make the Rectangle any less a stronghold of the devil as the years went by.

Daily In His Word

"You say, 'I am rich, and have become wealthy, and have need of nothing,' and you do not know that you are wretched and miserable and poor and blind and naked."

Revelation 3:17 NASB

Into this heart of the coarse part of the sin of Raymond the traveling evangelist and his brave little wife had pitched a good-sized tent and begun meetings. It was the spring of the year and the evenings were beginning to be pleasant. The evangelists had asked for the help of Christian people, and had received more than the usual amount of encouragement. But they felt a great need of more and better music. During the meetings on the Sunday just gone the assistant at the organ had been taken ill. The volunteers from the city were few and the voices were of ordinary quality.

"There will be a small meeting tonight, John," said his wife, as they entered the tent a little after seven o'clock and began to arrange the chairs and light up.

"Yes, I fear so." Mr. Gray was a small, energetic man, with a pleasant voice and the courage of a high-born fighter. He had already made friends in the neighborhood and one of his converts, a heavy-faced man who had just come in, began to help in the arranging of seats.

Daily In His Word

Wait patiently for the LORD. Be brave and courageous. Yes, wait patiently for the LORD.

PSALM 27:14 NLT

It was after eight o'clock when Alexander Powers opened the door of his office and started for home. He was going to take a car at the corner of the Rectangle. But he was roused by a voice coming from the tent.

It was the voice of Rachel Winslow. It struck through his consciousness of struggle over his own question that had sent him into the Divine Presence for an answer. He had not yet reached a conclusion. He was tortured with uncertainty. His whole previous course of action as a railroad man was the poorest possible preparation for anything sacrificial. And he could not yet say what he would do in the matter.

Hark! What was she singing? How did Rachel Winslow happen to be down here? Several windows near by went up. Some men quarreling near a saloon stopped and listened. Other figures were walking rapidly in the direction of the Rectangle and the tent. Surely Rachel Winslow had never sung like that in the First Church. It was a marvelous voice. What was it she was singing?

Daily In His Word

Oh come, let us sing to the LORD! Let us shout joyfully to the Rock of our salvation. Let us come before His presence with thanksgiving; let us shout joyfully to Him with psalms.

PSALM 95:1–2 NKJV

Again Alexander Powers, superintendent of the machine shops, paused and listened,

> *"Where He leads me I will follow,*
> *Where He leads me I will follow,*
> *Where He leads me I will follow,*
> *I'll go with Him, with Him.*
>
> *All the way!"*

The brutal, coarse, impure life of the Rectangle stirred itself into new life as the song, as pure as the surroundings were vile, floated out and into saloon and den and foul lodging. Someone stumbled hastily by Alexander Powers and said in answer to a question: "De tent's beginning to run over tonight. That's what the talent calls music, eh?"

Daily In His Word

Sing to him; yes, sing his praises. Tell everyone about his miracles. Exult in his holy name; O worshipers of the LORD, rejoice!

PSALM 105:2–3 NLT

Chapter Eight

"If any man would come after me, let him deny himself and take up his cross daily and follow me."

Henry Maxwell paced his study back and forth. It was Wednesday and he had started to think out the subject of his evening service which fell upon that night. Out of one of his study windows he could see the tall chimney of the railroad shops. The top of the evangelist's tent just showed over the buildings around the Rectangle. He looked out of his window every time he turned in his walk. After a while he sat down at his desk and drew a large piece of paper toward him. After thinking several moments he wrote in large letters the following:

A NUMBER OF THINGS THAT JESUS WOULD PROBABLY DO IN THIS PARISH:

1) Live in a simple, plain manner, without needless luxury on the one hand or undue asceticism on the other. 2) Preach fearlessly to the hypocrites in the church, no matter what their social importance or wealth. 3) Show in some practical form His sympathy and love for the common people as well as for the well-to-do, educated, refined people who make up the majority of the parish. 4) Identify Himself with the great causes of humanity in some personal way that would call for self-denial and suffering. 5) Preach against the saloon in Raymond. 6) Become known as a friend and companion of the sinful people in the Rectangle. 7) Give up the summer trip to Europe this year. (I have been abroad twice and cannot claim any special need of rest. I am well and could forego this pleasure, using the money for someone who needs a vacation more than I do. There are probably plenty of such people in the city.)

Daily In His Word

We are debtors, not to the flesh, to live according to the flesh—for if you live according to the flesh, you will die; but if by the Spirit you put to death the deeds of the body, you will live.

ROMANS 8:12–13 NRSV

He was conscious, with a humility that was once a stranger to him, that his outline of Jesus' probable action was painfully lacking in depth and power, but he was seeking carefully for concrete shapes into which he might cast his thought of Jesus' conduct. Nearly every point he had put down, meant, for him, a complete overturning of the custom and habit of years in the ministry. In spite of that, he still searched deeper for sources of the Christlike spirit. He did not attempt to write any more, but sat at his desk absorbed in his effort to catch more and more the spirit of Jesus in his own life. He had forgotten the particular subject for his prayer meeting with which he had begun his morning study.

He was so absorbed over his thought that he did not hear the bell ring; he was roused by the servant who announced a caller. He had sent up his name, Mr. Gray.

Maxwell stepped to the head of the stairs and asked Gray to come up. So Gray came up and stated the reason for his call.

"I want your help, Mr. Maxwell. Of course you have heard what a wonderful meeting we had Monday night and last night. Miss Winslow has done more with her voice than I could do, and the tent won't hold the people."

Daily In His Word

Be imitators of God, therefore, as dearly loved children, and live a life of love, just as Christ loved us and gave himself up for us as a fragrant offering and sacrifice to God.

Ephesians 5:1–2 niv

I've heard of that. It is the first time the people there have heard her. It is no wonder they are attracted."

"It has been a wonderful revelation to us and a most encouraging event in our work. But I came to ask if you could not come down tonight and preach. I am suffering from a severe cold. I do not dare trust my voice again. I know it is asking a good deal from such a busy man. But, if you can't come, say so frankly, and I'll try somewhere else."

"I'm sorry, but it's my regular prayer meeting night," began Henry Maxwell. Then he flushed and added, "I shall be able to arrange it in some way so as to come down. You can count on me."

Gray thanked him earnestly and rose to go.

"Won't you stay a minute, Gray, and let us have a prayer together?"

"Yes," said Gray simply.

So the two men kneeled together in the study. Henry Maxwell prayed like a child. Gray was touched to tears as he knelt there. There was something almost pitiful in the way this man who had lived his ministerial life in such a narrow limit of exercise now begged for wisdom and strength to speak a message to the people in the Rectangle.

Daily In His Word

We have not stopped praying for you and asking God to fill you with the knowledge of his will through all spiritual wisdom and understanding.

Colossians 1:9 niv

Gray rose and held out his hand. "God bless you, Mr. Maxwell. I'm sure the Spirit will give you power tonight."

Henry Maxwell made no answer. He did not even trust himself to say that he hoped so. But he thought of his promise and it brought him a certain peace that was refreshing to his heart and mind alike.

So that is how it came about that when the First Church audience came into the lecture room that evening it met with another surprise. There was an unusually large number present. The prayer meetings ever since that remarkable Sunday morning had been attended as never before in the history of the First Church. Mr. Maxwell came at once to the point.

"I feel that I am called to go down to the Rectangle tonight, and I will leave it with you to say whether you will go on with this meeting here. I think perhaps the best plan would be for a few volunteers to go down to the Rectangle with me prepared to help in the after-meeting, if necessary, and the rest to remain here and pray that the Spirit power may go with us."

So half a dozen of the men went with the pastor, and the rest of the audience stayed in the lecture room.

Daily In His Word

And my speech and my preaching were not with persuasive words of human wisdom, but in demonstration of the Spirit and of power, that your faith should not be in the wisdom of men but in the power of God.

1 Corinthians 2:4–5 NKJV

Maxwell could not escape the thought as he left the room that probably in his entire church membership there might not be found a score of disciples who were capable of doing work that would successfully lead needy, sinful men into the knowledge of Christ. The thought did not linger in his mind to vex him as he went his way, but it was simply a part of his whole new conception of the meaning of Christian discipleship.

When he and his little company of volunteers reached the Rectangle, the tent was already crowded. They had difficulty in getting to the platform. Rachel was there with Virginia and Jasper Chase who had come instead of the Doctor tonight.

When the meeting began with a song in which Rachel sang the solo and the people were asked to join in the chorus, not a foot of standing room was left in the tent. The night was mild and the sides of the tent were up and a great border of faces stretched around, looking in and forming part of the audience. After the singing and a prayer by one of the city pastors who was present, Gray stated the reason for his inability to speak, and in his simple manner turned the service over to "Brother Maxwell of the First Church."

Daily In His Word
Therefore being justified by faith, we have peace with God through our Lord Jesus Christ: by whom also we have access by faith into this grace wherein we stand, and rejoice in hope of the glory of God.

ROMANS 5:1–2 KJV

W ho's de bloke?" asked a hoarse voice near the outside of the tent.

"De Fust Church parson. We've got de whole high-tone swell outfit tonight."

"Did you say Fust Church? I know him. My landlord's got a front pew up there," said another voice, and there was a laugh, for the speaker was a saloon keeper.

"Trow out de life line 'cross de dark wave!" began a drunken man near by, singing in such an unconscious imitation of a local traveling singer's nasal tone that roars of laughter and jeers of approval rose around him. The people in the tent turned in the direction of the disturbance. There were shouts of "Put him out!" "Give the Fust Church a chance!" "Song! Song! Give us another song!"

Henry Maxwell stood up, and a great wave of actual terror went over him. This was not like preaching to the well-dressed, respectable, good-mannered people up on the boulevard. He began to speak, but the confusion increased. Gray went down into the crowd but did not seem able to quiet it. Maxwell raised his arm and his voice. The crowd in the tent began to pay some attention, but the noise on the outside increased. In a few minutes the audience was beyond his control. He turned to Rachel with a sad smile.

"Sing something, Miss Winslow. They will listen to you," he said, and then sat down and covered his face with his hands.

Daily In His Word

Did not God choose the poor of this world to be rich in faith and heirs of the kingdom which He promised to those who love Him?
JAMES 2:5 NASB

It was Rachel's opportunity, and she was fully equal to it. Virginia was at the organ and Rachel asked her to play a few notes of the hymn.

> "Savior, I follow on,
> Guided by Thee,
> Seeing not yet the hand
> That leadeth me.
> Hushed be my heart and still
> Fear I no farther ill,
> Only to meet Thy will,
> My will shall be."

Rachel had not sung the first line before the people in the tent were all turned toward her, hushed and reverent. Before she had finished the verse the Rectangle was subdued and tamed. It lay like some wild beast at her feet, and she sang it into harmlessness. Ah! What were the flippant, perfumed, critical audiences in concert halls compared with this dirty, drunken, impure, besotted mass of humanity that trembled and wept and grew strangely, sadly thoughtful under the touch of this divine ministry of this beautiful young woman!

Daily In His Word

"Heal the sick, raise the dead, cleanse the lepers, cast out demons. Freely you received, freely give."

Matthew 10:8 NASB

Mr. Maxwell, as he raised his head and saw the transformed mob, had a glimpse of something that Jesus would probably do with a voice like Rachel Winslow's. Jasper Chase sat with his eyes on the singer, and his greatest longing as an ambitious author was swallowed up in his thought of what Rachel Winslow's love might sometime mean to him. And over in the shadow outside stood the last person any one might have expected to see at a gospel tent service—Rollin Page, who, jostled on every side by rough men and women who stared at the swell in fine clothes, seemed careless of his surroundings and at the same time evidently swayed by the power that Rachel possessed. He had just come over from the club. Neither Rachel nor Virginia saw him that night.

The song was over. Maxwell rose again. This time he felt calmer. What would Jesus do? He spoke as he thought once he never could speak. Who were these people? They were immortal souls. What was Christianity? A calling of sinners, not the righteous, to repentance. How would Jesus speak? What would He say? He could not tell all that His message would include, but he felt sure of a part of it. And in that certainty he spoke on.

Daily In His Word

" 'I desire compassion, and not sacrifice,' for I did not come to call the righteous, but sinners."

MATTHEW 9:13 NASB

Never before had he felt "compassion for the multitude." What had the multitude been to him during his ten years in the First Church but a vague, dangerous, dirty, troublesome factor in society, outside of the church and of his reach, an element that caused him occasionally an unpleasant twinge of conscience, a factor in Raymond that was talked about at associations as the "masses," in papers written by the brethren in attempts to show why the "masses" were not being reached. But tonight as he faced the masses he asked himself whether, after all, this was not just about such a multitude as Jesus faced oftenest, and he felt the genuine emotion of love for a crowd which is one of the best indications a preacher ever has that he is living close to the heart of the world's eternal Life. It is easy to love an individual sinner, especially if he is personally picturesque or interesting. To love a multitude of sinners is distinctively a Christlike quality.

When the meeting closed, there was no special interest shown. No one stayed to the after-meeting. The people rapidly melted away from the tent, and the saloons, which had been experiencing a dull season while the meetings progressed, again drove a thriving trade. The Rectangle, as if to make up for lost time, started in with vigor on its usual night debauch. Maxwell and his little party, including Virginia, Rachel, and Jasper Chase, walked down past the row of saloons and dens until they reached the corner where the cars passed.

Daily In His Word

He healed people of every sort of disease and illness. He felt great pity for the crowds that came, because their problems were so great and they didn't know where to go for help.

MATTHEW 9:35–36 NLT

This is a terrible spot," said the minister as he stood waiting for their car. "I never realized that Raymond had such a festering sore. It does not seem possible that this is a city full of Christian disciples."

"Do you think any one can ever remove this great curse of drink?" asked Jasper Chase.

"I have thought lately as never before of what Christian people might do to remove the curse of the saloon. Why don't we all act together against it? Why don't the Christian pastors and the church members of Raymond move as one man against the traffic? What would Jesus do? Would He keep silent? Would He vote to license these causes of crime and death?"

He was talking to himself more than to the others. He remembered that he had always voted for license, and so had nearly all his church members. What would Jesus do? Could he answer that question? Would the Master preach and act against the saloon if He lived today? How would He preach and act? Suppose it was not popular to preach against license? Suppose the Christian people thought it was all that could be done to license the evil and so get revenue from the necessary sin? Or suppose the church members themselves owned the property where the saloons stood—what then? He knew that those were the facts in Raymond. What would Jesus do?

Daily In His Word

"Where are your accusers? Didn't even one of them condemn you?" "No, Lord," she said. And Jesus said, "Neither do I. Go and sin no more."

JOHN 8:10–11 NLT

He went up into his study the next morning with that question only partly answered. He thought of it all day. He was still thinking of it and reaching certain real conclusions when the evening *News* came. His wife brought it up and sat down a few minutes while he read to her.

The evening *News* was at present the most sensational paper in Raymond. That is to say, it was being edited in such a remarkable fashion that its subscribers had never been so excited over a newspaper before. First they had noticed the absence of the prize fight, and gradually it began to dawn upon them that the *News* no longer printed accounts of crime with detailed descriptions or scandals in private life. Then they noticed that the advertisements of liquor and tobacco were dropped, together with certain others of a questionable character. The discontinuance of the Sunday paper caused the greatest comment of all, and now the character of the editorials was creating the greatest excitement. A quotation from the Monday paper of this week will show what Edward Norman was doing to keep his promise. The editorial was headed:

THE MORAL SIDE OF POLITICAL QUESTIONS

Daily In His Word
Who are they that fear the Lord? He will teach them the way that they should choose.

PSALM 25:12 NRSV

The editor of the News has always advocated the principles of the great political party at present in power and has heretofore discussed all political questions from the standpoint of expediency, or of belief in the party as opposed to other political organizations. Hereafter, to be perfectly honest with all our readers, the editor will present and discuss all political questions from the standpoint of right and wrong. In other words, the first question asked in this office about any political question will not be, "Is it in the interests of our party?" or, "Is it according to the principles laid down by our party in its platform?" but the question first asked will be, "Is this measure in accordance with the spirit and teachings of Jesus as the author of the greatest standard of life known to men?" That is, to be perfectly plain, the moral side of every political question will be considered its most important side, and the ground will be distinctly taken that nations as well as individuals are under the same law to do all things to the glory of God as the first rule of action.

The same principle will be observed in this office toward candidates for places of responsibility and trust in the republic. Regardless of party politics the editor of the News will do all in his power to bring the best men into power and will not knowingly help to support for office any candidate who is unworthy, no matter how much he may be endorsed by the party. The first question asked about the man and about the measures will be, "Is he the right man for the place?" "Is he a good man with ability?" "Is the measure right?"

Daily In His Word

Godliness exalts a nation, but sin is a disgrace to any people.

PROVERBS 14:34 NLT

There had been more of this, but we have quoted enough to show the character of the editorial. Hundreds of men in Raymond had read it and rubbed their eyes in amazement. A good many of them had promptly written to the *News*, telling the editor to stop their paper. The paper still came out, however, and was eagerly read all over the city. At the end of a week Edward Norman knew very well that he was fast losing a large number of subscribers. He faced the conditions calmly, although Clark, the managing editor, grimly anticipated ultimate bankruptcy, especially since Monday's editorial.

Tonight, as Maxwell read to his wife, he could see in almost every column evidences of Norman's conscientious obedience to his promise. There was an absence of slangy, sensational scare heads. The reading matter under the headlines was in perfect keeping with them. He noticed in two columns that the reporters' name appeared signed at the bottom. And there was a distinct advance in the dignity and style of their contributions.

"So Norman is beginning to get his reporters to sign their work. He has talked with me about that. It is a good thing. It fixes responsibility for items where it belongs and raises the standard of work done. A good thing all around for the public and the writers."

Daily In His Word
Wealth is worthless in the day of wrath,
but righteousness delivers from death.

PROVERBS 11:4 NIV

Maxwell suddenly paused. His wife looked up from some work she was doing. He was reading something with the utmost interest. "Listen to this, Mary," he said, after a moment while his lip trembled:

> *"This morning, Alexander Powers, Superintendent of the L. and T. R. R. shops in this city, handed in his resignation to the road and gave as his reason the fact that certain proofs had fallen into his hands of the violation of the Interstate Commerce Law and also of the state law which has recently been framed to prevent and punish railroad pooling for the benefit of certain favored shippers. Mr. Powers states in his resignation that he can no longer consistently withhold the information he possesses against the road. He will be a witness against it. He has placed his evidence against the company in the hands of the Commission and it is now for them to take action upon it.*

Daily In His Word

It is better to be godly and have little than to be evil and possess much. For the strength of the wicked will be shattered, but the LORD takes care of the godly.

PSALM 37:16–17 NLT

The News *wishes to express itself on this action of Mr. Powers. In the first place he has nothing to gain by it. He has lost a very valuable place voluntarily, when by keeping silent he might have retained it. In the second place, we believe his action ought to receive the approval of all thoughtful, honest citizens who believe in seeing law obeyed and lawbreakers brought to justice. In a case like this, where evidence against a railroad company is generally understood to be almost impossible to obtain, it is the general belief that the officers of the road are often in possession of incriminating facts but do not consider it to be any of their business to inform the authorities that the law is being defied. The entire result of this evasion of responsibility on the part of those who are responsible is demoralizing to every young man connected with the road. The editor of the* News *recalls the statement made by a prominent railroad official in this city a little while ago, that nearly every clerk in a certain department of the road understood that large sums of money were made by shrewd violations of the Interstate Commerce Law, was ready to admire the shrewdness with which it was done, and declared that they would all do the same thing if they were high enough in railroad circles to attempt it."*

Daily In His Word

And what does the LORD *require of you? To act justly and to love mercy and to walk humbly with your God.*

MICAH 6:8 NIV

CHAPTER NINE

Henry Maxwell finished reading and dropped the paper.

"I must go and see Powers. This is the result of his promise."

He rose, and as he was going out, his wife said: "Do you think, Henry, that Jesus would have done that?"

Maxwell paused a moment. Then he answered slowly, "Yes, I think He would. At any rate, Powers has decided so and each one of us who made the promise understands that he is not deciding Jesus' conduct for any one else, only for himself."

"How about his family? How will Mrs. Powers and Celia be likely to take it?"

"Very hard, I've no doubt. That will be Powers's cross in this matter. They will not understand his motive."

Maxwell went out and walked over to the next block where Superintendent Powers lived. To his relief, Powers himself came to the door.

The two men shook hands silently. They instantly understood each other without words. There had never before been such a bond of union between the minister and his parishioner.

Daily In His Word

For the word of the cross is foolishness to those who are perishing, but to us who are being saved it is the power of God.

1 CORINTHIANS 1:18 NASB

Wat are you going to do?" Henry Maxwell asked after they had talked over the facts in the case.

"You mean another position? I have no plans yet. I can go back to my old work as a telegraph operator. My family will not suffer, except in a social way."

Powers spoke calmly and sadly. Henry Maxwell did not need to ask him how the wife and daughter felt. He knew well enough that the superintendent had suffered deepest at that point.

"There is one matter I wish you would see to," said Powers after awhile, "and that is, the work begun at the shops. So far as I know, the company will not object to that going on. It is one of the contradictions of the railroad world that Y. M. C. A.'s and other Christian influences are encouraged by the roads, while all the time the most unchristian and lawless acts may be committed in the official management of the roads themselves. Of course it is well understood that it pays a railroad to have in its employ men who are temperate, honest, and Christian. So I have no doubt the master mechanic will have the same courtesy shown him in the use of the room. But what I want you to do, Mr. Maxwell, is to see that my plan is carried out. Will you?"

Daily In His Word

The work of righteousness will be peace, and the service of righteousness, quietness and confidence forever.

Isaiah 32:17 NASB

Y ou understand what it was in general. You made a very favorable impression on the men. Go down there as often as you can. Get Milton Wright interested to provide something for the furnishing and expense of the coffee plant and reading tables. Will you do it?"

"Yes," replied Henry Maxwell. He stayed a little longer. Before he went away, he and the superintendent had a prayer together, and they parted with that silent hand grasp that seemed to them like a new token of their Christian discipleship and fellowship.

The pastor of the First Church went home stirred deeply by the events of the week. Gradually the truth was growing upon him that the pledge to do as Jesus would was working out a revolution in his parish and throughout the city. Every day added to the serious results of obedience to that pledge. Maxwell did not pretend to see the end. He was, in fact, only now at the very beginning of events that were destined to change the history of hundreds of families not only in Raymond but throughout the entire country. As he thought of Edward Norman and Rachel and Mr. Powers, and of the results that had already come from their actions, he could not help a feeling of intense interest in the probable effect if all the persons in the First Church who had made the pledge, faithfully kept it. Would they all keep it, or would some of them turn back when the cross became too heavy?

Daily In His Word

The Lord is not slack concerning His promise, as some count slackness, but is longsuffering toward us, not willing that any should perish but that all should come to repentance.

2 Peter 3:9 nkjv

He was asking this question the next morning as he sat in his study when the president of the Endeavor Society of his church called to see him.

"I suppose I ought not to trouble you with my case," said young Morris coming at once to his errand, "but I thought, Mr. Maxwell, that you might advise me a little."

"I'm glad you came. Go on, Fred." He had known the young man ever since his first year in the pastorate and loved and honored him for his consistent, faithful service in the church.

"Well, the fact is, I am out of a job. You know I've been doing reporter work on the morning *Sentinel* since I graduated last year. Well, last Saturday Mr. Burr asked me to go down the road Sunday morning and get the details of that train robbery at the Junction and write the thing up for the extra edition that came out Monday morning, just to get the start of the *News*. I refused to go, and Burr gave me my dismissal. He was in a bad temper, or I think perhaps he would not have done it. He has always treated me well before. Now, do you think Jesus would have done as I did? I ask because the other fellows say I was a fool not to do the work. I want to feel that a Christian acts from motives that may seem strange to others sometimes, but not foolish. What do you think?"

Daily In His Word

The foolishness of God is wiser than man's wisdom, and the weakness of God is stronger than man's strength.

1 Corinthians 1:25 NIV

I think you kept your promise, Fred. I cannot believe Jesus would do newspaper reporting on Sunday as you were asked to do it."

"Thank you, Mr. Maxwell. I felt a little troubled over it, but the longer I think it over the better I feel."

Morris rose to go, and his pastor rose and laid a loving hand on the young man's shoulder. "What are you going to do, Fred?"

"I don't know yet. I have thought some of going to Chicago or some large city."

"Why don't you try the *News*?"

"They are all supplied. I have not thought of applying there."

Maxwell thought a moment. "Come down to the *News* office with me, and let us see Norman about it."

So a few minutes later Edward Norman received into his room the minister and young Morris, and Maxwell briefly told the cause of the errand.

"I can give you a place on the *News*," said Norman with his keen look softened by a smile that made it winsome. "I want reporters who won't work Sundays. And what is more, I am making plans for a special kind of reporting which I believe you can develop because you are in sympathy with what Jesus would do."

Daily In His Word

"Maintain justice and do what is right, for my salvation is close at hand and my righteousness will soon be revealed."

Isaiah 56:1 NIV

He assigned Morris a definite task, and Maxwell started back to his study, feeling that kind of satisfaction (and it is a very deep kind) which a man feels when he has been even partly instrumental in finding an unemployed person a remunerative position.

He had intended to go right to his study, but on his way home he passed by one of Milton Wright's stores. He thought he would simply step in and shake hands with his parishioner and bid him Godspeed in what he had heard he was doing to put Christ into his business. But when he went into the office, Wright insisted on detaining him to talk over some of his new plans. Maxwell asked himself if this was the Milton Wright he used to know, eminently practical, businesslike, according to the regular code of the business world and viewing every thing first and foremost from the standpoint of, "Will it pay?"

"There is no use to disguise the fact, Mr. Maxwell, that I have been compelled to revolutionize the entire method of my business since I made that promise. I have been doing a great many things during the last twenty years in this store that I know Jesus would not do. But that is a small item compared with the number of things I begin to believe Jesus would do. My sins of commission have not been as many as those of omission in business relations."

Daily In His Word

Be devoted to one another in brotherly love; give preference to one another in honor; not lagging behind in diligence, fervent in Spirit, serving the Lord.

ROMANS 12:10–11 NASB

W hat was the first change you made?" He felt as if his sermon could wait for him in his study. As the interview with Milton Wright continued, he was not so sure but that he had found material for a sermon without going back to his study.

"I think the first change I had to make was in my thought of my employees. I came down here Monday morning after that Sunday and asked myself, 'What would Jesus do in His relation to these clerks, bookkeepers, office-boys, draymen, salesmen? Would He try to establish some sort of personal relation to them different from that which I have sustained all these years?' I soon answered this by saying, 'Yes.' Then came the question of what that relation would be and what it would lead me to do. I did not see how I could answer it to my satisfaction without getting all my employees together and having a talk with them. So I sent invitations to all of them, and we had a meeting out there in the warehouse Tuesday night. A good many things came out of that meeting. I can't tell you all. I tried to talk with the men as I imagined Jesus might. It was hard work, for I have not been in the habit of it and must have made some mistakes. But I can hardly make you believe, Mr. Maxwell, the effect of that meeting on some of the men. Before it closed I saw more than a dozen of them with tears on their faces."

Daily In His Word

As they listen, their secret thoughts will be laid bare, and they will fall down on their knees and worship God, declaring, "God is really here among you."

1 CORINTHIANS 14:25 NLT

I kept asking, 'What would Jesus do?' and the more I asked it the farther along it pushed me into the most intimate and loving relations with the men who have worked for me all these years. Every day something new is coming up and I am right now in the midst of a reconstruction of the entire business so far as its motive for being conducted is concerned. I am so practically ignorant of all plans for cooperation and its application to business that I am trying to get information from every possible source. I have lately made a special study of the life of Titus Salt, the great mill owner of Bradford, England, who afterward built that model town on the banks of the Aire. There is a good deal in his plans that will help me. But I have not yet reached definite conclusions in regard to all the details. I am not enough used to Jesus' methods. But see here."

Wright eagerly reached up into one of the pigeon holes of his desk and took out a paper.

"I have sketched out what seems to me like a program such as Jesus might go by in a business like mine. I want you to tell me what you think of it."

Daily In His Word

Never pay back evil for evil to anyone. Do things in such a way that everyone can see you are honorable. Do your part to live in peace with everyone, as much as possible.

ROMANS 12:17–18 NLT

"WHAT JESUS WOULD PROBABLY DO IN MILTON WRIGHT'S PLACE AS A BUSINESSMAN:

> *1) He would engage in the business first of all for the purpose of glorifying God, and not for the primary purpose of making money. 2) All money that might be made he would never regard as his own, but as trust funds to be used for the good of humanity. 3) His relations with all the persons in his employ would be the most loving and helpful. He could not help thinking of all of them in the light of souls to be saved. This thought would always be greater than his thought of making money in the business. 4) He would never do a single dishonest or questionable thing or try in any remotest way to get the advantage of anyone else in the same business. 5) The principle of unselfishness and helpfulness in the business would direct all its details. 6) Upon this principle he would shape the entire plan of his relations to his employees, to the people who were his customers and to the general business world with which he was connected."*

Henry Maxwell read this over slowly. It reminded him of his own attempts the day before to put into a concrete form his thought of Jesus' probable action. He was very thoughtful as he looked up and met Wright's eager gaze.

Daily In His Word
"Let your light so shine before men, that they may see your good works and glorify your Father in heaven."
MATTHEW 5:16 NKJV

Do you believe you can continue to make your business pay on these lines?"

"I do. Intelligent unselfishness ought to be wiser than intelligent selfishness, don't you think? If the men who work as employees begin to feel a personal share in the profits of the business and, more than that, a personal love for themselves on the part of the firm, won't the result be more care, less waste, more diligence, more faithfulness?"

"Yes, I think so. A good many other businessmen don't, do they? I mean as a general thing. How about your relations to the selfish world that is not trying to make money on Christian principles?"

"That complicates my action, of course."

"Does your plan contemplate what is coming to be known as cooperation?"

"Yes, as far as I have gone, it does. As I told you, I am studying out my details carefully. I am absolutely convinced that Jesus in my place would be absolutely unselfish. He would love all these men in His employ. He would consider the main purpose of all the business to be a mutual helpfulness, and would conduct it all so that God's kingdom would be evidently the first object sought. On those general principles, as I say, I am working. I must have time to complete the details."

Daily In His Word

Therefore judge nothing before the time, until the Lord come, who both will bring to light the hidden things of darkness, and will make manifest the counsels of the hearts: and then shall every man have praise of God.

1 CORINTHIANS 4:5 KJV

W hen Maxwell finally left he was profoundly impressed with the revolution that was being wrought already in the business. As he passed out of the store he caught something of the new spirit of the place. There was no mistaking the fact that Milton Wright's new relations to his employees were beginning even so soon, after less than two weeks, to transform the entire business. This was apparent in the conduct and faces of the clerks.

"If he keeps on he will be one of the most influential preachers in Raymond," said Maxwell to himself when he reached his study. The question rose as to his continuance in this course when he began to lose money by it, as was possible. He prayed that the Holy Spirit, who had shown Himself with growing power in the company of First Church disciples, might abide long with them all. And with that prayer on his lips and in his heart he began the preparation of a sermon in which he was going to present to his people on Sunday the subject of the saloon in Raymond, as he now believed Jesus would do.

Daily In His Word

Create in me a clean heart, O God, and renew a steadfast spirit within me. Do not cast me away from Your presence, and do not take Your Holy Spirit from me.

Psalm 51:10–11 NKJV

He had never preached against the saloon in this way before. He knew that the things he should say would lead to serious results. Nevertheless, he went on with his work, and every sentence he wrote or shaped was preceded with the question, "Would Jesus say that?" Once in the course of his study, he went down on his knees. No one except himself could know what that meant to him. When had he done that in his preparation of sermons, before the change that had come into his thought of discipleship? As he viewed his ministry now, he did not dare preach without praying long for wisdom. He no longer thought of his dramatic delivery and its effect on his audience. The great question with him now was, "What would Jesus do?"

Saturday night at the Rectangle witnessed some of the most remarkable scenes that Mr. Gray and his wife had ever known. The meetings had intensified with each night of Rachel's singing. A stranger passing through the Rectangle in the daytime might have heard a good deal about the meetings in one way and another. It cannot be said that up to that Saturday night there was any appreciable lack of oaths and impurity and heavy drinking. The Rectangle would not have acknowledged that it was growing any better or that even the singing had softened its outward manner. It had too much local pride in being "tough." But in spite of itself there was a yielding to a power it had never measured and did not know enough to resist beforehand.

Daily In His Word

All of your works will thank you, LORD, and your faithful followers will bless you. They will talk together about the glory of your kingdom; they will celebrate examples of your power.

PSALM 145:10–11 NLT

Gray had recovered his voice so that by Saturday he was able to speak. The fact that he was obliged to use his voice carefully made it necessary for the people to be very quiet if they wanted to hear. Gradually they had come to understand that this man was talking these many weeks and giving his time and strength to give them a knowledge of a Savior, all out of a perfectly unselfish love for them. Tonight the great crowd was as quiet as Henry Maxwell's decorous audience ever was. The fringe around the tent was deeper and the saloons were practically empty. The Holy Spirit had come at last, and Gray knew that one of the great prayers of his life was going to be answered.

And Rachel—her singing was the best, most wonderful, that Virginia or Jasper Chase had ever known. They came together again tonight, this time with Dr. West, who had spent all his spare time that week in the Rectangle with some charity cases. Virginia was at the organ, Jasper sat on a front seat looking up at Rachel, and the Rectangle swayed as one man towards the platform as she sang:

> "Just as I am, without one plea,
> But that Thy blood was shed for me,
> And that Thou bidst me come to Thee,
> O Lamb of God, I come, I come."

Daily In His Word

The Spirit is God's guarantee that he will give us everything he promised and that he has purchased us to be his own people. This is just one more reason for us to praise our glorious God.

EPHESIANS 1:14 NLT

Gray hardly said a word. He stretched out his hand with a gesture of invitation. And down the two aisles of the tent, broken, sinful creatures, men and women, stumbled towards the platform. One woman out of the street was near the organ. Virginia caught the look of her face, and for the first time in the life of the rich girl the thought of what Jesus was to the sinful woman came with a suddenness and power that was like nothing but a new birth. Virginia left the organ, went to her, looked into her face, and caught her hands in her own. The other girl trembled, then fell on her knees sobbing, with her head down upon the back of the rude bench in front of her, still clinging to Virginia. And Virginia, after a moment's hesitation, kneeled down by her, and the two heads were bowed close together.

Daily In His Word

Be thou exalted, LORD, in thine own strength: so will we sing and praise thy power.

PSALM 21:13 KJV

But when the people had crowded in a double row all about the platform, most of them kneeling and crying, a man in evening dress, different from the others, pushed through the seats and came and kneeled down by the side of the drunken man who had disturbed the meeting when Maxwell spoke. He kneeled within a few feet of Rachel Winslow, who was still singing softly. And as she turned for a moment and looked in his direction, she was amazed to see the face of Rollin Page! For a moment her voice faltered. Then she went on:

> *"Just as I am, thou wilt receive,*
> *Wilt welcome, pardon, cleanse, relieve,*
> *Because Thy promise I believe,*
> *O Lamb of God, I come, I come."*

Daily In His Word

"Worthy is the Lamb who was slain to receive power and riches and wisdom, and strength and honor and glory and blessing!"
REVELATION 5:12 NKJV

Chapter Ten

"If any man serve me, let him follow me."

It was nearly midnight before the services at the Rectangle closed. Gray stayed up long into Sunday morning, praying and talking with a little group of converts who in the great experiences of their new life, clung to the evangelist with a personal helplessness that made it as impossible for him to leave them as if they had been depending upon him to save them from physical death. Among these converts was Rollin Page.

Virginia and her uncle had gone home about eleven o'clock, and Rachel and Jasper Chase had gone with them as far as the avenue where Virginia lived. Dr. West had walked on a little way with them to his own home, and Rachel and Jasper had then gone on together to her mother's.

That was a little after eleven. It was now striking midnight, and Jasper Chase sat in his room staring at the papers on his desk and going over the last half hour with painful persistence.

He had told Rachel Winslow of his love for her, and she had not given him her love in return.

Daily In His Word
Think of more ways to encourage one another to outbursts of love and good deeds.

Hebrews 10:24 nlt

It would be difficult to know what was most powerful in the impulse that had moved him to speak to her tonight. He had yielded to his feelings without any special thought of results to himself, because he had felt so certain that Rachel would respond to his love. He tried to recall the impression she made on him when he first spoke to her.

Never had her beauty and her strength influenced him as tonight. While she was singing he saw and heard no one else. The tent swarmed with a confused crowd of faces and he knew he was sitting there hemmed in by a mob of people, but they had no meaning to him. He felt powerless to avoid speaking to her. He knew he should speak when they were alone.

Now that he had spoken, he felt that he had misjudged either Rachel or the opportunity. He knew, or thought he knew, that she had begun to care something for him. It was no secret between them that the heroine of Jasper's first novel had been his own ideal of Rachel and the hero in the story was himself, and they had loved each other in the book, and Rachel had not objected. No one else knew. The names and characters had been drawn with a subtle skill that revealed to Rachel, when she received a copy of the book from Jasper, the fact of his love for her, and she had not been offended. That was nearly a year ago.

Daily In His Word

Love does no wrong to anyone,
so love satisfies all of God's requirements.
Romans 13:10 nlt

Tonight he recalled the scene between them with every inflection and movement unerased from his memory. He even recalled the fact that he began to speak just at that point on the avenue where, a few days before, he had met Rachel walking with Rollin Page. He had wondered at the time what Rollin was saying.

"Rachel," Jasper had said, and it was the first time he had ever spoken her first name, "I never knew till tonight how much I loved you. Why should I try to conceal any longer what you have seen me look? You know I love you as my life. I can no longer hide it from you if I would."

The first intimation he had of a repulse was the trembling of Rachel's arm in his. She had allowed him to speak and had neither turned her face toward him nor away from him. She had looked straight on, and her voice was sad but firm and quiet when she spoke.

"Why do you speak to me now? I cannot bear it—after what we have seen tonight."

Daily In His Word

Dear friends, let us love one another, for love comes from God.

1 JOHN 4:7 NIV

Why—what—" he had stammered and then was silent.

Rachel withdrew her arm from his but still walked near him. Then he had cried out with the anguish of one who begins to see a great loss facing him where he expected a great joy.

"Rachel! Do you not love me? Is not my love for you as sacred as anything in all of life itself?"

She had walked silent for a few steps after that. They passed a street lamp. Her face was pale and beautiful. He had made a movement to clutch her arm and she had moved a little farther from him.

"No," she had replied. "There was a time I—cannot answer for that you—should not have spoken to me—now."

He had seen in these words his answer. He was extremely sensitive. Nothing short of a joyous response to his own love would ever have satisfied him. He could not think of pleading with her.

"Sometime—when I am more worthy?" he had asked in a low voice, but she did not seem to hear, and they had parted at her home, and he recalled vividly the fact that no goodnight had been said.

Daily In His Word

Whoever does not love does not know God, because God is love.

1 JOHN 4:8 NIV

Now as he went over the brief but significant scene he lashed himself for his foolish precipitancy. He had not reckoned on Rachel's tense, passionate absorption of all her feeling in the scenes at the tent which were so new in her mind. But he did not know her well enough even yet to understand the meaning of her refusal. When the clock in the First Church struck one he was still sitting at his desk staring at the last page of manuscript of his unfinished novel.

Rachel went up to her room and faced her evening's experience with conflicting emotions. Had she ever loved Jasper Chase? Yes. No. One moment she felt that her life's happiness was at stake over the result of her action. Another, she had a strange feeling of relief that she had spoken as she had. There was one great, overmastering feeling in her. The response of the wretched creatures in the tent to her singing, the swift, powerful, awesome presence of the Holy Spirit had affected her as never in all her life before. The moment Jasper had spoken her name and she realized that he was telling her of his love she had felt a sudden revulsion for him, as if he should have respected the supernatural events they had just witnessed. She felt as if it was not the time to be absorbed in anything less than the divine glory of those conversions.

Daily In His Word
Grace to all who love our Lord Jesus Christ with an undying love.
Ephesians 6:24 niv

The thought that all the time she was singing, with the one passion of her soul to touch the conscience of that tent full of sin, Jasper Chase had been unmoved by it except to love her for herself, gave her a shock as of irreverence on her part as well as on his. She could not tell why she felt as she did, only she knew that if he had not told her tonight she would still have felt the same toward him as she always had. What was that feeling? What had he been to her? Had she made a mistake? She went to her bookcase and took out the novel which Jasper had given her. Her face deepened in color as she turned to certain passages which she had read often and which she knew Jasper had written for her. She read them again. Somehow they failed to touch her strongly. She closed the book and let it lie on the table. She gradually felt that her thought was busy with the sights she had witnessed in the tent. Those faces, men and women, touched for the first time with the Spirit's glory—what a wonderful thing life was after all! The complete regeneration revealed in the sight of drunken, vile, debauched humanity kneeling down to give itself to a life of purity and Christlikeness—oh, it was surely a witness to the superhuman in the world!

Daily In His Word

He saved us, not because of any works of righteousness that we had done, but according to his mercy, through the water of rebirth and renewal by the Holy Spirit.

Titus 3:5 NRSV

And the face of Rollin Page by the side of that miserable wreck out of the gutter! She could recall as if she now saw it, Virginia crying, with her arms about her brother just before she left the tent, and Mr. Gray kneeling close by, and the girl Virginia had taken into her heart while she whispered something to her before she went out. All these pictures drawn by the Holy Spirit in the human tragedies brought to a climax there in the most abandoned spot in all Raymond, stood out in Rachel's memory now, a memory so recent that her room seemed for the time being to contain all the actors and their movements.

"No! No!" she said aloud. "He had no right to speak after all that! He should have respected the place where our thoughts should have been. I am sure I do not love him—not enough to give him my life!"

And after she had thus spoken, the evening's experience at the tent came crowding in again, thrusting out all other things. It is perhaps the most striking evidence of the tremendous spiritual factor which had now entered the Rectangle that Rachel felt, even when the great love of a strong man had come very near to her, that the spiritual manifestation moved her with an agitation far greater than anything Jasper had felt for her personally or she for him.

Daily In His Word

And this is love, that we walk after his commandments. This is the commandment.

2 JOHN 6 KJV

The people of Raymond awoke Sunday morning to a growing knowledge of events which were beginning to revolutionize many of the regular, customary habits of the town. Alexander Powers's action in the matter of the railroad frauds had created a sensation not only in Raymond but throughout the country. Edward Norman's daily changes of policy in the conduct of his paper had startled the community and caused more comment than any recent political event. Rachel Winslow's singing at the Rectangle meetings had made a stir in society and excited the wonder of all her friends.

Virginia's conduct, her presence every night with Rachel, her absence from the usual circle of her wealthy, fashionable acquaintances, had furnished a great deal of material for gossip and question. In addition to these events which centered about these persons who were so well known, there had been all through the city in very many homes and in business and social circles strange happenings. Nearly one hundred persons in Henry Maxwell's church had made the pledge to do everything after asking: "What would Jesus do?" and the result had been, in many cases, unheard-of actions. The city was stirred as it had never been before.

Daily In His Word

Purify me from my sins, and I will be clean; wash me, and I will be whiter than snow.

PSALM 51:7 NLT

As a climax to the week's events had come the spiritual manifestation at the Rectangle and the announcement which came to most people before church time of the actual conversion at the tent of nearly fifty of the worst characters in that neighborhood, together with the conversion of Rollin Page, the well-known society and club man.

It is no wonder that under the pressure of all this the First Church of Raymond came to the morning service in a condition that made it quickly sensitive to any large truth. Perhaps nothing had astonished the people more than the great change that had come over the minister, since he had proposed to them the imitation of Jesus in conduct. The dramatic delivery of his sermons no longer impressed them. The self-satisfied, contented, easy attitude of the fine figure and refined face in the pulpit had been displaced by a manner that could not be compared with the old style of his delivery. The sermon had become a message. It was no longer delivered. It was brought to them with a love, an earnestness, a passion, a desire, a humility that poured its enthusiasm about the truth and made the speaker no more prominent than he had to be as the living voice of God.

Daily In His Word

Preach the word of God. Be persistent, whether the time is favorable or not. Patiently correct, rebuke, and encourage your people with good teaching.

2 Timothy 4:2 nlt

His prayers were unlike any the people had heard before. They were often broken, even once or twice they had been actually ungrammatical in a phrase or two. When had Henry Maxwell so far forgotten himself in a prayer as to make a mistake of that sort? He knew that he had often taken as much pride in the diction and delivery of his prayers as of his sermons. Was it possible he now so abhorred the elegant refinement of a formal public petition that he purposely chose to rebuke himself for his previous precise manner of prayer? It is more likely that he had no thought of all that. His great longing to voice the needs and wants of his people made him unmindful of an occasional mistake. It is certain that he had never prayed so effectively as he did now.

There are times when a sermon has a value and power due to conditions in the audience rather than to anything new or startling or eloquent in the words said or arguments presented. Such conditions faced Henry Maxwell this morning as he preached against the saloon, according to his purpose determined on the week before. He had no new statements to make about the evil influence of the saloon in Raymond. What new facts were there?

Daily In His Word

The prayer of the righteous is powerful and effective.

JAMES 5:16 NRSV

He had no startling illustrations of the power of the saloon in business or politics. What could he say that had not been said by temperance orators a great many times? The effect of his message this morning owed its power to the unusual fact of his preaching about the saloon at all, together with the events that had stirred the people. He had never in the course of his ten years' pastorate mentioned the saloon as something to be regarded in the light of an enemy, not only to the poor and tempted, but to the business life of the place and the church itself. He spoke now with a freedom that seemed to measure his complete sense of conviction that Jesus would speak so. At the close he pleaded with the people to remember the new life that had begun at the Rectangle. The regular election of city officers was near at hand. The question of license would be an issue in the election. What of the poor creatures surrounded by the hell of drink while just beginning to feel the joy of deliverance from sin? Who could tell what depended on their environment? Was there one word to be said by the Christian disciple, businessman, citizen, in favor of continuing the license to crime and shame-producing institutions? Was not the most Christian thing they could do to act as citizens in the matter, fight the saloon at the polls, elect good men to the city offices, and clean the municipality?

Daily In His Word

So then you are no longer strangers and aliens, but you are fellow citizens with the saints, and are of God's household.

Ephesians 2:19 nasb

H̲ow much had prayers helped to make Raymond better while votes and actions had really been on the side of the enemies of Jesus? Would not Jesus do this? What disciple could imagine Him refusing to suffer or to take up His cross in this matter? How much had the members of the First Church ever suffered in an attempt to imitate Jesus? Was Christian discipleship a thing of conscience simply, of custom, of tradition? Where did the suffering come in? Was it necessary in order to follow Jesus' steps to go up Calvary as well as the Mount of Transfiguration?

His appeal was stronger at this point than he knew. It is not too much to say that the spiritual tension of the people reached its highest point right there. The imitation of Jesus which had begun with the volunteers in the church was working like leaven in the organization, and Henry Maxwell would even thus early in his life have been amazed if he could have measured the extent of desire on the part of his people to take up the cross.

Daily In His Word

My brethren, take the prophets, who spoke in the name of the Lord, as an example of suffering and patience. Indeed we count them blessed who endure.

JAMES 5:10–11 NKJV

While he was speaking this morning, before he closed with a loving appeal to the discipleship of two thousand years' knowledge of the Master, many a man and woman in the church was saying as Rachel had said so passionately to her mother: "I want to do something that will cost me something in the way of sacrifice." "I am hungry to suffer something." Truly, Mazzini was right when he said that no appeal is quite so powerful in the end as the call: "Come and suffer."

The service was over, the great audience had gone, and Maxwell again faced the company gathered in the lecture room as on the two previous Sundays. He had asked all to remain who had made the pledge of discipleship, and any others who wished to be included. The after-service seemed now to be a necessity. As he went in and faced the people there, his heart trembled. There were at least one hundred present. The Holy Spirit was never before so manifest. He missed Jasper Chase. But all the others were present. He asked Milton Wright to pray. The very air was charged with divine possibilities. What could resist such a baptism of power? How had they lived all these years without it?

Daily In His Word

For God did not give us a spirit of timidity, but a spirit of power, of love and of self-discipline.

2 Timothy 1:7 niv

Chapter Eleven

Donald Marsh, president of Lincoln College, walked home with Mr. Maxwell.

"I have reached one conclusion, Maxwell," said Marsh, speaking slowly. "I have found my cross and it is a heavy one, but I shall never be satisfied until I take it up and carry it." Maxwell was silent and the President went on.

"Your sermon today made clear to me what I have long been feeling I ought to do. 'What would Jesus do in my place?' I have asked the question repeatedly since I made my promise. I have tried to satisfy myself that He would simply go on as I have done, attending to the duties of my college work, teaching the classes in ethics and philosophy. But I have not been able to avoid the feeling that He would do something more. That something is what I do not want to do. It will cause me genuine suffering to do it. I dread it with all my soul. You may be able to guess what it is."

"Yes, I think I know. It is my cross too. I would almost rather do any thing else."

Daily In His Word
And being found in fashion as a man, he humbled himself, and became obedient unto death, even the death of the cross.

Philippians 2:8 KJV

Donald Marsh looked surprised, then relieved. Then he spoke sadly but with great conviction: "Maxwell, you and I belong to a class of professional men who have always avoided the duties of citizenship. We have lived in a little world of literature and scholarly seclusion, doing work we have enjoyed and shrinking from the disagreeable duties that belong to the life of the citizen. I confess with shame that I have purposely avoided the responsibility that I owe to this city personally. I understand that our city officials are a corrupt, unprincipled set of men, controlled in large part by the whiskey element and thoroughly selfish so far as the affairs of city government are concerned. Yet all these years I, with nearly every teacher in the college, have been satisfied to let other men run the municipality and have lived in a little world of my own, out of touch and sympathy with the real world of the people. 'What would Jesus do?' I have even tried to avoid an honest answer. I can no longer do so. My plain duty is to take a personal part in this coming election, go to the primaries, throw the weight of my influence, whatever it is, toward the nomination and election of good men, and plunge into the very depths of the entire horrible whirlpool of deceit, bribery, political trickery, and saloonism as it exists in Raymond today."

Daily In His Word

"The servant is not even thanked, because he is merely doing what he is supposed to do. In the same way, when you obey me you should say, 'We are not worthy of praise. We are servants who have simply done our duty.' "

LUKE 17:9–10 NLT

I would sooner walk up to the mouth of a cannon any time than do this. I dread it because I hate the touch of the whole matter. I would give almost any thing to be able to say, 'I do not believe Jesus would do anything of the sort.' But I am more and more persuaded that He would. This is where the suffering comes for me. It would not hurt me half so much to lose my position or my home. I loathe the contact with this municipal problem. I would so much prefer to remain quietly in my scholastic life with my classes in ethics and philosophy. But the call has come to me so plainly that I cannot escape. 'Donald Marsh, follow me. Do your duty as a citizen of Raymond at the point where your citizenship will cost you something. Help to cleanse this municipal stable, even if you do have to soil your aristocratic feelings a little.' Maxwell, this is my cross, I must take it up or deny my Lord."

"You have spoken for me also," replied Maxwell with a sad smile. "Why should I, simply because I am a minister, shelter myself behind my refined, sensitive feelings, and like a coward refuse to touch, except in a sermon possibly, the duty of citizenship?"

Daily In His Word

And it came to pass, that, as Jesus sat at meat in his house, many publicans and sinners sat also together with Jesus and his disciples: for there were many, and they followed him.
MARK 2:15 KJV

I am unused to the ways of the political life of the city. I have never taken an active part in any nomination of good men. There are hundreds of ministers like me. As a class we do not practice in the municipal life the duties and privileges we preach from the pulpit. 'What would Jesus do?' I am now at a point where, like you, I am driven to answer the question one way. My duty is plain. I must suffer. All my parish work, all my little trials or self-sacrifices are as nothing to me compared with the breaking into my scholarly, intellectual, self-contained habits, of this open, coarse, public fight for a clean city life. I could go and live at the Rectangle the rest of my life and work in the slums for a bare living, and I could enjoy it more than the thought of plunging into a fight for the reform of this whiskey-ridden city. It would cost me less. But, like you, I have been unable to shake off my responsibility. The answer to the question 'What would Jesus do?' in this case leaves me no peace except when I say, Jesus would have me act the part of a Christian citizen. Marsh, as you say, we professional men, ministers, professors, artists, literary men, scholars, have almost invariably been political cowards. We have avoided the sacred duties of citizenship either ignorantly or selfishly. Certainly Jesus in our age would not do that. We can do no less than take up this cross, and follow Him."

Daily In His Word

A final word: Be strong with the Lord's mighty power. Put on all of God's armor so that you will be able to stand firm against all strategies and tricks of the Devil.

Ephesians 6:10–11 NLT

The two men walked on in silence for a while. Finally President Marsh said: "We do not need to act alone in this matter. With all the men who have made the promise we certainly can have companionship, and strength even, of numbers. Let us organize the Christian forces of Raymond for the battle against rum and corruption. We certainly ought to enter the primaries with a force that will be able to do more than enter a protest. It is a fact that the saloon element is cowardly and easily frightened in spite of its lawlessness and corruption. Let us plan a campaign that will mean something because it is organized righteousness. Jesus would use great wisdom in this matter. He would employ means. He would make large plans. Let us do so. If we bear this cross let us do it bravely, like men."

They talked over the matter a long time and met again the next day in Maxwell's study to develop plans.

Daily In His Word

Before me every knee will bow; by me every tongue will swear. They will say of me, "In the LORD alone are righteousness and strength."

ISAIAH 45:23–24 NIV

The city primaries were called for Friday. Rumors of strange and unknown events to the average citizen were current that week in political circles throughout Raymond. The Crawford system of balloting for nominations was not in use in the state, and the primary was called for a public meeting at the courthouse.

The citizens of Raymond will never forget that meeting. It was so unlike any political meeting ever held in Raymond before that there was no attempt at comparison. The special officers to be nominated were mayor, city council, chief of police, city clerk, and city treasurer.

The evening *News* in its Saturday edition gave a full account of the primaries, and in the editorial columns Edward Norman spoke with a directness and conviction that the Christian people of Raymond were learning to respect deeply, because it was so evidently sincere and unselfish.

Daily In His Word

Act as free men and do not use your freedom as a covering for evil, but use it as bondslaves of God.

1 PETER 2:16 NASB

A part of that editorial is also a part of this history. We quote the following:

> It is safe to say that never before in the history of Raymond was there a primary like the one in the courthouse last night. It was, first of all, a complete surprise to the city politicians who have been in the habit of carrying on the affairs of the city as if they owned them, and everyone else was simply a tool or a cipher. The overwhelming surprise of the wire pullers last night consisted in the fact that a large number of the citizens of Raymond who have heretofore taken no part in the city's affairs, entered the primary and controlled it, nominating some of the best men for all the offices to be filled at the coming election.
>
> It was a tremendous lesson in good citizenship. President Marsh of Lincoln College, who never before entered a city primary, and whose face was not even known to the ward politicians, made one of the best speeches ever made in Raymond. It was almost ludicrous to see the faces of the men who for years have done as they pleased, when President Marsh rose to speak. Many of them asked, "Who is he?" The consternation deepened as the primary proceeded and it became evident that the oldtime ring of city rulers was outnumbered.

Daily In His Word

Remind the people to be subject to rulers and authorities, to be obedient, to be ready to do whatever is good.

TITUS 3:1 NIV

Rev. Henry Maxwell of the First Church, Milton Wright, Alexander Powers, Professors Brown, Willard, and Park of Lincoln College, Dr. West, Rev. George Main of the Pilgrim Church, Dean Ward of the Holy Trinity, and scores of well-known businessmen and professional men, most of them church members, were present, and it did not take long to see that they had all come with the one direct and definite purpose of nominating the best men possible. Most of those men had never before been seen in a primary. They were complete strangers to the politicians. But they had evidently profited by the politician's methods and were able by organized and united effort to nominate the entire ticket.

As soon as it became plain that the primary was out of their control, the regular ring withdrew in disgust and nominated another ticket. The News simply calls the attention of all decent citizens to the fact that this last ticket contains the names of whiskey men, and the line is sharply and distinctly drawn between the saloon and corrupt management such as we have known for years; and a clean, honest, capable, businesslike city administration, such as every good citizen ought to want.

Daily In His Word

Let the elders who rule well be counted worthy of double honor, especially those who labor in the word and doctrine.

1 TIMOTHY 5:17 NKJV

It is not necessary to remind the people of Raymond that the question of local option comes up at the election. That will be the most important question on the ticket. The crisis of our city affairs has been reached. The issue is squarely before us. Shall we continue the rule of rum and boodle and shameless incompetency, or shall we, as President Marsh said in his noble speech, rise as good citizens and begin a new order of things, cleansing our city of the worst enemy known to municipal honesty and doing what lies in our power to do with the ballot to purify our civic life?

The News *is positively and without reservation on the side of the new movement. We shall henceforth do all in our power to drive out the saloon and destroy its political strength. We shall advocate the election of the men nominated by the majority of citizens met in the first primary and we call upon all Christians, church members, lovers of right, purity, temperance, and the home, to stand by President Marsh and the rest of the citizens who have thus begun a long-needed reform in our city.*

Daily In His Word

Do not be deceived: Neither the sexually immoral nor idolaters nor adulterers nor male prostitutes nor homosexual offenders nor thieves nor the greedy nor drunkards nor slanderers nor swindlers will inherit the kingdom of God.

1 CORINTHIANS 6:9–10 NIV

President Marsh read this editorial and thanked God for Edward Norman. At the same time he understood well enough that every other paper in Raymond was on the other side. He did not underestimate the importance and seriousness of the fight which was only just begun. It was no secret that the *News* had lost enormously since it had been governed by the standard of "What would Jesus do?" And the question was, would the Christian people of Raymond stand by it? Would they make it possible for Norman to conduct a daily Christian paper? Or would the desire for what is called news in the way of crime, scandal, political partisanship of the regular sort, and a dislike to champion so remarkable a reform in journalism, influence them to drop the paper and refuse to give it their financial support? That was, in fact, the question Edward Norman was asking even while he wrote that Saturday editorial. He knew well enough that his actions expressed in that editorial would cost him very heavily from the hands of many businessmen in Raymond. And still, as he drove his pen over the paper, he asked another question, "What would Jesus do?" That question had become a part of this whole life now. It was greater than any other.

Daily In His Word

God stands in the congregation of the mighty; He judges among the gods. How long will you judge unjustly, and show partiality to the wicked? Selah. Defend the poor and fatherless; do justice to the afflicted and needy.

Psalm 82:1–3 nkjv

But for the first time in its history Raymond had seen the professional men, the teachers, the college professors, the doctors, the ministers, take political action and put themselves definitely and sharply in public antagonism to the evil forces that had so long controlled the machine of municipal government. The fact itself was astounding. President Marsh acknowledged to himself with a feeling of humiliation, that never before had he known what civic righteousness could accomplish. From that Friday night's work he dated for himself and his college a new definition of the worn phrase "the scholar in politics." Education for him and those who were under his influence ever after meant some element of suffering. Sacrifice must now enter into the factor of development.

At the Rectangle that week the tide of spiritual life rose high, and as yet showed no signs of flowing back. Rachel and Virginia went every night. Virginia was rapidly reaching a conclusion with respect to a large part of her money. She had talked it over with Rachel and they had been able to agree that if Jesus had a vast amount of money at His disposal He might do with some of it as Virginia planned.

Daily In His Word

This suffering is all part of what God has called you to. Christ, who suffered for you, is your example. Follow in his steps.

1 Peter 2:21 nlt

At any rate they felt that whatever He might do in such case would have as large an element of variety in it as the differences in persons and circumstances. There could be no one fixed Christian way of using money. The rule that regulated its use was unselfish utility.

But meanwhile the glory of the Spirit's power possessed all their best thought. Night after night that week witnessed miracles as great as walking on the sea or feeding the multitude with a few loaves and fishes. For what greater miracle is there than a regenerate humanity? The transformation of these coarse, brutal, sottish lives into praying, rapturous lovers of Christ, struck Rachel and Virginia every time with the feeling that people may have had when they saw Lazarus walk out of the tomb. It was an experience full of profound excitement for them.

Daily In His Word

"Very truly, I tell you, no one can see the kingdom of God without being born from above."

JOHN 3:3 NRSV

Rollin Page came to all the meetings. There was no doubt of the change that had come over him. Rachel had not yet spoken much with him. He was wonderfully quiet. It seemed as if he was thinking all the time. Certainly he was not the same person. He talked more with Gray than with any one else. He did not avoid Rachel, but he seemed to shrink from any appearance of seeming to renew the acquaintance with her. Rachel found it even difficult to express to him her pleasure at the new life he had begun to know. He seemed to be waiting to adjust himself to his previous relations before this new life began. He had not forgotten those relations. But he was not yet able to fit his consciousness into new ones.

The end of the week found the Rectangle struggling hard between two mighty opposing forces. The Holy Spirit was battling with all His supernatural strength against the saloon devil which had so long held a jealous grasp on its slaves. If the Christian people of Raymond once could realize what the contest meant to the souls newly awakened to a purer life it did not seem possible that the election could result in the old system of license. But that remained yet to be seen.

Daily In His Word

Therefore submit to God. Resist the devil and he will flee from you. Draw near to God and He will draw near to you.
JAMES 4:7–8 NKJV

The horror of the daily surroundings of many of the converts was slowly burning its way into the knowledge of Virginia and Rachel, and every night as they went uptown to their luxurious homes they carried heavy hearts.

"A good many of these poor creatures will go back again," Gray would say with sadness too deep for tears. "The environment does have a good deal to do with the character. It does not stand to reason that these people can always resist the sight and smell of the devilish drink about them. O Lord, how long shall Christian people continue to support by their silence and their ballots the greatest form of slavery known in America?"

He asked the question, and did not have much hope of an immediate answer. There was a ray of hope in the action of Friday night's primary, but what the result would be he did not dare to anticipate. The whiskey forces were organized, alert, aggressive, roused into unusual hatred by the events of the last week at the tent and in the city.

Daily In His Word

Be sober, be vigilant; because your adversary the devil walks about like a roaring lion, seeking whom he may devour.

1 PETER 5:8 NKJV

Would the Christian forces act as a unit against the saloon? Or would they be divided on account of their business interests or because they were not in the habit of acting all together as the whiskey power always did? That remained to be seen. Meanwhile the saloon reared itself about the Rectangle like some deadly viper hissing and coiling, ready to strike its poison into any unguarded part.

Saturday afternoon as Virginia was just stepping out of her house to go and see Rachel to talk over her new plans, a carriage drove up containing three of her fashionable friends. Virginia went out to the driveway and stood there talking with them. They had not come to make a formal call but wanted Virginia to go driving with them up on the boulevard. There was a band concert in the park. The day was too pleasant to be spent indoors.

"Where have you been all this time, Virginia?" asked one of the girls, tapping her playfully on the shoulder with a red silk parasol. "We hear that you have gone into the show business. Tell us about it."

Virginia colored, but after a moment's hesitation she frankly told something of her experience at the Rectangle. The girls in the carriage began to be really interested.

Daily In His Word
"I know full well that false teachers, like vicious wolves, will come in among you after I leave, not sparing the flock."
Acts 20:29 NLT

I tell you, girls, let's go 'slumming' with Virginia this afternoon instead of going to the band concert. I've never been down to the Rectangle. I've heard it's an awful wicked place and lots to see. Virginia will act as guide, and it would be"—"real fun" she was going to say, but Virginia's look made her substitute the word "interesting."

Virginia was angry. At first thought she said to herself she would never go under such circumstances. The other girls seemed to be of the same mind with the speaker. They chimed in with earnestness and asked Virginia to take them down there.

Suddenly she saw in the idle curiosity of the girls an opportunity. They had never seen the sin and misery of Raymond. Why should they not see it, even if their motive in going down there was simply to pass away an afternoon?

Daily In His Word

My friends, if anyone is detected in a transgression, you who have received the Spirit should restore such a one in a spirit of gentleness. Take care that you yourselves are not tempted.

GALATIANS 6:1 NRSV

CHAPTER TWELVE

*"For I come to set a man at variance against his father,
and the daughter against her mother, and the daughter-in-law
against her mother-in-law; and a man's foes shall be
they of his own household."*

*"Be ye therefore imitators of God, as beloved children;
and walk in love, even as Christ also loved you."*

Hadn't we better take a policeman along?" said one of the girls with a nervous laugh. "It really isn't safe down there, you know."

"There's no danger," said Virginia briefly.

"Is it true that your brother Rollin has been converted?" asked the first speaker, looking at Virginia curiously. It impressed her during the drive to the Rectangle that all three of her friends were regarding her with close attention as if she were peculiar.

"Yes, he certainly is."

"I understand he is going around to the clubs talking with his old friends there, trying to preach to them. Doesn't that seem funny?" said the girl with the red silk parasol.

Daily In His Word
Stay away from a foolish man, for you will not find knowledge on his lips.

PROVERBS 14:7 NIV

Virginia did not answer, and the other girls were beginning to feel sober as the carriage turned into a street leading to the Rectangle. As they neared the district they grew more and more nervous. The sights and smells and sounds which had become familiar to Virginia struck the senses of these refined, delicate society girls as something horrible. As they entered farther into the district, the Rectangle seemed to stare as with one great, bleary, beer-soaked countenance at this fine carriage with its load of fashionably dressed young women. "Slumming" had never been a fad with Raymond society, and this was perhaps the first time that the two had come together in this way. The girls felt that instead of seeing the Rectangle they were being made the objects of curiosity. They were frightened and disgusted.

"Let's go back. I've seen enough," said the girl who was sitting with Virginia.

Daily In His Word

The wisdom of the prudent is to give thought to their ways.

Proverbs 14:8 niv

They were at that moment just opposite a notorious saloon and gambling house. The street was narrow and the sidewalk crowded. Suddenly, out of the door of this saloon a young woman reeled. She was singing in a broken, drunken sob that seemed to indicate that she partly realized her awful condition, "Just as I am, without one plea—," and as the carriage rolled past she leered at it, raising her face so that Virginia saw it very close to her own. It was the face of the girl who had kneeled sobbing, that night with Virginia kneeling beside her and praying for her.

"Stop!" cried Virginia, motioning to the driver who was looking around. The carriage stopped, and in a moment she was out and had gone up to the girl and taken her by the arm. "Loreen!" she said, and that was all. The girl looked into her face, and her own changed into a look of utter horror. The girls in the carriage were smitten into helpless astonishment. The saloonkeeper had come to the door of the saloon and was standing there looking on with his hands on his hips. And the Rectangle from its windows, its saloon steps, its filthy sidewalk, gutter and roadway, paused, and with undisguised wonder stared at the two girls.

Daily In His Word

Awake, drunkards, and weep; and wail, all you wine drinkers.
Joel 1:5 nasb

Over the scene the warm sun of spring poured its mellow light. A faint breath of music from the bandstand in the park floated into the Rectangle. The concert had begun, and the fashion and wealth of Raymond were displaying themselves up town on the boulevard.

When Virginia left the carriage and went up to Loreen she had no definite idea as to what she would do or what the result of her action would be. She simply saw a soul that had tasted of the joy of a better life slipping back again into its old hell of shame and death. And before she had touched the drunken girl's arm she had asked only one question, "What would Jesus do?" That question was becoming with her, as with many others, a habit of life.

She looked around now as she stood close by Loreen, and the whole scene was cruelly vivid to her. She thought first of the girls in the carriage.

"Drive on; don't wait for me. I am going to see my friend home," she said calmly enough.

The girl with the red parasol seemed to gasp at the word "friend," when Virginia spoke it. She did not say anything.

The other girls seemed speechless.

Daily In His Word
"Blessed are the merciful, for they will be shown mercy."

MATTHEW 5:7 NIV

Go on. I cannot go back with you," said Virginia. The driver started the horses slowly. One of the girls leaned a little out of the carriage.

"Can't we—that is—do you want our help? Couldn't you—"

"No, no!" exclaimed Virginia. "You cannot be of any help to me."

The carriage moved on and Virginia was alone with her charge. She looked up and around. Many faces in the crowd were sympathetic. They were not all cruel or brutal. The Holy Spirit had softened a good deal of the Rectangle.

"Where does she live?" asked Virginia.

No one answered. It occurred to Virginia afterward when she had time to think it over, that the Rectangle showed a delicacy in its sad silence that would have done credit to the boulevard. For the first time it flashed across her that the immortal being who was flung like wreckage upon the shore of this early hell called the saloon, had no place that could be called home. The girl suddenly wrenched her arm from Virginia's grasp. In doing so she nearly threw Virginia down.

"You shall not touch me! Leave me! Let me go to hell! That's where I belong! The devil is waiting for me. See him!" she exclaimed hoarsely. She turned and pointed with a shaking finger at the saloonkeeper. The crowd laughed. Virginia stepped up to her and put her arm about her.

Daily In His Word

. . .and that they will come to their senses and escape from the trap of the devil, who has taken them captive to do his will.

2 TIMOTHY 2:26 NIV

Loreen," she said firmly, "come with me. You do not belong to hell. You belong to Jesus and He will save you. Come."

The girl suddenly burst into tears. She was only partly sobered by the shock of meeting Virginia.

Virginia looked around again. "Where does Mr. Gray live?" she asked. She knew that the evangelist boarded somewhere near the tent. A number of voices gave the direction.

"Come, Loreen, I want you to go with me to Mr. Gray's," she said, still keeping her hold of the swaying, trembling creature who moaned and sobbed and now clung to her as firmly as before she had repulsed her.

So the two moved on through the Rectangle toward the evangelist's lodging place. The sight seemed to impress the Rectangle seriously. It never took itself seriously when it was drunk, but this was different. The fact that one of the richest, most beautifully dressed girls in all Raymond was taking care of one of the Rectangle's most noted characters, who reeled along under the influence of liquor, was a fact astounding enough to throw more or less dignity and importance about Loreen herself.

Daily In His Word
But the Lord our God is merciful and forgiving, even though we have rebelled against him.

DANIEL 9:9 NLT

The event of Loreen's stumbling through the gutter dead drunk always made the Rectangle laugh and jest. But Loreen staggering along with a young lady from the society circles uptown supporting her, was another thing. The Rectangle viewed it with soberness and more or less wondering admiration.

When they finally reached Mr. Gray's lodging place the woman who answered Virginia's knock said that both Mr. and Mrs. Gray were out somewhere and would not be back until six o'clock.

Virginia had not planned anything farther than a possible appeal to the Grays, either to take charge of Loreen for a while or find some safe place for her until she was sober. She stood now at the door after the woman had spoken, and she was really at a loss to know what to do. Loreen sank down stupidly on the steps and buried her face in her arms. Virginia eyed the miserable figure of the girl with a feeling that she was afraid would grow into disgust.

Finally a thought possessed her that she could not escape. What was to hinder her from taking Loreen home with her? Why should not this homeless, wretched creature, reeking with the fumes of liquor, be cared for in Virginia's own home instead of being consigned to strangers in some hospital or house of charity?

Daily In His Word

The generous prosper and are satisfied; those who refresh others will themselves be refreshed.

PROVERBS 11:25 NLT

Virginia really knew very little about any such places of refuge. As a matter of fact, there were two or three such institutions in Raymond, but it is doubtful if any of them would have taken a person like Loreen in her present condition. But that was not the question with Virginia just now. "What would Jesus do with Loreen?" That was what Virginia faced, and she finally answered it by touching the girl again.

"Loreen, come. You are going home with me. We will take the car here at the corner."

Loreen staggered to her feet and, to Virginia's surprise, made no trouble. She had expected resistance or a stubborn refusal to move. When they reached the corner and took the car it was nearly full of people going uptown. Virginia was painfully conscious of the stare that greeted her and her companion as they entered. But her thought was directed more and more to the approaching scene with her grandmother. What would Madam Page say?

Daily In His Word

The eternal God is thy refuge,
and underneath are the everlasting arms.

DEUTERONOMY 33:27 KJV

Loreen was nearly sober now. But she was lapsing into a state of stupor. Virginia was obliged to hold fast to her arm. Several times the girl lurched heavily against her, and as the two went up the avenue a curious crowd of so-called civilized people turned and gazed at them. When she mounted the steps of her handsome house Virginia breathed a sigh of relief, even in the face of the interview with the grandmother, and when the door shut and she was in the wide hall with her homeless outcast, she felt equal to anything that might now come.

Madam Page was in the library. Hearing Virginia come in, she came into the hall. Virginia stood there supporting Loreen, who stared stupidly at the rich magnificence of the furnishings around her.

"Grandmother," Virginia spoke without hesitation and very clearly, "I have brought one of my friends from the Rectangle. She is in trouble and has no home. I am going to care for her here a little while."

Madam Page glanced from her granddaughter to Loreen in astonishment.

Daily In His Word

He said to His mother, "Woman, behold your son!" Then He said to the disciple, "Behold your mother!" And from that hour the disciple took her to his own home.

JOHN 19:26–27 NKJV

Did you say she is one of your friends?" she asked in a cold, sneering voice that hurt Virginia more than anything she had yet felt.

"Yes, I said so." Virginia's face flushed, but she seemed to recall a verse that Mr. Gray had used for one of his recent sermons, "A friend of publicans and sinners." Surely, Jesus would do this that she was doing.

"Do you know what this girl is?" asked Madam Page, in an angry whisper, stepping near Virginia.

"I know very well. She is an outcast. You need not tell me, Grandmother. I know it even better than you do. She is drunk at this minute. But she is also a child of God. I have seen her on her knees, repentant. And I have seen hell reach out its horrible fingers after her again. And by the grace of Christ I feel that the least that I can do is to rescue her from such peril. Grandmother, we call ourselves Christians. Here is a poor, lost human creature without a home, slipping back into a life of misery and possibly eternal loss, and we have more than enough. I have brought her here, and I shall keep her."

Daily In His Word

The Son of man came eating and drinking, and they say, Behold a man gluttonous, and a winebibber, a friend of publicans and sinners.

MATTHEW 11:19 KJV

Madam Page glared at Virginia and clenched her hands. All this was contrary to her social code of conduct. How could society excuse familiarity with the scum of the streets? What would Virginia's action cost the family in the way of criticism and loss of standing, and all that long list of necessary relations which people of wealth and position must sustain to the leaders of society? To Madam Page society represented more than the church or any other institution. It was a power to be feared and obeyed. The loss of its good-will was a loss more to be dreaded than anything except the loss of wealth itself.

She stood erect and stern and confronted Virginia, fully roused and determined. Virginia placed her arm about Loreen and calmly looked her grandmother in the face.

"You shall not do this, Virginia! You can send her to the asylum for helpless women. We can pay all the expenses. We cannot afford for the sake of our reputations to shelter such a person."

"Grandmother, I do not wish to do anything that is displeasing to you, but I must keep Loreen here tonight, and longer if it seems best."

Daily In His Word

"Which of these three do you think was a neighbor to the man who fell into the hands of robbers?" The expert in the law replied, "The one who had mercy on him." Jesus told him, "Go and do likewise."

LUKE 10:36–37 NIV

Then you can answer for the consequences! I do not stay in the same house with a miserable—," Madam Page lost her self-control. Virginia stopped her before she could speak the next word.

"Grandmother, this house is mine. It is your home with me as long as you choose to remain. But in this matter I must act as I fully believe Jesus would in my place. I am willing to bear all that society may say or do. Society is not my God. By the side of this poor soul I do not count the verdict of society as of any value."

"I shall not stay here, then!" said Madam Page. She turned suddenly and walked to the end of the hall. She then came back, and going up to Virginia said, with an emphasis that revealed her intensive excitement of passion, "You can always remember that you have driven your grandmother out of your house in favor of a drunken woman." Then, without waiting for Virginia to reply, she turned again and went upstairs. Virginia called a servant and soon had Loreen cared for. She was fast lapsing into a wretched condition. During the brief scene in the hall she had clung to Virginia so hard that her arm was sore from the clutch of the girl's fingers.

Daily In His Word

"Do not judge, or you too will be judged. For in the same way you judge others, you will be judged, and with the measure you use, it will be measured to you."

Matthew 7:1–2 niv

Chapter Thirteen

When the bell rang for tea she went down and her grandmother did not appear. She sent a servant to her room who brought back word that Madam Page was not there. A few minutes later Rollin came in. He brought word that his grandmother had taken the evening train for the South. He had been at the station to see some friends off, and had by chance met his grandmother as he was coming out. She had told him her reason for going.

Virginia and Rollin comforted each other at the tea table, looking at each other with earnest, sad faces.

"Rollin," said Virginia, and for the first time, almost, since his conversion she realized what a wonderful thing her brother's changed life meant to her, "do you blame me? Am I wrong?"

"No, dear, I cannot believe you are. This is very painful for us. But if you think this poor creature owes her safety and salvation to your personal care, it was the only thing for you to do. O Virginia, to think that we have all these years enjoyed our beautiful home and all these luxuries selfishly, forgetful of the multitudes like this woman! Surely Jesus in our places would do what you have done."

Daily In His Word

And do not neglect doing good and sharing, for with such sacrifices God is pleased.

Hebrews 13:16 nasb

And so Rollin comforted Virginia and counseled with her that evening. And of all the wonderful changes that she henceforth was to know on account of her great pledge, nothing affected her so powerfully as the thought of Rollin's change of life. Truly, this man in Christ was a new creature. Old things were passed away. Behold, all things in him had become new.

Dr. West came that evening at Virginia's summons and did everything necessary for the outcast. She had drunk herself almost into delirium. The best that could be done for her now was quiet nursing and careful watching and personal love. So, in a beautiful room, with a picture of Christ walking by the sea hanging on the wall, where her bewildered eyes caught daily something more of its hidden meaning, Loreen lay, tossed she hardly knew how into this haven, and Virginia crept nearer the Master than she had ever been, as her heart went out towards this wreck which had thus been flung torn and beaten at her feet.

Meanwhile the Rectangle awaited the issue of the election with more than usual interest; and Mr. Gray and his wife wept over the poor, pitiful creatures who, after a struggle with surroundings that daily tempted them, too often wearied of the struggle and, like Loreen, threw up their arms and went whirling over the cataract into the boiling abyss of their previous condition.

Daily In His Word
But God forbid that I should boast except in the cross of our Lord Jesus Christ, by whom the world has been crucified to me, and I to the world. For in Christ Jesus neither circumcision nor uncircumcision avails anything, but a new creation.

Galatians 6:14–15 nkjv

The after-meeting at the First Church was now eagerly established. Henry Maxwell went into the lecture room on the Sunday succeeding the week of the primary, and was greeted with an enthusiasm that made him tremble at first for its reality. He noted again the absence of Jasper Chase, but all the others were present, and they seemed drawn very close together by a bond of common fellowship that demanded and enjoyed mutual confidences. It was the general feeling that the spirit of Jesus was the spirit of very open, frank confession of experience. It seemed the most natural thing in the world, therefore, for Edward Norman to be telling all the rest of the company about the details of his newspaper.

"The fact is, I have lost a great deal of money during the last three weeks. I cannot tell just how much. I am losing a great many subscribers every day."

"What do the subscribers give as their reason for dropping the paper?" asked Mr. Maxwell. All the rest were listening eagerly.

"There are a good many different reasons. Some say they want a paper that prints all the news; meaning, by that, the crime details, sensations like prize fights, scandals and horrors of various kinds. Others object to the discontinuance of the Sunday edition."

Daily In His Word

That which we have seen and heard we declare to you, that you also may have fellowship with us; and truly our fellowship is with the Father and with His Son Jesus Christ.

1 JOHN 1:3 NKJV

I have lost hundreds of subscribers by that action, although I have made satisfactory arrangements with many of the old subscribers by giving them even more in the extra Saturday edition than they formerly had in the Sunday issue. My greatest loss has come from a falling off in advertisements, and from the attitude I have felt obliged to take on political questions. The last action has really cost me more than any other. The bulk of my subscribers are intensely partisan. I may as well tell you all frankly that if I continue to pursue the plan which I honestly believe Jesus would pursue in the matter of political issues and their treatment from a non-partisan and moral standpoint, the *News* will not be able to pay its operating expenses unless one factor in Raymond can be depended on."

He paused a moment and the room was very quiet. Virginia seemed specially interested. Her face glowed with interest. It was like the interest of a person who had been thinking hard of the same thing which Norman went on to mention.

"That one factor is the Christian element in Raymond."

Daily In His Word

Who is there to harm you if you prove zealous for what is good?

1 Peter 3:13 nasb

Say the *News* has lost heavily from the dropping off of people who do not care for a Christian daily, and from others who simply look upon a newspaper as a purveyor of all sorts of material to amuse or interest them, are there enough genuine Christian people in Raymond who will rally to the support of a paper such as Jesus would probably edit? Or are the habits of the church people so firmly established in their demand for the regular type of journalism that they will not take a paper unless it is stripped largely of the Christian and moral purpose? I may say in this fellowship gathering that owing to recent complications in my business affairs outside of my paper I have been obliged to lose a large part of my fortune. I had to apply the same rule of Jesus' probable conduct to certain transactions with other men who did not apply it to their conduct, and the result has been the loss of a great deal of money. As I understand the promise we made, we were not to ask any question about 'Will it pay?' but all our action was to be based on the one question, 'What would Jesus do?'"

Daily In His Word

. . .for whom I have suffered the loss of all things, and do count them but dung, that I may win Christ.

Philippians 3:8 KJV

Acting on that rule of conduct, I have been obliged to lose nearly all the money I have accumulated in my paper. It is not necessary for me to go into details. There is no question with me now, after the three weeks' experience I have had, that a great many men would lose vast sums of money under the present system of business if this rule of Jesus was honestly applied. I mention my loss here because I have the fullest faith in the final success of a daily paper conducted on the lines I have recently laid down, and I had planned to put into it my entire fortune in order to win final success. As it is now, unless, as I said, the Christian people of Raymond, the church members and professing disciples, will support the paper with subscriptions and advertisements, I cannot continue its publication on the present basis."

Virginia asked a question. She had followed Mr. Norman's confession with the most intense eagerness.

"Do you mean that a Christian daily ought to be endowed with a large sum like a Christian college in order to make it pay?"

"That is exactly what I mean."

Daily In His Word

But whatever things were gain to me, those things I have counted as loss for the sake of Christ.

Philippians 3:7 NASB

I had laid out plans for putting into the *News* such a variety of material in such a strong and truly interesting way that it would more than make up for whatever was absent from its columns in the way of unchristian matter. But my plans called for a very large output of money. I am very confident that a Christian daily such as Jesus would approve, containing only what He would print, can be made to succeed financially if it is planned on the right lines. But it will take a large sum of money to work out the plans."

"How much, do you think?" asked Virginia quietly.

Edward Norman looked at her keenly, and his face flushed a moment as an idea of her purpose crossed his mind. He had known her when she was a little girl in the Sunday school, and he had been on intimate business relations with her father.

"I should say half a million dollars in a town like Raymond could be well spent in the establishment of a paper such as we have in mind," he answered. His voice trembled a little. The keen look on his grizzled face flashed out with a stern but thoroughly Christian anticipation of great achievements in the world of newspaper life, as it had opened up to him within the last few seconds.

"Then," said Virginia, speaking as if the thought was fully considered, "I am ready to put that amount of money into the paper on the one condition, of course, that it be carried on as it has been begun."

Daily In His Word

He does not put out his money at interest.

PSALM 15:5 NASB

Thank God!" exclaimed Mr. Maxwell softly. Norman was pale. The rest were looking at Virginia. She had more to say.

"Dear friends," she went on, and there was a sadness in her voice that made an impression on the rest that deepened when they thought it over afterwards, "I do not want any of you to credit me with an act of great generosity. I have come to know lately that the money which I have called my own is not mine, but God's. If I, as steward of His, see some wise way to invest His money, it is not an occasion for vainglory or thanks from anyone simply because I have proved in my administration of the funds He has asked me to use for His glory. I have been thinking of this very plan for some time. The fact is, dear friends, that in our coming fight with the whiskey power in Raymond—and it has only just begun— we shall need the *News* to champion the Christian side. You all know that all the other papers are for the saloon. As long as the saloon exists, the work of rescuing dying souls at the Rectangle is carried on at a terrible disadvantage. What can Mr. Gray do with his gospel meetings when half his converts are drinking people, daily tempted and enticed by the saloon on every corner? It would be giving up to the enemy to allow the *News* to fail."

Daily In His Word

Moreover it is required in stewards that one be found faithful.

1 CORINTHIANS 4:2 NKJV

I have great confidence in Mr. Norman's ability. I have not seen his plans, but I have the same confidence that he has in making the paper succeed if it is carried forward on a large enough scale. I cannot believe that Christian intelligence in journalism will be inferior to unchristian intelligence, even when it comes to making the paper pay financially. So that is my reason for putting this money—God's, not mine—into this powerful agent for doing as Jesus would do. If we can keep such a paper going for one year, I shall be willing to see that amount of money used in that experiment. Do not thank me. Do not consider my doing it a wonderful thing. What have I done with God's money all these years but gratify my own selfish personal desires? What can I do with the rest of it but try to make some reparation for what I have stolen from God? That is the way I look at it now. I believe it is what Jesus would do."

Over the lecture room swept that unseen yet distinctly felt wave of Divine Presence.

Daily In His Word

In Him you also trusted, after you heard the word of truth, the gospel of your salvation; in whom also, having believed, you were sealed with the Holy Spirit of promise.

EPHESIANS 1:13 NKJV

No one spoke for a while. Mr. Maxwell standing there, where the faces lifted their intense gaze into his, felt what he had already felt—a strange setting back out of the nineteenth century into the first, when the disciples had all things in common, and a spirit of fellowship must have flowed freely between them such as the First Church of Raymond had never before known. How much had his church membership known of this fellowship in daily interests before this little company had begun to do as they believed Jesus would do? It was with difficulty that he thought of his present age and surroundings. The same thought was present with all the rest, also. There was an unspoken comradeship such as they had never known. It was present with them while Virginia was speaking, and during the silence that followed. If it had been defined by any of them it would perhaps have taken some such shape as this: "If I shall, in the course of my obedience to my promise, meet with loss or trouble in the world, I can depend upon the genuine, practical sympathy and fellowship of any other Christian in this room who has, with me, made the pledge to do all things by the rule, 'What would Jesus do?'"

Daily In His Word

God will surely do this for you, for he always does just what he says, and he is the one who invited you into this wonderful friendship with his Son, Jesus Christ our Lord.

1 CORINTHIANS 1:9 NLT

All this, the distinct wave of spiritual power emphasized. It had the effect that a physical miracle may have had on the early disciples in giving them a feeling of confidence in the Lord that helped them to face loss and martyrdom with courage and even joy.

Before they went away this time there were several confidences like those of Edward Norman's. Some of the young men told of loss of places owing to their honest obedience to their promise. Alexander Powers spoke briefly of the fact that the Commission had promised to take action on his evidence at the earliest date possible.

Daily In His Word

"As a mother comforts her child, so will I comfort you."
ISAIAH 66:13 NIV

CHAPTER FOURTEEN

But more than any other feeling at this meeting rose the tide of fellowship for one another. Maxwell watched it, trembling for its climax which he knew was not yet reached. When it was, where would it lead them? He did not know, but he was not unduly alarmed about it. Only he watched with growing wonder the results of that simple promise as it was being obeyed in these various lives. Those results were already being felt all over the city. Who could measure their influence at the end of a year?

One practical form of this fellowship showed itself in the assurances which Edward Norman received of support for his paper. There was a general flocking toward him when the meeting closed, and the response to his appeal for help from the Christian disciples in Raymond was fully understood by this little company. The value of such a paper in the homes and in behalf of good citizenship, especially at the present crisis in the city, could not be measured. It remained to be seen what could be done now that the paper was endowed so liberally. But it still was true, as Norman insisted, that money alone could not make the paper a power. It must receive the support and sympathy of the Christians in Raymond before it could be counted as one of the great forces of the city.

Daily In His Word
You will be made rich in every way so that you can be generous on every occasion, and through us your generosity will result in thanksgiving to God.

2 CORINTHIANS 9:11 NIV

The week that followed this Sunday meeting was one of great excitement in Raymond. It was the week of the election. President Marsh, true to his promise, took up his cross and bore it manfully, but with shuddering, with groans and even tears, for his deepest conviction was touched, and he tore himself out of the scholarly seclusion of years with a pain and anguish that cost him more than anything he had ever done as a follower of Christ. With him were a few of the college professors who had made the pledge in the First Church. Their experience and suffering were the same as his; for their isolation from all the duties of citizenship had been the same. The same was also true of Henry Maxwell, who plunged into the horror of this fight against whiskey and its allies with a sickening dread of each day's new encounter with it. For never before had he borne such a cross. He staggered under it, and in the brief intervals when he came in from the work and sought the quiet of his study for rest, the sweat broke out on his forehead, and he felt the actual terror of one who marches into unseen, unknown horrors. Looking back on it afterwards he was amazed at his experience. He was not a coward, but he felt the dread that any man of his habits feels when confronted suddenly with a duty which carries with it the doing of certain things so unfamiliar that the actual details connected with it betray his ignorance and fill him with the shame of humiliation.

Daily In His Word

The building where they were meeting shook,
and they were all filled with the Holy Spirit.
And they preached God's message with boldness.

Acts 4:31 nlt

When Saturday, the election day, came, the excitement rose to its height. An attempt was made to close all the saloons. It was only partly successful. There was a great deal of drinking going on all day. The Rectangle boiled and heaved and cursed and turned its worst side out to the gaze of the city. Gray had continued his meetings during the week, and the results had been even greater than he had dared to hope. When Saturday came, it seemed to him that the crisis in his work had been reached. The Holy Spirit and the Satan of rum seemed to rouse up to a desperate conflict. The more interest in the meetings, the more ferocity and vileness outside. The saloon men no longer concealed their feelings. Open threats of violence were made. Once during the week Gray and his little company of helpers were assailed with missiles of various kinds as they left the tent late at night. The police sent down a special force, and Virginia and Rachel were always under the protection of either Rollin or Dr. West. Rachel's power in song had not diminished. Rather, with each night, it seemed to add to the intensity and reality of the Spirit's presence.

Gray had at first hesitated about having a meeting that night. But he had a simple rule of action, and was always guided by it. The Spirit seemed to lead him to continue the meeting, and so Saturday night he went on as usual.

Daily In His Word

"Don't be afraid of those who want to kill you. They can only kill your body; they cannot touch your soul."

Matthew 10:28 NLT

The excitement all over the city had reached its climax when the polls closed at six o'clock. Never before had there been such a contest in Raymond. The issue of license or no-license had never been an issue under such circumstances. Never before had such elements in the city been arrayed against each other. It was an unheard-of thing that the president of Lincoln College, the pastor of the First Church, the dean of the Cathedral, the professional men living in fine houses on the boulevard, should come personally into the wards, and by their presence and their example represent the Christian conscience of the place. The ward politicians were astonished at the sight. However, their astonishment did not prevent their activity. The fight grew hotter every hour, and when six o'clock came neither side could have guessed at the result with any certainty. Every one agreed that never before had there been such an election in Raymond, and both sides awaited the announcement of the result with the greatest interest.

Daily In His Word

In God I have put my trust;
I will not fear what flesh can do unto me.

Psalm 56:4 kjv

It was after ten o'clock when the meeting at the tent was closed. It had been a strange and, in some respects, a remarkable meeting. Maxwell had come down again at Gray's request. He was completely worn out by the day's work, but the appeal from Gray came to him in such a form that he did not feel able to resist it. President Marsh was also present. He had never been to the Rectangle, and his curiosity was aroused from what he had noticed of the influence of the evangelist in the worst part of the city. Dr. West and Rollin had come with Rachel and Virginia; and Loreen, who still stayed with Virginia, was present near the organ, in her right mind, sober, with a humility and dread of herself that kept her as close to Virginia as a faithful dog. All through the service she sat with bowed head, weeping a part of the time, sobbing when Rachel sang the song, "I was a wandering sheep," clinging with almost visible, tangible yearning to the one hope she had found, listening to prayer and appeal and confession all about her like one who was a part of a new creation, yet fearful of her right to share in it fully.

Daily In His Word

For ye were as sheep going astray; but are now returned unto the Shepherd and Bishop of your souls.

1 Peter 2:25 KJV

The tent had been crowded. As on some other occasions, there was more or less disturbance on the outside. This had increased as the night advanced, and Gray thought it wise not to prolong the service.

Once in a while a shout as from a large crowd swept into the tent. The returns from the election were beginning to come in, and the Rectangle had emptied every lodging house, den and hovel into the streets.

In spite of these distractions Rachel's singing kept the crowd in the tent from dissolving. There were a dozen or more conversions. Finally the people became restless and Gray closed the service, remaining a little while with the converts.

Rachel, Virginia, Loreen, Rollin and the Doctor, President Marsh, Mr. Maxwell and Dr. West went out together, intending to go down to the usual waiting place for their car. As they came out of the tent they were at once aware that the Rectangle was trembling on the verge of a drunken riot, and as they pushed through the gathering mobs in the narrow streets they began to realize that they themselves were objects of great attention.

"There he is—the bloke in the tall hat! He's the leader! shouted a rough voice. President Marsh, with his erect, commanding figure, was conspicuous in the little company.

Daily In His Word

Behold, I send you forth as sheep in the midst of wolves: be ye therefore wise as serpents, and harmless as doves.

Matthew 10:16 KJV

How has the election gone? It is too early to know the result yet, isn't it?" He asked the question aloud, and a man answered:

"They say second and third wards have gone almost solid for no-license. If that is so, the whiskey men have been beaten."

"Thank God! I hope it is true!" exclaimed Maxwell. "Marsh, we are in danger here. Do you realize our situation? We ought to get the ladies to a place of safety."

"That is true," said Marsh gravely. At that moment a shower of stones and other missiles fell over them. The narrow street and sidewalk in front of them was completely choked with the worst elements of the Rectangle.

"This looks serious," said Maxwell. With Marsh and Rollin and Dr. West he started to go forward through a small opening, Virginia, Rachel, and Loreen following close and sheltered by the men, who now realized something of their danger. The Rectangle was drunk and enraged. It saw in Marsh and Maxwell two of the leaders in the election contest which had perhaps robbed them of their beloved saloon.

"Down with the aristocrats!" shouted a shrill voice, more like a woman's than a man's. A shower of mud and stones followed. Rachel remembered afterwards that Rollin jumped directly in front of her and received on his head and chest a number of blows that would probably have struck her if he had not shielded her from them.

Daily In His Word

Let us behave decently, as in the daytime,
not in orgies and drunkenness.

ROMANS 13:13 NIV

And just then, before the police reached them, Loreen darted forward in front of Virginia and pushed her aside, looking up and screaming. It was so sudden that no one had time to catch the face of the one who did it. But out of the upper window of a room, over the very saloon where Loreen had come out a week before, someone had thrown a heavy bottle. It struck Loreen on the head and she fell to the ground. Virginia turned and instantly kneeled down by her. The police officers by that time had reached the little company.

President Marsh raised his arm and shouted over the howl that was beginning to rise from the wild beast in the mob.

"Stop! You've killed a woman!" The announcement partly sobered the crowd.

"Is it true?" Maxwell asked it, as Dr. West kneeled on the other side of Loreen, supporting her.

"She's dying!" said Dr. West briefly.

Loreen opened her eyes and smiled at Virginia, who wiped the blood from her face and then bent over and kissed her. Loreen smiled again, and the next minute her soul was in Paradise.

Daily In His Word

"Death is swallowed up in victory." "O Death, where is your sting? O Hades, where is your victory?"

1 Corinthians 15:54–55 NKJV

CHAPTER FIFTEEN

"He that followeth me shall not walk in darkness."

The body of Loreen lay in state at the Page mansion on the avenue. It was Sunday morning and the clear, sweet spring air, just beginning to breathe over the city the perfume of early blossoms in the woods and fields, swept over the casket from one of the open windows at the end of the grand hall. The church bells were ringing and people on the avenue going by to service turned curious, inquiring looks up at the great house and then went on, talking of the recent events which had so strangely entered into and made history in the city.

At the First Church, Mr. Maxwell, bearing on his face marks of the scene he had been through, confronted an immense congregation, and spoke to it with a passion and a power that came so naturally out of the profound experiences of the day before that his people felt for him something of the old feeling of pride they once had in his dramatic delivery. Only this was with a different attitude. And all through his impassioned appeal this morning, there was a note of sadness and rebuke and stern condemnation that made many of the members pale with self-accusation or with inward anger.

Daily In His Word

For the eyes of the Lord are over the righteous, and his ears are open unto their prayers: but the face of the Lord is against them that do evil.

1 PETER 3:12 KJV

For Raymond had awakened that morning to the fact that the city had gone for license after all. The rumor at the Rectangle that the second and third wards had gone no-license proved to be false. It was true that the victory was won by a very meager majority. But the result was the same as if it had been overwhelming. Raymond had voted to continue for another year the saloon. The Christians of Raymond stood condemned by the result. More than a hundred professing Christian disciples had failed to go to the polls, and many more than that number had voted with the whiskey men. If all the church members of Raymond had voted against the saloon, it would today be outlawed instead of crowned king of the municipality. For that had been the fact in Raymond for years. The saloon ruled. No one denied that. What would Jesus do? And this woman who had been brutally struck down by the very hand that had assisted so eagerly to work her earthly ruin what of her? Was it anything more than the logical sequence of the whole horrible system of license, that for another year the very saloon that received her so often and compassed her degradation, from whose very spot the weapon had been hurled that struck her dead, would, by the law which the Christian people of Raymond voted to support, perhaps open its doors tomorrow and damn a hundred Loreens before the year had drawn to its bloody close?

Daily In His Word

God is a righteous judge, and a God
who has indignation every day.

PSALM 7:11 NRSV

All this, with a voice that rang and trembled and broke in sobs of anguish for the result, did Henry Maxwell pour out upon his people that Sunday morning. And men and women wept as he spoke. President Marsh sat there, his usual erect, handsome, firm, bright self-confident bearing all gone; his head bowed upon his breast, the great tears rolling down his cheeks, unmindful of the fact that never before had he shown outward emotion in a public service. Edward Norman near by sat with his clear-cut, keen face erect, but his lip trembled and he clutched the end of the pew with a feeling of emotion that struck deep into his knowledge of the truth as Maxwell spoke it. No man had given or suffered more to influence public opinion that week than Norman. The thought that the Christian conscience had been aroused too late or too feebly, lay with a weight of accusation upon the heart of the editor. What if he had begun to do as Jesus would have done, long ago? Who could tell what might have been accomplished by this time! And up in the choir, Rachel Winslow, with her face bowed on the railing of the oak screen, gave way to a feeling which she had not allowed yet to master her, but it so unfitted her for her part that when Mr. Maxwell finished and she tried to sing the closing solo after the prayer, her voice broke, and for the first time in her life she was obliged to sit down, sobbing, and unable to go on.

Daily In His Word

And this is the victory that conquers the world, our faith. Who is it that conquers the world but the one who believes that Jesus is the Son of God?

1 JOHN 5:4–5 NRSV

Over the church, in the silence that followed this strange scene, sobs and the noise of weeping arose. When had the First Church yielded to such a baptism of tears? What had become of its regular, precise, conventional order of service, undisturbed by any vulgar emotion and unmoved by any foolish excitement? But the people had lately had their deepest convictions touched. They had been living so long on their surface feelings that they had almost forgotten the deeper wells of life. Now that they had broken the surface, the people were convicted of the meaning of their discipleship.

Mr. Maxwell did not ask, this morning, for volunteers to join those who had already pledged to do as Jesus would. But when the congregation had finally gone, and he had entered the lecture room, it needed but a glance to show him that the original company of followers had been largely increased. The meeting was tender; it glowed with the Spirit's presence; it was alive with strong and lasting resolve to begin a war on the whiskey power in Raymond that would break its reign forever.

Daily In His Word

Keep me as the apple of Your eye; hide me under the shadow of Your wings, from the wicked who oppress me.

PSALM 17:8–9 NKJV

Since the first Sunday when the first company of volunteers had pledged themselves to do as Jesus would do, the different meetings had been characterized by distinct impulses or impressions. Today, the entire force of the gathering seemed to be directed to this one large purpose. It was a meeting full of broken prayers of contrition, of confession, of strong yearning for a new and better city life. And all through it ran one general cry for deliverance from the saloon and its awful curse.

But if the First Church was deeply stirred by the events of the last week, the Rectangle also felt moved strangely in its own way. The death of Loreen was not in itself so remarkable a fact. It was her recent acquaintance with the people from the city that lifted her into special prominence and surrounded her death with more than ordinary importance. Every one in the Rectangle knew that Loreen was at this moment lying in the Page mansion up on the avenue. Exaggerated reports of the magnificence of the casket had already furnished material for eager gossip. The Rectangle was excited to know the details of the funeral. Would it be public? What did Miss Page intend to do?

Daily In His Word

We were burdened beyond measure, above strength, so that we despaired even of life. Yes, we had the sentence of death in ourselves, that we should not trust in ourselves but in God who raises the dead.

2 CORINTHIANS 1:8–9 NKJV

The Rectangle had never before mingled even in this distant personal manner with the aristocracy on the boulevard. The opportunities for doing so were not frequent. Gray and his wife were besieged by inquirers who wanted to know what Loreen's friends and acquaintances were expected to do in paying their last respects to her. For her acquaintance was large and many of the recent converts were among her friends.

So that is how it happened that Monday afternoon, at the tent, the funeral service of Loreen was held before an immense audience that choked the tent and overflowed beyond all previous bounds. Gray had gone up to Virginia's and, after talking it over with her and Maxwell, the arrangement had been made.

"I am and always have been opposed to large public funerals," said Gray, whose complete wholesome simplicity of character was one of its great sources of strength; "but the cry of the poor creatures who knew Loreen is so earnest that I do not know how to refuse this desire to see her and pay her poor body some last little honor. What do you think, Mr. Maxwell? I will be guided by your judgment in the matter. I am sure that whatever you and Miss Page think best, will be right."

Daily In His Word

"Be careful not to do your 'acts of righteousness' before men, to be seen by them. If you do, you will have no reward from your Father in heaven."

Matthew 6:1 niv

I feel as you do," replied Mr. Maxwell. "Under the circumstances I have a great distaste for what seems like display at such times. But this seems different. The people at the Rectangle will not come here to service. I think the most Christian thing will be to let them have the service at the tent. Do you think so, Miss Virginia?"

"Yes," said Virginia. "Poor soul! I do not know but that some time I shall know she gave her life for mine. We certainly cannot and will not use the occasion for vulgar display. Let her friends be allowed the gratification of their wishes. I see no harm in it."

So the arrangements were made, with some difficulty, for the service at the tent; and Virginia with her uncle and Rollin, accompanied by Maxwell, Rachel and President Marsh, and the quartet from the First Church, went down and witnessed one of the strange things of their lives.

It happened that that afternoon a somewhat noted newspaper correspondent was passing through Raymond on his way to an editorial convention in a neighboring city. He heard of the contemplated service at the tent and went down. His description of it was written in a graphic style that caught the attention of very many readers the next day.

Daily In His Word

He came and preached peace to you who were far away and peace to those who were near.

Ephesians 2:17 niv

A fragment of his account belongs to this part of the history of Raymond:

> *There was a very unique and unusual funeral service held here this afternoon at the tent of an evangelist, Rev. John Gray, down in the slum district known as the Rectangle. The occasion was caused by the killing of a woman during an election riot last Saturday night. It seems she had been recently converted during the evangelist's meetings, and was killed while returning from one of the meetings in company with other converts and some of her friends. She was a common street drunkard, and yet the services at the tent were as impressive as any I ever witnessed in a metropolitan church over the most distinguished citizen.*
>
> *In the first place, a most exquisite anthem was sung by a trained choir. It struck me, of course—being a stranger in the place—with considerable astonishment to hear voices like those one naturally expects to hear only in great churches or concerts, at such a meeting as this. But the most remarkable part of the music was a solo sung by a strikingly beautiful young woman, a Miss Winslow who, if I remember right, is the young singer who was sought for by Crandall the manager of National Opera, and who for some reason refused to accept his offer to go on the stage.*

Daily In His Word

I will sing about your power. I will shout with joy each morning because of your unfailing love. For you have been my refuge, a place of safety in the day of distress.

Psalm 59:16 NLT

She had a most wonderful manner in singing, and everybody was weeping before she had sung a dozen words. That, of course, is not so strange an effect to be produced at a funeral service, but the voice itself was one of thousands. I understand Miss Winslow sings in the First Church of Raymond and could probably command almost any salary as a public singer. She will probably be heard from soon. Such a voice could win its way anywhere.

The service aside from the singing was peculiar. The evangelist, a man of apparently very simple, unassuming style, spoke a few words, and he was followed by a fine-looking man, the Rev. Henry Maxwell, pastor of the First Church of Raymond. Mr. Maxwell spoke of the fact that the dead woman had been fully prepared to go, but he spoke in a peculiarly sensitive manner of the effect of the liquor business on the lives of men and women like this one. Raymond, of course, being a railroad town and the center of the great packing interests for this region, is full of saloons. I caught from the minister's remarks that he had only recently changed his views in regard to license. He certainly made a very striking address, and yet it was in no sense inappropriate for a funeral.

Daily In His Word

For the mind set on the flesh is death, but the mind set on the Spirit is life and peace.

Romans 8:6 nasb

Then followed what was perhaps the queer part of this strange service. The women in the tent, at least a large part of them up near the coffin, began to sing in a soft, tearful way, 'I was a wandering sheep.' Then while the singing was going on, one row of women stood up and walked slowly past the casket, and as they went by, each one placed a flower of some kind upon it. Then they sat down and another row filed past, leaving their flowers. All the time the singing continued softly like rain on a tent cover when the wind is gentle. It was one of the simplest and at the same time one of the most impressive sights I ever witnessed. The sides of the tent were up, and hundreds of people who could not get in, stood outside, all as still as death itself, with wonderful sadness and solemnity for such rough looking people. There must have been a hundred of these women, and I was told many of them had been converted at the meetings just recently. I cannot describe the effect of that singing. Not a man sang a note. All women's voices, and so soft, and yet so distinct, that the effect was startling.

Daily In His Word

Weeping may last for the night, but a shout of joy comes in the morning.

Psalm 30:5 nasb

*The service closed with another solo by Miss
Winslow, who sang, 'There were ninety and nine.'
And then the evangelist asked them all to bow their
heads while he prayed. I was obliged in order to
catch my train to leave during the prayer, and the
last view I caught of the service as the train went
by the shops was a sight of the great crowd pouring
out of the tent and forming in open ranks while the
coffin was borne out by six of the women. It is a long
time since I have seen such a picture in this unpoetic
Republic.*

If Loreen's funeral impressed a passing stranger like this, it is not difficult to imagine the profound feelings of those who had been so intimately connected with her life and death. Nothing had ever entered the Rectangle that had moved it so deeply as Loreen's body in that coffin. And the Holy Spirit seemed to bless with special power the use of this senseless clay. For that night He swept more than a score of lost souls, mostly women, into the fold of the Good Shepherd.

Daily In His Word

Jesus is the great Shepherd of the sheep by an everlasting covenant, signed with his blood. To him be glory forever and ever.

HEBREWS 13:20-21 NLT

CHAPTER SIXTEEN

No one in all Raymond, including the Rectangle, felt Loreen's death more keenly than Virginia. It came like a distinct personal loss to her. That short week while the girl had been in her home had opened Virginia's heart to a new life. She was talking it over with Rachel the day after the funeral. Thee were sitting in the hall of the Page mansion.

"I am going to do something with my money to help those women to a better life." Virginia looked over to the end of the hall where, the day before, Loreen's body had lain. "I have decided on a good plan, as it seems to me. I have talked it over with Rollin. He will devote a large part of his money also to the same plan."

"How much money have you, Virginia, to give in this way?" asked Rachel. Once, she would never have asked such a personal question. Now, it seemed as natural to talk frankly about money as about anything else that belonged to God.

"I have available for use at least four hundred and fifty-thousand dollars. Rollin has as much more. It is one of his bitter regrets now that his extravagant habits of life before his conversion practically threw away half that father left him. We are both eager to make all the reparation in our power. 'What would Jesus do with this money?'"

Daily In His Word

For the love of money is the root of all evil: which while some coveted after, they have erred from the faith, and pierced themselves through with many sorrows.

1 TIMOTHY 6:10 KJV

W e want to answer that question honestly and wisely. The money I shall put into the *News* is, I am confident, in a line with His probable action. It is as necessary that we have a Christian daily paper in Raymond, especially now that we have the saloon influence to meet, as it is to have a church or a college. So I am satisfied that the five hundred thousand dollars that Mr. Norman will know how to use so well will be a powerful factor in Raymond to do as Jesus would.

"About my other plan, Rachel, I want you to work with me. Rollin and I are going to buy up a large part of the property in the Rectangle. The field where the tent now is, has been in litigation for years. We mean to secure the entire tract as soon as the courts have settled the title. For some time I have been making a special study of the various forms of college settlements and residence methods of Christian work and institutional church work in the heart of great city slums. I do not know that I have yet been able to tell just what is the wisest and most effective kind of work that can be done in Raymond. But I do know this much. My money—I mean God's, which he wants me to use—can build wholesome lodging houses, refuges for poor women, asylums for shop girls, safety for many and many a lost girl like Loreen."

Daily In His Word

The LORD is a refuge for the oppressed,
a stronghold in times of trouble.

PSALM 9:9 NIV

$\mathbf{A}$nd I do not want to be simply a dispenser of this money. God help me! I do want to put myself into the problem. But you know, Rachel, I have a feeling all the time that all that limitless money and limitless personal sacrifice can possibly do, will not really lessen very much the awful condition at the Rectangle as long as the saloon is legally established there. I think that is true of any Christian work now being carried on in any great city. The saloon furnishes material to be saved faster than the settlement or residence or rescue mission work can save it."

Virginia suddenly rose and paced the hall. Rachel answered sadly, and yet with a note of hope in her voice:

"It is true. But, Virginia, what a wonderful amount of good can be done with this money! And the saloon cannot always remain here. The time must come when the Christian forces in the city will triumph."

Virginia paused near Rachel, and her pale, earnest face lighted up.

"I believe that too. The number of those who have promised to do as Jesus would is increasing. If we once have, say, five hundred such disciples in Raymond, the saloon is doomed."

Daily In His Word
LORD, how long shall the wicked,
how long shall the wicked triumph?
PSALM 94:3 KJV

But now, dear, I want you to look at your part in this plan for capturing and saving the Rectangle. Your voice is a power. I have had many ideas lately. Here is one of them. You could organize among the girls a Musical Institute; give them the benefit of your training. There are some splendid voices in the rough there. Did any one ever hear such singing as that yesterday by those women? Rachel, what a beautiful opportunity! You shall have the best of material in the way of organs and orchestras that money can provide, and what cannot be done with music to win souls there into higher and purer and better living?"

Before Virginia had ceased speaking Rachel's face was perfectly transformed with the thought of her life work. It flowed into her heart and mind like a flood, and the torrent of her feeling overflowed in tears that could not be restrained. It was what she had dreamed of doing herself. It represented to her something that she felt was in keeping with a right use of her talent.

"Yes," she said, as she rose and put her arm about Virginia, while both girls in the excitement of their enthusiasm paced the hall. "Yes, I will gladly put my life into that kind of service. I do believe that Jesus would have me use my life in this way. Virginia, what miracles can we not accomplish in humanity if we have such a lever as consecrated money to move things with!"

Daily In His Word

I know thy works, and charity, and service, and faith, and thy patience, and thy works.

Revelation 2:19 KJV

Add to it consecrated personal enthusiasm like yours, and it certainly can accomplish great things," said Virginia smiling. And before Rachel could reply, Rollin came in.

He hesitated a moment, and then was passing out of the hall into the library when Virginia called him back and asked some questions about his work.

Rollin came back and sat down, and together the three discussed their future plans. Rollin was apparently entirely free from embarrassment in Rachel's presence while Virginia was with them, only his manner with her was almost precise, if not cold. The past seemed to have been entirely absorbed in his wonderful conversion. He had not forgotten it, but he seemed to be completely caught up for this present time in the purpose of his new life. After a while Rollin was called out, and Rachel and Virginia began to talk of other things.

Daily In His Word
It [God's grace] teaches us to say "No" to ungodliness
and worldly passions, and to live self-controlled,
upright and godly lives in this present age.
Titus 2:12 niv

By the way, what has become of Jasper Chase?" Virginia asked the question innocently, but Rachel flushed and Virginia added with a smile, "I suppose he is writing another book. Is he going to put you into this one, Rachel? You know I always suspected Jasper Chase of doing that very thing in his first story."

"Virginia," Rachel spoke with the frankness that had always existed between the two friends, "Jasper Chase told me the other night that he—in fact—he proposed to me—or he would, if—"

Rachel stopped and sat with her hands clasped on her lap, and there were tears in her eyes.

"Virginia, I thought a little while ago I loved him, as he said he loved me. But when he spoke, my heart felt repelled, and I said what I ought to say. I told him no. I have not seen him since. That was the night of the first conversions at the Rectangle."

"I am glad for you," said Virginia quietly.

Daily In His Word

"As the Father has loved me, so have I loved you. Now remain in my love."

John 15:9 niv

Why?" asked Rachel a little startled.

"Because I have never really liked Jasper Chase. He is too cold and—I do not like to judge him, but I have always distrusted his sincerity in taking the pledge at the church with the rest."

Rachel looked at Virginia thoughtfully.

"I have never given my heart to him I am sure. He touched my emotions, and I admired his skill as a writer. I have thought at times that I cared a good deal for him. I think perhaps if he had spoken to me at any other time than the one he chose, I could easily have persuaded myself that I loved him. But not now."

Again Rachel paused suddenly, and when she looked up at Virginia again there were tears on her face. Virginia came to her and put her arm about her tenderly.

When Rachel had left the house, Virginia sat in the hall thinking over the confidence her friend had just shown her. There was something still to be told, Virginia felt sure from Rachel's manner, but she did not feel hurt that Rachel had kept back something. She was simply conscious of more on Rachel's mind than she had revealed.

Daily In His Word

Husbands, love your wives, just as Christ loved the church and gave himself up for her.

Ephesians 5:25 niv

Very soon Rollin came back, and he and Virginia, arm in arm as they had lately been in the habit of doing, walked up and down the long hall. It was easy for their talk to settle finally upon Rachel because of the place she was to occupy in the plans which were being made for the purchase of property at the Rectangle.

"Did you ever know of a girl of such really gifted powers in vocal music who was willing to give her life to the people as Rachel is going to do? She is going to give music lessons in the city, have private pupils to make her living, and then give the people in the Rectangle the benefit of her culture and her voice."

"It is certainly a very good example of self-sacrifice," replied Rollin a little stiffly.

Virginia looked at him a little sharply. "But don't you think it is a very unusual example? Can you imagine—," here Virginia named half a dozen famous opera singers, "—doing anything of this sort?"

"No, I cannot," Rollin answered briefly. "Neither can I imagine Miss—," he spoke the name of the girl with the red parasol who had begged Virginia to take the girls to the Rectangle, "doing what you are doing, Virginia."

"Any more than I can imagine Mr.—," Virginia spoke the name of a young society leader, "going about to the clubs doing your work, Rollin." The two walked on in silence for the length of the hall.

Daily In His Word

Let love be without dissimulation. Abhor that which is evil; cleave to that which is good.

Romans 12:9 KJV

Coming back to Rachel," began Virginia, "Rollin, why do you treat her with such a distinct, precise manner? I think, Rollin—pardon me if I hurt you—that she is annoyed by it. You need to be on easy terms. I don't think Rachel likes this change."

Rollin suddenly stopped. He seemed deeply agitated. He took his arm from Virginia's and walked alone to the end of the hall. Then he returned, with his hands behind him, and stopped near his sister and said, "Virginia, have you not learned my secret?"

Virginia looked bewildered, then over her face the unusual color crept, showing that she understood.

"I have never loved any one but Rachel Winslow." Rollin spoke calmly enough now. "That day she was here when you talked about her refusal to join the concert company, I asked her to be my wife, out there on the avenue. She refused me, as I knew she would. And she gave as her reason the fact that I had no purpose in life, which was true enough. Now that I have a purpose, now that I am a new man, don't you see, Virginia, how impossible it is for me to say anything? I owe my very conversion to Rachel's singing."

Daily In His Word

"Truly I say to you, unless you are converted and become like children, you will not enter the kingdom of heaven."

MATTHEW 18:3 NASB

And yet that night while she sang I can honestly say that, for the time being, I never thought of her voice except as God's message. I believe that all my personal love for her was for the time merged into a personal love to my God and my Saviour." Rollin was silent, then he went on with more emotion. "I still love her, Virginia. But I do not think she ever could love me." He stopped and looked his sister in the face with a sad smile.

"I don't know about that," said Virginia to herself. She was noting Rollin's handsome face, his marks of dissipation nearly all gone now, the firm lips showing manhood and courage, the clear eyes looking into hers frankly, the form strong and graceful. Rollin was a man now. Why should not Rachel come to love him in time? Surely the two were well fitted for each other, especially now that their purpose in life was moved by the same Christian force.

Daily In His Word

Be on your guard; stand firm in the faith; be men of courage; be strong.

1 CORINTHIANS 16:13 NIV

CHAPTER SEVENTEEN

T he next day she went down to the *News* office to see Edward Norman and arrange the details of her part in the establishment of the paper on its new foundation. Mr. Maxwell was present at this conference, and the three agreed that whatever Jesus would do in detail as editor of a daily paper, He would be guided by the same general principles that directed His conduct as the Savior of the world.

"I have tried to put down here in concrete form some of the things that it has seemed to me Jesus would do," said Edward Norman. He read from a paper lying on his desk, and Maxwell was reminded again of his own effort to put into written form his own conception of Jesus' probable action, and also of Milton Wright's same attempt in his business.

"I have headed this, 'What would Jesus do as Edward Norman, editor of a daily newspaper in Raymond?'

> *"1. He would never allow a sentence or a picture in his paper that could be called bad or coarse or impure in any way.*

Daily In His Word

Be an example to the believers in word, in conduct, in love, in spirit, in faith, in purity.

1 TIMOTHY 4:12 NKJV

"2. He would probably conduct the political part of the paper from the standpoint of nonpartisan patriotism, always looking upon all political questions in the light of their relation to the Kingdom of God, and advocating measures from the standpoint of their relation to the welfare of the people, always on the basis of 'What is right?' never on the basis of 'What is for the best interests of this or that party?' In other words, He would treat all political questions as he would treat every other subject, from the standpoint of the advancement of the Kingdom of God on earth."

Edward Norman looked up from the reading a moment. "You understand that is my opinion of Jesus' probable action on political matters in a daily paper. I am not passing judgment on other newspapermen who may have a different conception of Jesus' probable action from mine. I am simply trying to answer honestly, 'What would Jesus do as Edward Norman?' And the answer I find is what I have put down."

Daily In His Word

"But seek first the kingdom of God and His righteousness, and all these things shall be added to you."

MATTHEW 6:33 NKJV

"3. The end and aim of a daily paper conducted by Jesus would be to do the will of God. That is, His main purpose in carrying on a newspaper would not be to make money, or gain political influence; but His first and ruling purpose would be to so conduct his paper that it would be evident to all his subscribers that He was trying to seek first the Kingdom of God by means of His paper. This purpose would be as distinct and unquestioned as the purpose of a minister or a missionary or any unselfish martyr in Christian work anywhere.

"4. All questionable advertisements would be impossible.

"5. The relations of Jesus to the employees of the paper would be of the most loving character."

"So far as I have gone," said Norman again looking up, "I am of opinion that Jesus would employ practically some form of cooperation that would represent the idea of a mutual interest in a business where all were to move together for the same great end. I am working out such a plan, and I am confident it will be successful."

Daily In His Word
"The time is fulfilled, and the kingdom of God is at hand. Repent, and believe in the gospel."

MARK 1:15 NKJV

At any rate, once introduce the element of personal love into a business like this, take out the selfish principle of doing it for personal profits to a man or company, and I do not see any way except the most loving personal interest between editors, reporters, pressmen, and all who contribute anything to the life of the paper. And that interest would be expressed not only in the personal love and sympathy but in a sharing with the profits of the business."

> "6. As editor of a daily paper today, Jesus would give large space to the work of the Christian world. He would devote a page possibly to the facts of Reform, of sociological problems, of institutional church work and similar movements.

> "7. He would do all in His power in His paper to fight the saloon as an enemy of the human race and an unnecessary part of our civilization. He would do this regardless of public sentiment in the matter and, of course, always regardless of its effect upon His subscription list."

Again Edward Norman looked up. "I state my honest conviction on this point. Of course, I do not pass judgment on the Christian men who are editing other kinds of papers today. But as I interpret Jesus, I believe He would use the influence of His paper to remove the saloon entirely from the political and social life of the nation."

Daily In His Word
Each one's work will become clear.

1 CORINTHIANS 3:13 NKJV

"8. *Jesus would not issue a Sunday edition.*

"9. *He would print the news of the world that people ought to know. Among the things they do not need to know, and which would not be published, would be accounts of brutal prize fights, long accounts of crimes, scandals in private families, or any other human events which in any way would conflict with the first point mentioned in this outline.*

"10. *If Jesus had the amount of money to use on a paper which we have, He would probably secure the best and strongest Christian men and women to cooperate with him in the matter of contributions. That will be my purpose, as I shall be able to show you in a few days.*

"11. *Whatever the details of the paper might demand as the paper developed along its definite plan, the main principle that guided it would always be the establishment of the Kingdom of God in the world. This large general principle would necessarily shape all the detail.*"

Daily In His Word

He went through every city and village, preaching and bringing the glad tidings of the kingdom of God.

Luke 8:1 nkjv

Edward Norman finished reading the plan. He was very thoughtful.

"I have merely sketched a faint outline. I have a hundred ideas for making the paper powerful that I have not thought out fully as yet. This is simply suggestive. I have talked it over with other newspaper men. Some of them say I will have a weak, namby-pamby Sunday school sheet. If I get out something as good as a Sunday school it will be pretty good. Why do men, when they want to characterize something as particularly feeble, always use a Sunday school as a comparison, when they ought to know that the Sunday school is one of the strongest, most powerful influences in our civilization in this country today? But the paper will not necessarily be weak because it is good. Good things are more powerful than bad. The question with me is largely one of support from the Christian people of Raymond. There are over twenty thousand church members here in this city. If half of them will stand by the *News* its life is assured. What do you think, Maxwell, of the probability of such support?"

Daily In His Word

"I have shown you in every way, by laboring like this, that you must support the weak. And remember the words of the Lord Jesus, that He said 'It is more blessed to give than to receive.'"

Acts 20:35 NKJV

I don't know enough about it to give an intelligent answer. I believe in the paper with all my heart. If it lives a year, as Miss Virginia said, there is no telling what it can do. The great thing will be to issue such a paper, as near as we can judge, as Jesus probably would, and put into it all the elements of Christian brains, strength, intelligence and sense; and command respect for freedom from bigotry, fanaticism, narrowness and anything else that is contrary to the spirit of Jesus. Such a paper will call for the best that human thought and action is capable of giving. The greatest minds in the world would have their powers taxed to the utmost to issue a Christian daily."

"Yes," Edward Norman spoke humbly. "I shall make a great many mistakes, no doubt. I need a great deal of wisdom. But I want to do as Jesus would. 'What would He do?' I have asked it, and shall continue to do so, and abide by the results."

"I think we are beginning to understand," said Virginia, "the meaning of that command, 'Grow in the grace and knowledge of our Lord and Savior Jesus Christ.' I am sure I do not know all that He would do in detail until I know Him better."

Daily In His Word

We. . .do not cease to pray for you, and to ask that you may be filled with the knowledge of His will in all wisdom and spiritual understanding.

Colossians 1:9 NKJV

T hat is very true," said Henry Maxwell. "I am beginning to understand that I cannot interpret the probable action of Jesus until I know better what His spirit is. The greatest question in all of human life is summed up when we ask, 'What would Jesus do?' if, as we ask it, we also try to answer it from a growth in knowledge of Jesus himself. We must know Jesus before we can imitate Him."

When the arrangement had been made between Virginia an Edward Norman, he found himself in possession of the sum of five hundred thousand dollars to use for the establishment of a Christian daily paper. When Virginia and Maxwell had gone, Norman closed his door and, alone with the Divine Presence, asked like a child for help from his all-powerful Father. All through his prayer as he knelt before his desk ran the promise, "If any man lack wisdom, let him ask of God who giveth to all men liberally and upbraideth not, and it shall be given him." Surely his prayer would be answered, and the kingdom advanced through this instrument of God's power, this mighty press, which had become so largely degraded to the base uses of man's avarice and ambition.

Daily In His Word

For the LORD gives wisdom; from His mouth
come knowledge and understanding.

PROVERBS 2:6 NASB

Two months went by. They were full of action and of results in the city of Raymond and especially in the First Church. In spite of the approaching heat of the summer season, the after-meeting of the disciples who had made the pledge to do as Jesus would do, continued with enthusiasm and power. Gray had finished his work at the Rectangle, and an outward observer going through the place could not have seen any difference in the old conditions, although there was an actual change in hundreds of lives. But the saloons, dens, hovels, gambling houses, still ran, overflowing their vileness into the lives of fresh victims to take the place of those rescued by the evangelist. And the devil recruited his ranks very fast.

Henry Maxwell did not go abroad. Instead of that, he took the money he had been saving for the trip and quietly arranged for a summer vacation for a whole family living down in the Rectangle, who had never gone outside of the foul district of the tenements. The pastor of the First Church will never forget the week he spent with this family making the arrangements. He went down into the Rectangle one hot day when something of the terrible heat in the horrible tenements was beginning to be felt, and helped the family to the station, and then went with them to a beautiful spot on the coast where, in the home of a Christian woman, the bewildered city tenants breathed for the first time in years the cool salt air, and felt blow about them the pine-scented fragrance of a new lease of life.

Daily In His Word

What is desirable in a man is his kindness,
and it is better to be a poor man than a liar.

PROVERBS 19:22 NASB

There was a sickly babe with the mother, and three other children, one a cripple. The father, who had been out of work until he had been, as he afterwards confessed to Maxwell, several times on the edge of suicide, sat with the baby in his arms during the journey, and when Maxwell started back to Raymond, after seeing the family settled, the man held his hand at parting, and choked with his utterance, and finally broke down, to Maxwell's great confusion. The mother, a wearied, worn-out woman who had lost three children the year before from a fever scourge in the Rectangle, sat by the car window all the way and drank in the delights of sea and sky and field. It all seemed a miracle to her.

And Maxwell, coming back into Raymond at the end of that week, feeling the scorching, sickening heat all the more because of his little taste of the ocean breezes, thanked God for the joy he had witnessed, and entered upon his discipleship with a humble heart, knowing for almost the first time in his life this special kind of sacrifice. For never before had he denied himself his regular summer trip away from the heat of Raymond, whether he felt in any great need of rest or not.

"It is a fact," he said in reply to several inquiries on the part of his church, "I do not feel in need of a vacation this year. I am very well and prefer to stay here."

Daily In His Word

He who gives to the poor will never want, but he who shuts his eyes will have many curses.

PROVERBS 28:27 NASB

It was with a feeling of relief that he succeeded in concealing from every one but his wife what he had done with this other family. He felt the need of doing anything of that sort without display or approval from others.

So the summer came on, and Maxwell grew into a large knowledge of his Lord. The First Church was still swayed by the power of the Spirit. Maxwell marveled at the continuance of His stay. He knew very well that from the beginning nothing but the Spirit's presence had kept the church from being torn asunder by the remarkable testing it had received of its discipleship. Even now there were many of the members among those who had not taken the pledge, who regarded the whole movement as Mrs. Winslow did, in the nature of a fanatical interpretation of Christian duty, and looked for the return of the old normal condition. Meanwhile the whole body of disciples was under the influence of the Spirit, and the pastor went his way that summer, doing his parish work in great joy, keeping up his meetings with the railroad men as he had promised Alexander Powers, and daily growing into a better knowledge of the Master.

Daily In His Word

The Spirit of the Lord will rest on Him, the spirit of wisdom and understanding, the spirit of counsel and strength, the spirit of knowledge and the fear of the Lord.

Isaiah 11:2 nasb

Early one afternoon in August, after a day of refreshing coolness following a long period of heat, Jasper Chase walked to his window in the apartment house on the avenue and looked out.

On his desk lay a pile of manuscript. Since that evening when he had spoken to Rachel Winslow he had not met her. His singularly sensitive nature—sensitive to the point of extreme irritability when he was thwarted—served to thrust him into an isolation that was intensified by his habits as an author.

All through the heat of summer he had been writing. His book was nearly done now. He had thrown himself into its construction with a feverish strength that threatened at any moment to desert him and leave him helpless. He had not forgotten his pledge made with the other church members at the First Church. It had forced itself upon his notice all through his writing, and ever since Rachel had said no to him, he had asked a thousand times, "Would Jesus do this? Would He write this story?" It was a social novel, written in a style that had proved popular. It had no purpose except to amuse.

Its moral teaching was not bad, but neither was it Christian in any positive way. Jasper Chase knew that such a story would probably sell. He was conscious of powers in this way that the social world petted and admired.

Daily In His Word

So teach us to number our days, that we may apply our hearts unto wisdom.

Psalm 90:12 KJV

What would Jesus do?" He felt that Jesus would never write such a book. The question obtruded on him at the most inopportune times. He became irascible over it. The standard of Jesus for an author was too ideal. Of course, Jesus would use His powers to produce something useful or helpful, or with a purpose. What was he, Jasper Chase, writing this novel for? Why, what nearly every writer wrote for—money, money, and fame as a writer. There was no secret with him that he was writing this new story with that object. He was not poor, and so had no great temptation to write for money. But he was urged on by his desire for fame as much as anything. He must write this kind of matter. But what would Jesus do? The question plagued him even more than Rachel's refusal. Was he going to break his promise? "Did the promise mean much after all?" he asked.

Daily In His Word

"Beware of the teachers of the law. They like to walk around in flowing robes and love to be greeted in the marketplaces and have the most important seats in the synagogues and the places of honor at banquets."

LUKE 20:46 NIV

As he stood at the window, Rollin Page came out of the clubhouse just opposite. Jasper noted his handsome face and noble figure as he started down the street. He went back to his desk and turned over some papers there. Then he came back to the window. Rollin was walking down past the block and Rachel Winslow was walking beside him. Rollin must have overtaken her as she was coming from Virginia's that afternoon.

Jasper watched the two figures until they disappeared in the crowd on the walk. Then he turned to his desk and began to write. When he had finished the last page of the last chapter of his book it was nearly dark. "What would Jesus do?" He had finally answered the question by denying his Lord. It grew darker in his room. He had deliberately chosen his course, urged on by his disappointment and loss.

Daily In His Word

Knowing that you were not redeemed with corruptible things, like silver or gold. . .but with the precious blood of Christ, as of a lamb without blemish and without spot.

1 PETER 1:18–19 NKJV

CHAPTER EIGHTEEN

"What is that to thee? Follow thou me."

Whenen Rollin started down the street the afternoon that Jasper stood looking out of his window he was not thinking of Rachel Winslow and did not expect to see her anywhere. He had come suddenly upon her as he turned into the avenue and his heart had leaped up at the sight of her. He walked along by her now, rejoicing after all in a little moment of this earthly love he could not drive out of his life.

"I have just been over to see Virginia," said Rachel. "She tells me the arrangements are nearly completed for the transfer of the Rectangle property."

"Yes. It has been a tedious case in the courts. Did Virginia show you all the plans and specifications for building?"

"We looked over a good many. It is astonishing to me where Virginia has managed to get all her ideas about this work."

"Virginia knows more now about Arnold Toynbee and East End London and Institutional Church work in America than a good many professional slum workers. She has been spending nearly all summer in getting information." Rollin was beginning to feel more at ease as they talked over this coming work of humanity. It was safe, common ground.

Daily In His Word

God is not unfair. He will not forget how hard you have worked for him and how you have shown your love to him by caring for other Christians, as you still do.

HEBREWS 6:10 NLT

Whhave you been doing all summer? I have not seen much of you," Rachel suddenly asked, and then her face warmed with its quick flush of tropical color as if she might have implied too much interest in Rollin or too much regret at not seeing him oftener.

"I have been busy," replied Rollin briefly.

"Tell me something about it," persisted Rachel. "You say so little. Have I a right to ask?"

She put the question very frankly, turning toward Rollin in real earnest.

"Yes, certainly," he replied, with a graceful smile. "I am not so certain that I can tell you much. I have been trying to find some way to reach the men I once knew and win them into more useful lives."

He stopped suddenly as if he were almost afraid to go on. Rachel did not venture to suggest anything.

"I have been a member of the same company to which you and Virginia belong," continued Rollin, beginning again. "I made the pledge to do as I believe Jesus would do, and it is in trying to answer this question that I have been doing my work."

"That is what I do not understand. Virginia told me about the other. It seems wonderful to think that you are trying to keep that pledge with us. But what can you do with the club men?"

Daily In His Word

Happy is the person who finds wisdom and gains understanding. For the profit of wisdom is better than silver, and her wages are better than gold.

Proverbs 3:13–14 NLT

Y ou have asked me a direct question and I shall have to answer it now," replied Rollin, smiling again. "You see, I asked myself after that night at the tent, you remember" (he spoke hurriedly and his voice trembled a little), "what purpose I could now have in my life to redeem it, to satisfy my thought of Christian discipleship? And the more I thought of it, the more I was driven to a place where I knew I must take up the cross. Did you ever think that of all the neglected beings in our social system none are quite so completely left alone as the fast young men who fill the clubs and waste their time and money as I used to? The churches look after the poor, miserable creatures like those in the Rectangle; they make some effort to reach the workingman, they have a large constituency among the average salary-earning people, they send money and missionaries to the foreign heathen, but the fashionable, dissipated young men around town, the club men, are left out of all plans for reaching and Christianizing. And yet no class of people need it more. I said to myself: 'I know these men, their good and their bad qualities. I have been one of them. I am not fitted to reach the Rectangle people. I do not know how. But I think I could possibly reach some of the young men and boys who have money and time to spend.' So that is what I have been trying to do. When I asked as you did, 'What would Jesus do?' that was my answer. It has been also my cross."

Daily In His Word
He that findeth his life shall lose it: and he that loseth his life for my sake shall find it.
MATTHEW 10:39 KJV

Rollin's voice was so low on this last sentence that Rachel had difficulty in hearing him above the noise around them, But she knew what he had said. She wanted to ask what his methods were. But she did not know how to ask him. Her interest in his plan was larger than mere curiosity. Rollin Page was so different now from the fashionable young man who had asked her to be his wife that she could not help thinking of him and talking with him as if he were an entirely new acquaintance.

They had turned off the avenue and were going up the street to Rachel's home. It was the same street where Rollin had asked Rachel why she could not love him. They were both stricken with a sudden shyness as they went on. Rachel had not forgotten that day and Rollin could not. She finally broke a long silence by asking what she had not found words for before.

"In your work with the club men, with your old acquaintances, what sort of reception do they give you? How do you approach them? What do they say?"

Rollin was relieved when Rachel spoke. He answered quickly, "Oh, it depends on the man. A good many of them think I am a crank."

Daily In His Word

"Most assuredly, I say to you, We speak what We know and testify what We have seen, and you do not receive Our witness."

JOHN 3:11 NKJV

I have kept my membership up and am in good standing in that way. I try to be wise and not provoke any unnecessary criticism. But you would be surprised to know how many of the men have responded to my appeal. I could hardly make you believe that only a few nights ago a dozen men became honestly and earnestly engaged in a conversation over religious matters. I have had the great joy of seeing some of the men give up bad habits and begin a new life. 'What would Jesus do?' I keep asking it. The answer comes slowly, for I am feeling my way slowly. One thing I have found out: The men are not fighting shy of me. I think that is a good sign. Another thing: I have actually interested some of them in the Rectangle work, and when it is started up they will give something to help make it more powerful. And in addition to all the rest, I have found a way to save several of the young fellows from going to the bad in gambling."

Rollin spoke with enthusiasm. His face was transformed by his interest in the subject which had now become a part of his real life. Rachel again noted the strong, manly tone of his speech. With it all she knew there was a deep, underlying seriousness which felt the burden of the cross even while carrying it with joy.

Daily In His Word

"There will be more joy in heaven over one sinner who repents than over ninety-nine just persons who need no repentance."
LUKE 15:7 NKJV

The next time she spoke it was with a swift feeling of justice due to Rollin and his new life.

"Do you remember I reproached you once for not having any purpose worth living for?" she asked, while her beautiful face seemed to Rollin more beautiful than ever when he had won sufficient self-control to look up. "I want to say, I feel the need of saying, in justice to you now, that I honor you for your courage and your obedience to the promise you have made as you interpret the promise. The life you are living is a noble one."

Rollin trembled. His agitation was greater than he could control. Rachel could not help seeing it. They walked along in silence. At last Rollin said, "I thank you. It has been worth more to me than I can tell you to hear you say that." He looked into her face for one moment. She read his love for her in that look, but he did not speak.

When they separated Rachel went into the house and, sitting down in her room, she put her face in her hands and said to herself, "I am beginning to know what it means to be loved by a noble man. I shall love Rollin Page after all. What am I saying! Rachel Winslow, have you forgotten—"

Daily In His Word

When it goes well with the righteous, the city rejoices.

PROVERBS 11:10 NASB

She rose and walked back and forth. She was deeply moved. Nevertheless, it was evident to herself that her emotion was not that of regret or sorrow. Somehow a glad new joy had come to her. She had entered another circle of experience, and later in the day she rejoiced with a very strong and sincere gladness that her Christian discipleship found room in this crisis for her feeling. It was indeed a part of it, for if she was beginning to love Rollin Page it was the Christian man she had begun to love; the other never would have moved her to this great change.

And Rollin, as he went back, treasured a hope that had been a stranger to him since Rachel had said no that day. In that hope he went on with his work as the days sped on, and at no time was he more successful in reaching and saving his old acquaintances than in the time that followed that chance meeting with Rachel Winslow.

Daily In His Word

This righteousness from God comes through faith in Jesus Christ to all who believe.

Romans 3:22 niv

The summer had gone and Raymond was once more facing the rigor of her winter season. Virginia had been able to accomplish a part of her plan for "capturing the Rectangle," as she called it. But the building of houses in the field, the transforming of its bleak, bare aspect into an attractive park, all of which was included in her plan, was a work too large to be completed that fall after she had secured the property. But a million dollars in the hands of a person who truly wants to do with it as Jesus would, ought to accomplish wonders for humanity in a short time, and Henry Maxwell, going over to the scene of the new work one day after a noon hour with the shop men, was amazed to see how much had been done outwardly.

Yet he walked home thoughtfully, and on his way he could not avoid the question of the continual problem thrust upon his notice by the saloon. How much had been done for the Rectangle after all? Even counting Virginia's and Rachel's work and Mr. Gray's, where had it actually counted in any visible quantity?

Daily In His Word

O love the LORD, all you His godly ones! The LORD preserves the faithful, and fully recompenses the proud doer.

PSALM 31:23 NASB

Of course, he said to himself, the redemptive work begun and carried on by the Holy Spirit in His wonderful displays of power in the First Church and in the tent meetings had its effect upon the life of Raymond. But as he walked past saloon after saloon and noted the crowds going in and coming out of them, as he saw the wretched dens, as many as ever apparently, as he caught the brutality and squalor and open misery and degradation on countless faces of men and women and children, he sickened at the sight. He found himself asking how much cleansing could a million dollars poured into this cesspool accomplish? Was not the living source of nearly all the human misery they sought to relieve untouched as long as the saloons did their deadly but legitimate work? What could even such unselfish Christian discipleship as Virginia's and Rachel's do to lessen the stream of vice and crime so long as the great spring of vice and crime flowed as deep and strong as ever? Was it not a practical waste of beautiful lives for these young women to throw themselves into this earthly hell, when for every soul rescued by their sacrifice the saloon made two more that needed rescue?

He could not escape the question. It was the same that Virginia had put to Rachel in her statement that, in her opinion, nothing really permanent would ever be done until the saloon was taken out of the Rectangle. Henry Maxwell went back to his parish work that afternoon with added convictions on the license business.

Daily In His Word

"Bad company corrupts character." Come back to your senses as you ought, and stop sinning; for there are some who are ignorant of God—I say this to your shame.

1 CORINTHIANS 15:33–34 NIV

B ut if the saloon was a factor in the problem of the life of Raymond, no less was the First Church and its little company of disciples who had pledged to do as Jesus would do. Henry Maxwell, standing at the very center of the movement, was not in a position to judge of its power as some one from the outside might have done. But Raymond itself felt the touch in very many ways, not knowing all the reasons for the change.

The winter was gone and the year was ended, the year which Henry Maxwell had fixed as the time during which the pledge should be kept to do as Jesus would do. Sunday, the anniversary of that one a year ago, was in many ways the most remarkable day that the First Church ever knew. It was more important than the disciples in the First Church realized. The year had made history so fast and so serious that the people were not yet able to grasp its significance. And the day itself which marked the completion of a whole year of such discipleship was characterized by such revelations and confessions that the immediate actors in the events themselves could not understand the value of what had been done, or the relation of their trial to the rest of the churches and cities of the country.

Daily In His Word

"Light has come into the world, but men loved darkness instead of light because their deeds were evil. . . . But whoever lives by the truth comes into the light, so that it may be seen plainly that what he has done has been done through God."

JOHN 3:19, 21 NIV

Chapter Nineteen

[Letter from Rev. Calvin Bruce, D.D., of the Nazareth Avenue Church, Chicago, to Rev. Philip A. Caxton, D.D., New York City.]

My Dear Caxton:

"It is late Sunday night, but I am so intensely awake and so overflowing with what I have seen and heard that I feel driven to write you now some account of the situation in Raymond as I have been studying it, and as it has apparently come to a climax today. So this is my only excuse for writing so extended a letter at this time.

"You remember Henry Maxwell in the Seminary. I think you said the last time I visited you in New York that you had not seen him since we graduated. He was a refined, scholarly fellow, you remember, and when he was called to the First Church of Raymond within a year after leaving the Seminary, I said to my wife, 'Raymond has made a good choice. Maxwell will satisfy them as a sermonizer.' He has been here eleven years, and I understand that up to a year ago he had gone on in the regular course of the ministry, giving good satisfaction and drawing good congregations."

Daily In His Word

And lovingkindness is Yours, O Lord, for You recompense a man according to his work.

Psalm 62:12 nasb

Hhis church was counted the largest and wealthiest church in Raymond. All the best people attended it, and most of them belonged. The quartet choir was famous for its music, especially for its soprano, Miss Winslow, of whom I shall have more to say; and, on the whole, as I understand the facts, Maxwell was in a comfortable berth, with a very good salary, pleasant surroundings, a not very exacting parish of refined, rich, respectable people—such a church and parish as nearly all the young men of the seminary in our time looked forward to as very desirable.

"But a year ago today Maxwell came into his church on Sunday morning, and at the close of the service made the astounding proposition that the members of his church volunteer for a year not to do anything without first asking the question, 'What would Jesus do?' and, after answering it, to do what in their honest judgment He would do, regardless of what the result might be to them.

"The effect of this proposition, as it has been met and obeyed by a number of members of the church, has been so remarkable that, as you know, the attention of the whole country has been directed to the movement."

Daily In His Word

For a wide door for effective service has opened to me, and there are many adversaries.

1 CORINTHIANS 16:9 NASB

I call it a 'movement' because from the action taken today, it seems probable that what has been tried here will reach out into the other churches and cause a revolution in methods, but more especially in a new definition of Christian discipleship.

"In the first place, Maxwell tells me he was astonished at the response to his proposition. Some of the most prominent members in the church made the promise to do as Jesus would. Among them were Edward Norman, editor of the *Daily News*, which has made such a sensation in the newspaper world; Milton Wright, one of the leading merchants in Raymond; Alexander Powers, whose action in the matter of the railroads against the interstate commerce laws made such a stir about a year ago; Miss Page, one of Raymond's leading society heiresses, who has lately dedicated her entire fortune, as I understand, to the Christian daily paper and the work of reform in the slum district known as the Rectangle; and Miss Winslow, whose reputation as a singer is now national, but who in obedience to what she has decided to be Jesus' probable action, has devoted her talent to volunteer work among the girls and women who make up a large part of the city's worst and most abandoned population."

Daily In His Word

"You are truly my disciples if you keep obeying my teachings. And you will know the truth, and the truth will set you free."
JOHN 8:31–32 NLT

In addition to these well-known people has been a gradually increasing number of Christians from the First Church and lately from other churches of Raymond. A large proportion of these volunteers who pledged themselves to do as Jesus would do comes from the Endeavor societies. The young people say that they have already embodied in their society pledge the same principle in the words, 'I promise Him that I will strive to do whatever He would have me do.' This is not exactly what is included in Maxwell's proposition, which is that the disciple shall try to do what Jesus would probably do in the disciple's place. But the result of an honest obedience to either pledge, he claims, will be practically the same, and he is not surprised that the largest numbers have joined the new discipleship from the Endeavor Society.

"I am sure the first question you will ask is, 'What has been the result of this attempt? What has it accomplished or how has it changed in any way the regular life of the church or the community?'

"You already know something, from reports of Raymond that have gone over the country, what the events have been. But one needs to come here and learn something of the changes in individual lives, and especially the change in the church life, to realize all that is meant by this following of Jesus' steps so literally."

Daily In His Word

Now your sins have been washed away, and you have been set apart for God.

1 CORINTHIANS 6:11 NLT

To tell all that would be to write a long story or series of stories. I am not in a position to do that, but I can give you some idea perhaps of what has been done as told me by friends here and by Maxwell himself.

"The result of the pledge upon the First Church has been twofold. It has brought upon a spirit of Christian fellowship which Maxwell tells me never before existed, and which now impresses him as being very nearly what the Christian fellowship of the apostolic churches must have been; and it has divided the church into two distinct groups of members. Those who have not taken the pledge regard the others as foolishly literal in their attempt to imitate the example of Jesus. Some of them have drawn out of the church and no longer attend, or they have removed their membership entirely to other churches. Some are an element of internal strife, and I heard rumors of an attempt on their part to force Maxwell's resignation. I do not know that this element is very strong in the church. It has been held in check by a wonderful continuance of spiritual power, which dates from the first Sunday the pledge was taken a year ago, and also by the fact that so many of the most prominent members have been identified with the movement."

Daily In His Word

And they continued steadfastly in the apostles' doctrine and fellowship, in the breaking of bread, and in prayers.

ACTS 2:42 NKJV

The effect on Maxwell is very marked. I heard him preach in our State Association four years ago. He impressed me at the time as having considerable power in dramatic delivery, of which he himself was somewhat conscious. His sermon was well written and abounded in what the Seminary students used to call 'fine passages.' The effect of it was what an average congregation would call 'pleasing.' This morning I heard Maxwell preach again, for the first time since then. I shall speak of that farther on. He is not the same man. He gives me the impression of one who has passed through a crisis of revolution. He tells me this revolution is simply a new definition of Christian discipleship. He certainly has changed many of his old habits and many of his old views. His attitude on the saloon question is radically opposite to the one he entertained a year ago. And in his entire thought of the ministry, his pulpit and parish work, I find he has made a complete change. So far as I can understand, the idea that is moving him on now is the idea that the Christianity of our times must represent a more literal imitation of Jesus, and especially in the element of suffering."

Daily In His Word

And when they had brought their ships to land, they forsook all, and followed him.

LUKE 5:11 KJV

He quoted to me in the course of our conversation several times the verses in Peter: 'For even hereunto were ye called, because Christ also suffered for you, leaving you an example, that ye would follow His steps.' He seems filled with the conviction that what our churches need today more than anything else is this factor of joyful suffering for Jesus in some form.

"I do not know as I agree with him, altogether; but, my dear Caxton, it is certainly astonishing to note the results of this idea as they have impressed themselves upon this city and this church.

"You ask how about the results on the individuals who have made this pledge and honestly tried to be true to it. Those results are, as I have said, a part of individual history and cannot be told in detail. Some of them I can give you so that you may see that this form of discipleship is not merely sentiment or fine posing for effect."

Daily In His Word

Forasmuch then as Christ hath suffered for us in the flesh, arm yourselves likewise with the same mind: for he that hath suffered in the flesh hath ceased from sin.

1 PETER 4:1 KJV

For instance, take the case of Mr. Powers, who was superintendent of the machine shops of the L. and T. R. R. here. When he acted upon the evidence which incriminated the road he lost his position, and more than that, I learn from my friends here, his family and social relations have become so changed that he and his family no longer appear in public. They have dropped out of the social circle where once they were so prominent. By the way, Caxton, I understand in this connection that the Commission, for one reason or another, postponed action on this case, and it is now rumored that the L. and T. R. R. will pass into a receiver's hands very soon. The president of the road who, according to the evidence submitted by Powers, was the principal offender, has resigned, and complications which have risen since point to the receivership. Meanwhile, the superintendent has gone back to his old work as a telegraph operator. I met him at the church yesterday. He impressed me as a man who had, like Maxwell, gone through a crisis in character. I could not help thinking of him as being good material for the church of the first century when the disciples had all things in common."

Daily In His Word
All who believed were together and had all things in common;
they would sell their possessions and goods and distribute
the proceeds to all, as any had need.

ACTS 2:44–45 NRSV

Or take the case of Mr. Norman, editor of the *Daily News*. He risked his entire fortune in obedience to what he believed was Jesus' action, and revolutionized his entire conduct of the paper at the risk of a failure. I send you a copy of yesterday's paper. I want you to read it carefully. To my mind it is one of the most interesting and remarkable papers ever printed in the United States. It is open to criticism, but what could any mere man attempt in this line that would be free from criticism. Take it all in all, it is so far above the ordinary conception of a daily paper that I am amazed at the result. He tells me that the paper is beginning to be read more and more by the Christian people of the city. He was very confident of its final success. Read his editorial on the money questions, also the one on the coming election in Raymond when the question of license will again be an issue. Both articles are of the best from his point of view. He says he never begins an editorial or, in fact, any part of his newspaper work without first asking, 'What would Jesus do?' The result is certainly apparent."

Daily In His Word

The godly give good advice to their friends;
the wicked lead them astray.

Proverbs 12:26 nlt

Then there is Milton Wright, the merchant. He has, I am told, so revolutionized his business that no man is more beloved today in Raymond. His own clerks and employees have an affection for him that is very touching. During the winter, while he was lying dangerously ill at his home, scores of clerks volunteered to watch and help in any way possible, and his return to his store was greeted with marked demonstrations. All this has been brought about by the element of personal love introduced into the business. This love is not mere words, but the business itself is carried on under a system of cooperation that is not a patronizing recognition of inferiors, but a real sharing in the whole business. Other men on the street look upon Milton Wright as odd. It is a fact, however, that while he has lost heavily in some directions, he has increased his business, and is today respected and honored as one of the best and most successful merchants in Raymond."

Daily In His Word

You are my portion, O LORD;
I have promised to obey your words.

PSALM 119:57 NIV

And there is Miss Winslow. She has chosen to give her great talent to the poor of the city. Her plans include a Musical Institute where choruses and classes in vocal music shall be a feature. She is enthusiastic over her life work. In connection with her friend Miss Page she has planned a course in music which, if carried out, will certainly do much to lift up the lives of the people down there. I am not too old, dear Caxton, to be interested in the romantic side of much that has also been tragic here in Raymond, and I must tell you that it is well understood here that Miss Winslow expects to be married this spring to a brother of Miss Page who was once a society leader and club man, and who was converted in a tent where his wife-that-is-to-be took an active part in the service. I don't know all the details of this little romance, but I imagine there is a story wrapped up in it, and it would make interesting reading if we only knew it all."

Daily In His Word

"We must work the works of Him who sent Me, as long as it is day; night is coming, when no one can work."

JOHN 9:4 NASB

These are only a few illustrations of results in individual lives owing to obedience to the pledge. I meant to have spoken of President Marsh of Lincoln College. He is a graduate of my alma mater and I knew him slightly when I was in the senior year. He has taken an active part in the recent municipal campaign, and his influence in the city is regarded as a very large factor in the coming election. He impressed me, as did all the other disciples in this movement, as having fought out some hard questions, and as having taken up some real burdens that have caused and still do cause that suffering of which Henry Maxwell speaks, a suffering that does not eliminate, but does appear to intensify, a positive and practical joy."

Daily In His Word

Bear one another's burdens, and thereby fulfill the law of Christ.

GALATIANS 6:2 NASB

CHAPTER TWENTY

But I am prolonging this letter, possibly to your weariness. I am unable to avoid the feeling of fascination which my entire stay here has increased. I want to tell you something of the meeting in the First Church today.

"As I said, I heard Maxwell preach. At his earnest request I had preached for him the Sunday before, and this was the first time I had heard him since the Association meeting four years ago. His sermon this morning was as different from his sermon then as if it had been thought out and preached by some one living on another planet. I was profoundly touched. I believe I actually shed tears once. Others in the congregation were moved like myself. His text was: 'What is that to thee? Follow thou Me.' It was a most unusually impressive appeal to the Christians of Raymond to obey Jesus' teachings and follow in His steps regardless of what others might do. I cannot give you even the plan of the sermon. It would take too long. At the close of the service there was the usual after meeting that has become a regular feature of the First Church. Into this meeting have come all those who made the pledge to do as Jesus would do, and the time is spent in mutual fellowship, confession, question as to what Jesus would do in special cases, and prayer that the one great guide of every disciple's conduct may be the Holy Spirit."

Daily In His Word

For the Holy Ghost shall teach you in the same hour what ye ought to say.

LUKE 12:12 KJV

Maxwell asked me to come into this meeting. Nothing in all my ministerial life, Caxton, has so moved me as that meeting. I never felt the Spirit's presence so powerfully. It was a meeting of reminiscences and of the most loving fellowship. I was irresistibly driven in thought back to the first years of Christianity. There was something about all this that was apostolic in its simplicity and Christ imitation.

"I asked questions. One that seemed to arouse more interest than any other was in regard to the extent of the Christian disciple's sacrifice of personal property. Maxwell tells me that so far no one has interpreted the spirit of Jesus in such a way as to abandon his earthly possessions, give away of his wealth, or in any literal way imitate the Christians of the order, for example, of St. Francis of Assisi. It was the unanimous consent, however, that if any disciple should feel that Jesus in his own particular case would do that, there could be only one answer to the question. Maxwell admitted that he was still to a certain degree uncertain as to Jesus' probable action when it came to the details of household living, the possession of wealth, the holding of certain luxuries. It is, however, very evident that many of these disciples have repeatedly carried their obedience to Jesus to the extreme limit, regardless of financial loss. There is no lack of courage or consistency at this point."

Daily In His Word
Teach me to do your will, for you are my God; may your good Spirit lead me on level ground.

PSALM 143:10 NIV

It is also true that some of the businessmen who took the pledge have lost great sums of money in this imitation of Jesus, and many have, like Alexander Powers, lost valuable positions owing to the impossibility of doing what they had been accustomed to do and at the same time what they felt Jesus would do in the same place. In connection with these cases it is pleasant to record the fact that many who have suffered in this way have been at once helped financially by those who still have means. In this respect I think it is true that these disciples have all things in common. Certainly such scenes as I witnessed at the First Church at that after service this morning I never saw in my church or in any other. I never dreamed that such Christian fellowship could exist in this age of the world. I was almost incredulous as to the witness of my own senses. I still seem to be asking myself if this is the close of the nineteenth century in America."

Daily In His Word

For I do not mean that others should be eased and you burdened; but by an equality, that now at this time your abundance may supply their lack, that their abundance also may supply your lack—that there may be equality.

2 CORINTHIANS 8:13–14 NKJV

But now, dear friend, I come to the real cause of this letter, the real heart of the whole question as the First Church of Raymond has forced it upon me. Before the meeting closed today steps were taken to secure the cooperation of all other Christian disciples in this country. I think Maxwell took this step after long deliberation. He said as much to me one day when we were discussing the effect of this movement upon the church in general.

" 'Why,' he said, 'suppose that the church membership generally in this country made this pledge and lived up to it! What a revolution it would cause in Christendom! But why not? Is it any more than the disciple ought to do? Has he followed Jesus, unless he is willing to do this? Is the test of discipleship any less today than it was in Jesus' time?'

"I do not know all that preceded or followed his thought of what ought to be done outside of Raymond, but the idea crystallized today in a plan to secure the fellowship of all the Christians in America. The churches, through their pastors, will be asked to form disciple gatherings like the one in the First Church. Volunteers will be called for in the great body of church members in the United States, who will promise to do as Jesus would do."

Daily In His Word

Jesus said to the people who believed in him, "You are truly my disciples if you keep obeying my teachings."

JOHN 8:31 NLT

Maxwell spoke particularly of the result of such general action on the saloon question. He is terribly in earnest over this. He told me that there was no question in his mind that the saloon would be beaten in Raymond at the election now near at hand. If so, they could go on with some courage to do the redemptive work begun by the evangelist and now taken up by the disciples in his own church. If the saloon triumphs again there will be a terrible and, as he thinks, unnecessary waste of Christian sacrifice. But, however we differ on that point, he convinced his church that the time had come for a fellowship with other Christians. Surely, if the First Church could work such changes in society and its surroundings, the church in general if combining such a fellowship, not of creed but of conduct, ought to stir the entire nation to a higher life and a new conception of Christian following."

Daily In His Word

"And everyone who has left houses or brothers or sisters or father or mother or children or fields for my sake will receive a hundred times as much and will inherit eternal life."

Matthew 19:29 niv

This is a grand idea, Caxton, but right here is where I find myself hesitating. I do not deny that the Christian disciple ought to follow Christ's steps as closely as these here in Raymond have tried to do. But I cannot avoid asking what the result would be if I ask my church in Chicago to do it. I am writing this after feeling the solemn, profound touch of the Spirit's presence, and I confess to you, old friend, that I cannot call up in my church a dozen prominent business or professional men who would make this trial at the risk of all they hold dear. Can you do any better in your church? What are we to say? That the churches would not respond to the call: 'Come and suffer?' Is our standard of Christian disciple-ship a wrong one? Or are we possibly deceiving ourselves, and would we be agreeably disappointed if we once asked our people to take such a pledge faithfully? The actual results of the pledge as obeyed here in Raymond are enough to make any pastor tremble, and at the same time long with yearning that they might occur in his own parish. Certainly never have I seen a church so signally blessed by the Spirit as this one. But—am I myself ready to take this pledge? I ask the question honestly, and I dread to face an honest answer."

Daily In His Word

Our responsibility is never to oppose the truth, but to stand for the truth at all times.

2 Corinthians 13:8 nlt

Iknow well enough that I should have to change very much in my life if I undertook to follow His steps so closely. I have called myself a Christian for many years. For the past ten years I have enjoyed a life that has had comparatively little suffering in it. I am, honestly I say it, living at a long distance from municipal problems and the life of the poor, the degraded, and the abandoned. What would the obedience to this pledge demand of me? I hesitate to answer. My church is wealthy, full of well-to-do, satisfied people. The standard of their discipleship is, I am aware, not of a nature to respond to the call of suffering or personal loss. I say, 'I am aware.' I may be mistaken. I may have erred in not stirring their deeper life. Caxton, my friend, I have spoken my inmost thought to you. Shall I go back to my people next Sunday and stand up before them in my large city church and say: 'Let us follow Jesus closer; let us walk in His steps where it will cost us something more than it is costing us now; let us pledge not to do anything without first asking, 'What would Jesus do?' If I should go before them with that message, it would be a strange and startling one to them. But why? Are we not ready to follow Him all the way? What is it to be a follower of Jesus? What does it mean to imitate Him? What does it mean to walk in His steps?"

Daily In His Word

Anyone who wants to do the will of God will know whether my teaching is from God or is merely my own. . . . Those who seek to honor the one who sent them are good and genuine.

JOHN 7:17–18 NLT

The Rev. Calvin Bruce, D. D., of the Nazareth Avenue Church, Chicago, let his pen fall on the table. He had come to the parting of the ways, and his question, he felt sure, was the question of many and many a man in the ministry and in the church. He went to his window and opened it. He was oppressed with the weight of his convictions and he felt almost suffocated with the air in the room. He wanted to see the stars and feel the breath of the world.

The night was very still. The clock in the First Church was just striking midnight. As it finished, a clear, strong voice down in the direction of the Rectangle came floating up to him as if borne on radiant pinions.

It was a voice of one of Gray's old converts, a night watchman at the packinghouses, who sometimes solaced his lonesome hours by a verse or two of some familiar hymn:

> *"Must Jesus bear the cross alone*
> *And all the world go free?*
> *No, there's a cross for every one,*
> *And there's a cross for me."*

Daily In His Word

"Any of you who does not give up everything he has cannot be my disciple."

Luke 14:33 NIV

T he Rev. Calvin Bruce turned away from the window and, after a little hesitation, he kneeled. "What would Jesus do?" That was the burden of his prayer. Never had he yielded himself so completely to the Spirit's searching revealing of Jesus. He was on his knees a long time. He retired and slept fitfully with many awakenings. He rose before it was clear dawn and threw open his window again. As the light in the east grew stronger he repeated to himself, "What would Jesus do? Shall I follow His steps?"

The sun rose and flooded the city with its power. When shall the dawn of a new discipleship usher in the conquering triumph of a closer walk with Jesus? When shall Christendom tread more closely the path he made?

"It is the way the Master trod; Shall not the servant tread it still?"

Daily In His Word

"You have already been cleansed by the word that I have spoken to you. Abide in me as I abide in you."

JOHN 15:3–4 NRSV

Chapter Twenty-one

"Master, I will follow Thee whithersoever Thou goest."

The Saturday afternoon matinee at the Auditorium in Chicago was just over and the usual crowd was struggling to get to its carriage before any one else. The Auditorium attendant was shouting out the numbers of different carriages and the carriage doors were slamming as the horses were driven rapidly up to the curb, held there impatiently by the drivers who had shivered long in the raw east wind and then let go to plunge for a few minutes into the river of vehicles that tossed under the elevated railway and finally went whirling off up the avenue.

"Now then, 624," shouted the Auditorium attendant, "624!" he repeated, and there dashed up to the curb a splendid span of black horses attached to a carriage having the monogram, "C. R. S." in gilt letters on the panel of the door.

Two girls stepped out of the crowd towards the carriage. The older one had entered and taken her seat, and the attendant was still holding the door open for the younger, who stood hesitating on the curb.

"Come, Felicia! What are you waiting for? I shall freeze to death!" called the voice from the carriage.

The girl outside of the carriage hastily unpinned a bunch of English violets from her dress and handed them to a small boy who was standing shivering on the edge of the sidewalk almost under the horses' feet.

Daily In His Word
Though he was rich, yet for your sakes he became poor, that ye through his poverty might be rich.

2 Corinthians 8:9 KJV

He took them, with a look of astonishment and a "Thank ye, lady!" and instantly buried a very grimy face in the bunch of perfume. The girl stepped into the carriage, the door shut with the incisive bang peculiar to well-made carriages of this sort, and in a few moments the coachman was speeding the horses rapidly up one of the boulevards.

"You are always doing some queer thing or other, Felicia," said the older girl as the carriage whirled on past the great residences already brilliantly lighted.

"Am I? What have I done that is queer now, Rose?" asked the other, looking up suddenly and turning her head towards her sister.

"Oh, giving those violets to that boy! He looked as if he needed a good hot supper more than a bunch of violets. It's a wonder you didn't invite him home with us. I shouldn't have been surprised if you had. You are always doing such queer things."

"Would it be queer to invite a boy like that to come to the house and get a hot supper?" Felicia asked the question softly and almost as if she were alone.

" 'Queer' isn't just the word, of course," replied Rose indifferently. "It would be what Madam Blanc calls 'outre.' Decidedly. Therefore you will please not invite him or others like him to hot suppers because I suggested it. Oh dear! I'm awfully tired."

She yawned, and Felicia silently looked out the window in the door.

Daily In His Word
She stretcheth out her hand to the poor; yea, she reacheth forth her hands to the needy.

Proverbs 31:20 kjv

The concert was stupid and the violinist was simply a bore. I don't see how you could sit so still through it all," Rose exclaimed a little impatiently.

"I liked the music," answered Felicia quietly.

"You like anything. I never saw a girl with so little critical taste."

Felicia colored slightly, but would not answer.

Rose yawned again and then hummed a fragment of a popular song. Then she exclaimed abruptly, "I'm sick of most everything. I hope *The Shadows of London* will be exciting tonight."

"The Shadows of Chicago," murmured Felicia.

" 'The 'Shadows of Chicago!' *The Shadows of London*, the play, the great drama with its wonderful scenery, the sensation of New York for two months. You know we have a box with the Delanos tonight."

Felicia turned her face towards her sister. Her great brown eyes were very expressive and not altogether free from a sparkle of luminous heat.

"And yet we never weep over the real thing on the actual stage of life. What are the 'Shadows of London' on the stage to the shadows of London or Chicago as they really exist? Why don't we get excited over the facts as they are?"

Daily In His Word

" 'You must love the Lord your God with all your heart, all your soul, all your strength, and all your mind.' And, 'Love your neighbor as yourself.' "

Luke 10:27 NLT

Because the actual people are dirty and disagreeable and it's too much bother, I suppose," replied Rose carelessly. "Felicia, you can never reform the world. What's the use? We're not to blame for the poverty and misery. There have always been rich and poor, and there always will be. We ought to be thankful we're rich."

"Suppose Christ had gone on that principle," replied Felicia, with unusual persistence. "Do you remember Dr. Bruce's sermon on that verse a few Sundays ago: 'For ye know the grace of our Lord Jesus Christ, that though he was rich yet for our sakes he became poor, that ye through his poverty might become rich'?"

"I remember it well enough," said Rose with some petulance, "and didn't Dr. Bruce go on to say that there is no blame attached to people who have wealth if they are kind and give to the needs of the poor? And I am sure that he himself is pretty comfortably settled. He never gives up his luxuries just because some people go hungry. What good would it do if he did? I tell you, Felicia, there will always be poor and rich in spite of all we can do. Ever since Rachel Winslow has written about those queer doings in Raymond you have upset the whole family. People can't live at that concert pitch all the time. You see if Rachel doesn't give it up soon. It's a great pity she doesn't come to Chicago and sing in the Auditorium concerts. She has received an offer. I'm going to write and urge her to come. I'm just dying to hear her sing."

Daily In His Word
Blessed is he that considereth the poor: the LORD will deliver him in time of trouble.

PSALM 41:1 KJV

Felicia looked out of the window and was silent. The carriage rolled on past two blocks of magnificent private residences and turned into a wide driveway under a covered passage, and the sisters hurried into the house. It was an elegant mansion of gray stone furnished like a palace, every corner of it warm with the luxury of paintings, sculpture, art and modern refinement.

The owner of it all, Mr. Charles R. Sterling, stood before an open grate fire smoking a cigar. He had made his money in grain speculation and railroad ventures and was reputed to be worth something over two millions. His wife was a sister of Mrs. Winslow of Raymond. She had been an invalid for several years. The two girls, Rose and Felicia, were the only children. Rose was twenty-one years old, fair, vivacious, educated in a fashionable college, just entering society and already somewhat cynical and indifferent. A very hard young lady to please, her father said, sometimes playfully, sometimes sternly. Felicia was nineteen, with a tropical beauty somewhat like her cousin, Rachel Winslow, with warm, generous impulses just waking into Christian feeling, capable of all sorts of expression, a puzzle to her father, a source of irritation to her mother, and with a great unsurveyed territory of thought and action in herself, of which she was more than dimly conscious. There was that in Felicia that would easily endure any condition in life if only the liberty to act fully on her conscientious convictions were granted her.

Daily In His Word
It was for freedom that Christ set us free;
therefore keep standing firm.
GALATIANS 5:1 NASB

Here's a letter for you, Felicia," said Mr. Sterling, handing it to her.

Felicia sat down and instantly opened the letter, saying as she did so, "It's from Rachel."

"Well, what's the latest news from Raymond?" asked Mr. Sterling, taking his cigar out of his mouth and looking at Felicia with half-shut eyes, as if he were studying her.

"Rachel says Dr. Bruce has been staying in Raymond for two Sundays and has seemed very much interested in Mr. Maxwell's pledge in the First Church."

"What does Rachel say about herself?" asked Rose, who was lying on a couch almost buried under elegant cushions.

"She is still singing at the Rectangle. Since the tent meetings closed, she sings in an old hall until the new buildings which her friend, Virginia Page, is putting up are completed.

"I must write Rachel to come to Chicago and visit us. She ought not to throw away her voice in that railroad town upon all those people who don't appreciate her."

Daily In His Word

Speaking to yourselves in psalms and hymns and spiritual songs, singing and making melody in your heart to the Lord.

EPHESIANS 5:19 KJV

M r. Sterling lighted a new cigar and Rose exclaimed, "Rachel is so queer. She might set Chicago wild with her voice if she sang in the Auditorium. And there she goes on throwing it away on people who don't know what they are hearing."

"Rachel won't come here unless she can do it and keep her pledge at the same time," said Felicia, after a pause.

"What pledge?" Mr. Sterling asked the question and then added hastily, "Oh, I know, yes! A very peculiar thing that. Alexander Powers used to be a friend of mine. We learned telegraphy in the same office. Made a great sensation when he resigned and handed over that evidence to the Interstate Commerce Commission. And he's back at his telegraph again. There have been queer doings in Raymond during the past year. I wonder what Dr. Bruce thinks of it on the whole. I must have a talk with him about it."

"He is at home and will preach tomorrow," said Felicia. "Perhaps he will tell us something about it."

There was silence for a minute. Then Felicia said abruptly, as if she had gone on with a spoken thought to some invisible hearer, "And what if he should propose the same pledge to the Nazareth Avenue Church?"

Daily In His Word

He has given us very great and precious promises, so that through them you may participate in the divine nature and escape the corruption of the world caused by evil desires.

2 PETER 1:4 NIV

Who? What are you talking about?" asked her father a little sharply.

"About Dr. Bruce. I say, what if he should propose to our church what Mr. Maxwell proposed to his, and ask for volunteers who would pledge themselves to do everything after asking the question, 'What would Jesus do?' "

"There's no danger of it," said Rose, rising suddenly from the couch as the tea bell rang.

"It's a very impracticable movement, to my mind," said Mr. Sterling shortly.

"I understand from Rachel's letter that the Raymond church is going to make an attempt to extend the idea of the pledge to other churches. If it succeeds it will certainly make great changes in the churches and in people's lives," said Felicia.

"Oh, well, let's have some tea first!" said Rose, walking into the dining room. Her father and Felicia followed, and the meal proceeded in silence.

Daily In His Word

So you must remain faithful to what you have been taught from the beginning.

1 JOHN 2:24 NLT

Mrs. Sterling had her meals served in her room. Mr. Sterling was preoccupied. He ate very little and excused himself early, and although it was Saturday night, he remarked as he went out that he should be down town on some special business.

"Don't you think father looks very much disturbed lately?" asked Felicia a little while after he had gone out.

"Oh, I don't know! I hadn't noticed anything unusual," replied Rose. After a silence she said: "Are you going to the play tonight, Felicia? Mrs. Delano will be here at half past seven. I think you ought to go. She will feel hurt if you refuse."

"I'll go. I don't care about it. I can see shadows enough without going to the play."

"That's a doleful remark for a girl nineteen years old to make," replied Rose. "But then you're queer in your ideas anyhow, Felicia. If you are going up to see mother, tell her I'll run in after the play if she is still awake."

Daily In His Word
But they do not know the LORD's thoughts or understand his plan.
Micah 4:12 NLT

CHAPTER TWENTY-TWO

Felicia started off to the play not very happy, but she was familiar with that feeling, only sometimes she was more unhappy than at others. Her feeling expressed itself tonight by a withdrawal into herself. When the company was seated in the box and the curtain had gone up Felicia was back of the others and remained for the evening by herself. Mrs. Delano, as chaperon for half a dozen young ladies, understood Felicia well enough to know that she was "queer," as Rose so often said, and she made no attempt to draw her out of her corner. And so the girl really experienced that night by herself one of the feelings that added to the momentum that was increasing the coming on of her great crisis.

The play was an English melodrama, full of startling situations, realistic scenery and unexpected climaxes. There was one scene in the third act that impressed even Rose Sterling.

It was midnight on Blackfriars Bridge. The Thames flowed dark and forbidden below. St. Paul's rose through the dim light imposing, its dome seeming to float above the buildings surrounding it. The figure of a child came upon the bridge and stood there for a moment peering about as if looking for someone. Several persons were crossing the bridge, but in one of the recesses about midway of the river a woman stood, leaning out over the parapet, with a strained agony of face and figure that told plainly of her intention.

Daily In His Word

When Jesus saw her weeping, and the Jews who had come along with her also weeping, he was deeply moved in spirit and troubled.

JOHN 11:33 NIV

Just as she was stealthily mounting the parapet to throw herself into the river, the child caught sight of her, ran forward with a shrill cry more animal than human, and seizing the woman's dress dragged back upon it with all her little strength. Then there came suddenly upon the scene two other characters who had already figured in the play—a tall, handsome, athletic gentleman dressed in the fashion, attended by a slim-figured lad who was as refined in dress and appearance as the little girl clinging to her mother, who was mournfully hideous in her rags and repulsive poverty. These two, the gentleman and the lad, prevented the attempted suicide, and after a tableau on the bridge, where the audience learned that the man and woman were brother and sister, the scene was transferred to the interior of one of the slum tenements in the East Side of London. Here the scene painter and carpenter had done their utmost to produce an exact copy of a famous court and alley well known to the poor creatures who make up a part of the outcast London humanity. The rags, the crowding, the vileness, the broken furniture, the horrible animal existence forced upon creatures made in God's image were so skillfully shown in this scene that more than one elegant woman in the theater, seated like Rose Sterling in a sumptuous box surrounded with silk hangings and velvet covered railing, caught herself shrinking back a little as if contamination were possible from the nearness of this piece of scenery. It was almost too realistic, and yet it had a horrible fascination for Felicia as she sat there alone, buried back in a cushioned seat and absorbed in thoughts that went far beyond the dialogue on the stage.

Daily In His Word

So God created man in his own image, in the image of God he created him; male and female he created them.

Genesis 1:27 NIV

From the tenement scene, the play shifted to the interior of a nobleman's palace, and almost a sigh of relief went up all over the house at the sight of the accustomed luxury of the upper classes. The contrast was startling. It was brought about by a clever piece of staging that allowed only a few moments to elapse between the slum and the palace scene. The dialogue went on, the actors came and went in their various roles, but upon Felicia the play made but one distinct impression. In realty the scenes on the bridge and in the slums were only incidents in the story of the play, but Felicia found herself living those scenes over and over. She had never philosophized about the causes of human misery; she was not old enough she had not the temperament that philosophizes. But she felt intensely, and this was not the first time she had felt the contrast thrust into her feeling between the upper and the lower conditions of human life. It had been growing upon her until it had made her what Rose called "queer," and other people in her circle of wealthy acquaintances called very unusual. It was simply the human problem in its extreme of riches and poverty, its refinement and its vileness, that was, in spite of her unconscious attempts to struggle against the facts, burning into her life the impression that would in the end either transform her into a woman of rare love and self-sacrifice for the world, or a miserable enigma to herself and all who knew her.

Daily In His Word

And do not be conformed to this world,
but be transformed by the renewing of your mind,
that you may prove what the will of God is.
Romans 12:2 NASB

Come, Felicia, aren't you going home?" said Rose. The play was over, the curtain down, and people were going noisily out, laughing and gossiping as if *The Shadows of London* were simply good diversion, as they were, put on the stage so effectively.

Felicia rose and went out with the rest quietly, and with the absorbed feeling that had actually left her in her seat oblivious of the play's ending. She was never absentminded, but often thought herself into a condition that left her alone in the midst of a crowd.

"Well, what did you think of it?" asked Rose when the sisters had reached home and were in the drawing room. Rose really had considerable respect for Felicia's judgment of a play.

"I thought it was a pretty fair picture of real life."

"I mean the acting," said Rose, annoyed.

"The bridge scene was well acted, especially the woman's part. I thought the man overdid the sentiment a little."

"Did you? I enjoyed that. And wasn't the scene between the two cousins funny when they first learned they were related? But the slum scene was horrible. I think they ought not to show such things in a play. They are too painful."

"They must be painful in real life, too," replied Felicia.

"Yes, but we don't have to look at the real thing. It's bad enough at the theatre where we pay for it."

Daily In His Word

He will have compassion on the poor and needy, and the lives of the needy he will save. He will rescue their life from oppression and violence.

Psalm 72:13–14 nasb

Rose went into the dining room and began to eat from a plate of fruit and cakes on the sideboard.

"Are you going up to see Mother?" asked Felicia after a while. She had remained in front of the drawing room fireplace.

"No," replied Rose from the other room. "I won't trouble her tonight. If you go in tell her I am too tired to be agreeable."

So Felicia turned into her mother's room as she went up the great staircase and down the upper hall. The light was burning there, and the servant who always waited on Mrs. Sterling was beckoning Felicia to come in.

"Tell Clara to go out," exclaimed Mrs. Sterling as Felicia came up to the bed.

Felicia was surprised, but she did as her mother bade her and then inquired how she was feeling.

"Felicia," said her mother, "can you pray?"

The question was so unlike any her mother had ever asked before that she was startled. But she answered, "Why, yes, mother. Why do you ask such a question?"

"Felicia, I am frightened. Your father—I have had such strange fears about him all day. Something is wrong with him. I want you to pray—"

"Now, here, Mother?"

"Yes. Pray, Felicia."

Daily In His Word

The Holy Spirit helps us in our distress. For we don't even know what we should pray for, nor how we should pray. But the Holy Spirit prays for us with groaning that cannot be expressed in words.

Romans 8:26 nlt

Felicia reached out her hand and took her mother's. It was trembling. Mrs. Sterling had never shown such tenderness for her younger daughter, and her strange demand now was the first real sign of any confidence in Felicia's character.

The girl kneeled, still holding her mother's trembling hand, and prayed. It is doubtful if she had ever prayed aloud before. She must have said in her prayer the words that her mother needed, for when it was silent in the room, the invalid was weeping softly and her nervous tension was over.

Felicia stayed some time. When she was assured that her mother would not need her any longer, she rose to go.

"Good night, Mother. You must let Clara call me if you feel badly in the night."

"I feel better now." Then as Felicia was moving away, Mrs. Sterling said, "Won't you kiss me, Felicia?"

Felicia went back and bent over her mother. The kiss was almost as strange to her as the prayer had been. When Felicia went out of the room her cheeks were wet with tears. She had not often cried since she was a little child.

Daily In His Word
"All that's required is that you really believe and do not doubt in your heart. Listen to me! You can pray for anything, and if you believe, you will have it."

MARK 11:23–24 NLT

Sunday morning at the Sterling mansion was generally very quiet. The girls usually went to church at eleven o'clock service. Mr. Sterling was not a member but a heavy contributor, and he generally went to church in the morning. This time he did not come down to breakfast and finally sent word by a servant that he did not feel well enough to go out. So Rose and Felicia drove up to the door of the Nazareth Avenue Church and entered the family pew alone.

When Dr. Bruce walked out of the room at the rear of the platform and went up to the pulpit to open the Bible as his custom was, those who knew him best did not detect anything unusual in his manner or his expression. He proceeded with the service as usual. He was calm and his voice was steady and firm. His prayer was the first intimation the people had of anything new or strange in the service. It is safe to say that the Nazareth Avenue Church had not heard Dr. Bruce offer such a prayer before during the twelve years he had been pastor there. How would a minister be likely to pray who had come out of a revolution in Christian feeling that had completely changed his definition of what was meant by following Jesus?

No one in Nazareth Avenue Church had any idea that the Rev. Calvin Bruce, D.D., the dignified, cultured, refined Doctor of Divinity, had within a few days been crying like a little child on his knees, asking for strength and courage and Christlikeness to speak his Sunday message; and yet the prayer was an unconscious involuntary disclosure of his soul's experience such as the Nazareth Avenue people had seldom heard, and never before from that pulpit.

Daily In His Word

For you have magnified Your word above all Your name. In the day when I cried out, You answered me, and made me bold with strength in my soul.

PSALM 138:2–3 NKJV

Chapter Twenty-three

I am just back from a visit to Raymond," Dr. Bruce began, "and I want to tell you something of my impressions of the movement there."

He paused and his look went out over his people with yearning for them and at the same time with a great uncertainty at his heart. How many of his rich, fashionable, refined, luxury-loving members would understand the nature of the appeal he was soon to make to them? He was altogether in the dark as to that. Nevertheless he had been through his desert, and had come out of it ready to suffer. He went on now after that brief pause and told them the story of his stay in Raymond. The people already knew something of that experiment in the First Church. The whole country had watched the progress of the pledge as it had become history in so many lives. Mr. Maxwell had at last decided that the time had come to seek the fellowship of other churches throughout the country. The new discipleship in Raymond had proved to be so valuable in its results that he wished the churches in general to share with the disciples in Raymond. Already there had begun a volunteer movement in many churches throughout the country, acting on their own desire to walk closer in the steps of Jesus. The Christian Endeavor Society had, with enthusiasm, in many churches taken the pledge to do as Jesus would do, and the result was already marked in a deeper spiritual life and a power in church influence that was like a new birth for the members.

Daily In His Word

That I may open my mouth boldly to make known the mystery of the gospel, for which I am an ambassador in chains; that in it I may speak boldly, as I ought to speak.

Ephesians 6:19–20 NKJV

All this Dr. Bruce told his people simply and with a personal interest that evidently led the way to the announcement which now followed. Felicia had listened to every word with strained attention. She sat there by the side of Rose, in contrast like fire beside snow, although even Rose was alert and as excited as she could be.

"Dear friends," he said, and for the first time since his prayer the emotion of the occasion was revealed in his voice and gesture, "I am going to ask that Nazareth Avenue Church take the same pledge that Raymond Church has taken. I know what this will mean to you and me. It will mean the complete change of very many habits. It will mean, possibly, social loss. It will mean very probably, in many cases, loss of money. It will mean suffering. It will mean what following Jesus meant in the first century, and then it meant suffering, loss, hardship, separation from everything un-Christian. But what does following Jesus mean? The test of discipleship is the same now as then. Those of us who volunteer in this church to do as Jesus would do, simply promise to walk in His steps as He gave us commandment."

Again he paused, and now the result of his announcement was plainly visible in the stir that went up over the, congregation. He added in a quiet voice that all who volunteered to make the pledge to do as Jesus would do, were asked to remain after the morning service.

Daily In His Word
And do not forget to do good and to share with others, for with such sacrifices God is pleased.

Hebrews 13:16 niv

Instantly he proceeded with his sermon. His text was, "Master, I will follow Thee whithersoever Thou goest." It was a sermon that touched the deep springs of conduct; it was a revelation to the people of the definition their pastor had been learning; it took them back to the first century of Christianity; above all, it stirred them below the conventional thought of years as to the meaning and purpose of church membership. It was such a sermon as a man can preach once in a lifetime, and with enough in it for people to live on all through the rest of their lifetime.

The service closed in a hush that was slowly broken. People rose here and there, a few at a time. There was a reluctance in the movements of some that was very striking. Rose, however, walked straight out of the pew, and as she reached the aisle she turned her head and beckoned to Felicia. By that time the congregation was rising all over the church. "I am going to stay," she said, and Rose had heard her speak in the same manner on other occasions, and knew that her resolve could not be changed. Nevertheless she went back into the pew two or three steps and faced her.

"Felicia," she whispered, and there was a flush of anger on her cheeks, "this is folly. What can you do? You will bring some disgrace on the family. What will father say? Come!"

Daily In His Word

Suppose ye that I am come to give peace on earth? I tell you, Nay; but rather division: For from henceforth there shall be five in one house divided, three against two, and two against three.

Luke 12:51–52 KJV

Felicia looked at her but did not answer at once. Her lips were moving with a petition that came from the depth of feeling that measured a new life for her. She shocked her head.

"No, I am going to stay. I shall take the pledge. I am ready to obey it. You do not know why I am doing this."

Rose gave her one look and then turned and went out of the pew, and down the aisle. She did not even stop to talk with her acquaintances. Mrs. Delano was going out of the church just as Rose stepped into the vestibule.

"So you are not going to join Dr. Bruce's volunteer company?" Mrs. Delano asked, in a queer tone that made Rose redden.

"No, are you? It is simply absurd. I have always regarded that Raymond movement as fanatical. You know cousin Rachel keeps us posted about it."

"Yes, I understand it is resulting in a great deal of hardship in many cases. For my part, I believe Dr. Bruce has simply provoked disturbance here. It will result in splitting our church. You see if it isn't so. There are scores of people in the church who are so situated that they can't take such a pledge and keep it. I am one of them," added Mrs. Delano as she went out with Rose.

Daily In His Word

You are to lead clean, innocent lives, as children of God in a dark world full of crooked and perverse people.

PHILIPPIANS 2:15 NLT

W hen Rose reached home, her father was standing in his usual attitude before the open fireplace, smoking a cigar.

"Where is Felicia?" he asked as Rose came in.

"She stayed to an after-meeting," replied Rose shortly. She threw off her wraps and was going upstairs when Mr. Sterling called after her.

"An after-meeting? What do you mean?"

"Dr. Bruce asked the church to take the Raymond pledge."

Mr. Sterling took his cigar out of his mouth and twirled it nervously between his fingers.

"I didn't expect that of Dr. Bruce. Did many of the members stay?"

"I don't know. I didn't," replied Rose, and she went upstairs leaving her father standing in the drawing room.

After a few moments he went to the window and stood there looking out at the people driving on the boulevard. His cigar had gone out, but he still fingered it nervously. Then he turned from the window and walked up and down the room. A servant stepped across the hall and announced dinner and he told her to wait for Felicia. Rose came downstairs and went into the library. And still Mr. Sterling paced the drawing room restlessly.

Daily In His Word

"Hear, O Israel! The LORD is our God, the LORD alone. And you must love the LORD your God with all your heart, all your soul, and all your strength."

DEUTERONOMY 6:4–5 NLT

He had finally wearied of the walking apparently, and throwing himself into a chair was brooding over something deeply when Felicia came in.

He rose and faced her. Felicia was evidently very much moved by the meeting from which she had just come. At the same time she did not wish to talk too much about it. Just as she entered the drawing room, Rose came in from the library.

"How many stayed?" she asked. Rose was curious. At the same time she was skeptical of the whole movement in Raymond.

"About a hundred," replied Felicia gravely. Mr. Sterling looked surprised. Felicia was going out of the room, but he called to her: "Do you really mean to keep the pledge?" he asked.

Felicia colored. Over her face and neck the warm blood flowed and she answered, "You would not ask such a question, father, if you had been at the meeting." She lingered a moment in the room, then asked to be excused from dinner for a while and went up to see her mother.

Daily In His Word

For the love of money is at the root of all kinds of evil. And some people, craving money, have wandered from the faith and pierced themselves with many sorrows.

1 Timothy 6:10 nlt

No one but they two ever knew what that interview between Felicia and her mother was. It is certain that she must have told her mother something of the spiritual power that had awed every person present in the company of disciples who faced Dr. Bruce in that meeting after the morning service. It is also certain that Felicia had never before known such an experience, and would never have thought of sharing it with her mother if it had not been for the prayer the evening before. Another fact is also known of Felicia's experience at this time. When she finally joined her father and Rose at the table she seemed unable to tell them much about the meeting. There was a reluctance to speak of it as one might hesitate to attempt a description of a wonderful sunset to a person who never talked about anything but the weather.

When that Sunday in the Sterling mansion was drawing to a close and the soft, warm lights throughout the dwelling were glowing through the great windows, in a corner of her room, where the light was obscure, Felicia kneeled, and when she raised her face and turned it towards the light, it was the face of a woman who had already defined for herself the greatest issues of earthly life.

Daily In His Word

Evildoers shall be cut off; but those who wait on the LORD, they shall inherit the earth.

PSALM 37:9 NKJV

That same evening, after the Sunday evening service, Dr. Bruce was talking over the events of the day with his wife. They were of one heart and mind in the matter, and faced their new future with all the faith and courage of new disciples. Neither was deceived as to the probable results of the pledge to themselves or to the church.

They had been talking but a little while when the bell rang and Dr. Bruce going to the door exclaimed, as he opened it: "It is you, Edward! Come in."

There came into the hall a commanding figure. The Bishop was of extraordinary height and breadth of shoulder, but of such good proportions that there was no thought of ungainly or even of unusual size. The impression the Bishop made on strangers was, first, that of great health, and then of great affection.

He came into the parlor and greeted Mrs. Bruce, who after a few moments was called out of the room, leaving the two men together. The Bishop sat in a deep, easy chair before the open fire. There was just enough dampness in the early spring of the year to make an open fire pleasant.

"Calvin, you have taken a very serious step today," he finally said, lifting his large dark eyes to his old college classmate's face. "I heard of it this afternoon. I could not resist the desire to see you about it tonight."

Daily In His Word

Better a poor man whose walk is blameless
than a fool whose lips are perverse.

Proverbs 19:1 niv

I'm glad you came." Dr. Bruce laid a hand on the Bishop's shoulder. "You understand what this means, Edward?"

"I think I do. Yes, I am sure." The Bishop spoke very slowly and thoughtfully. He sat with his hands clasped together. Over his face, marked with lines of consecration and service and the love of men, a shadow crept, a shadow not caused by the firelight. Once more he lifted his eyes toward his old friend.

"Calvin, we have always understood each other. Ever since our paths led us in different ways in church life we have walked together in Christian fellowship—"

"It is true," replied Dr. Bruce with an emotion he made no attempt to conceal or subdue. "Thank God for it. I prize your fellowship more than any other man's. I have always known what it meant, though it has always been more than I deserve."

The Bishop looked affectionately at his friend. But the shadow still rested on his face. After a pause he spoke again: "The new discipleship means a crisis for you in your work. If you keep this pledge to do all things as Jesus would do—as I know you will—it requires no prophet to predict some remarkable changes in your parish." The Bishop looked wistfully at his friend and then continued: "In fact, I do not see how a perfect upheaval of Christianity, as we now know it, can be prevented if the ministers and churches generally take the Raymond pledge and live it out."

Daily In His Word
A friend loves at all times, and a brother is born for adversity.
PROVERBS 17:17 NIV

He paused as if he were waiting for his friend to say something, to ask some question. But Bruce did not know of the fire that was burning in the Bishop's heart over the very question that Maxwell and himself had fought out.

"Now, in my church, for instance," continued the Bishop, "it would be rather a difficult matter, I fear, to find very many people who would take a pledge like that and live up to it. Martyrdom is a lost art with us. Our Christianity loves its ease and comfort too well to take up anything so rough and heavy as a cross. And yet what does following Jesus mean? What is it to walk in His steps?"

The Bishop was soliloquizing now and it is doubtful if he thought, for the moment, of his friend's presence. For the first time there flashed into Dr. Bruce's mind a suspicion of the truth. What if the Bishop would throw the weight of his great influence on the side of the Raymond movement? He had the following of the most aristocratic, wealthy, fashionable people, not only in Chicago, but in several large cities. What if the Bishop should join this new discipleship!

The thought was about to be followed by the word. Dr. Bruce had reached out his hand and with the familiarity of lifelong friendship had placed it on the Bishop's shoulder and was about to ask a very important question, when they were both startled by the violent ringing of the bell.

Daily In His Word

They asked each other, "Were not our hearts burning within us while he talked with us on the road and opened the Scriptures to us?"

LUKE 24:32 NIV

Mrs. Bruce had gone to the door and was talking with some one in the hall. There was a loud exclamation and then, as the Bishop rose and Bruce was stepping toward the curtain that hung before the entrance to the parlor, Mrs. Bruce pushed it aside. Her face was white and she was trembling.

"O Calvin! Such terrible news! Mr. Sterling—oh, I cannot tell it! What a blow to those girls!"

"What is it?" Mr. Bruce advanced with the Bishop into the hall and confronted the messenger, a servant from the Sterlings. The man was without his hat and had evidently run over with the news, as Dr. Bruce lived nearest of any intimate friends of the family.

"Mr. Sterling shot himself, sir, a few minutes ago. He killed himself in his bedroom. Mrs. Sterling—"

"I will go right over, Edward. Will you go with me? The Sterlings are old friends of yours."

The Bishop was very pale, but calm as always. He looked his friend in the face and answered: "Aye, Calvin, I will go with you not only to this house of death, but also the whole way of human sin and sorrow, please God."

Daily In His Word

"And whoever compels you to go one mile, go with him two."

Matthew 5:41 nkjv

CHAPTER TWENTY-FOUR

"These are they which follow the Lamb whithersoever He goeth."

When Dr. Bruce and the Bishop entered the Sterling mansion everything in the usually well appointed household was in the greatest confusion and terror. The great rooms downstairs were empty, but overhead were hurried footsteps and confused noises. One of the servants ran down the grand staircase with a look of horror on her face just as the Bishop and Dr. Bruce were starting to go up.

"Miss Felicia is with Mrs. Sterling," the servant stammered in answer to a question, and then burst into a hysterical cry and ran through the drawing-room and out of doors.

At the top of the staircase the two men were met by Felicia. She walked up to Dr. Bruce at once and put both hands in his. The Bishop then laid his hand on her head and the three stood there a moment in perfect silence. The Bishop had known Felicia since she was a little child. He was the first to break the silence.

"The God of all mercy be with you, Felicia, in this dark hour. Your mother—"

The Bishop hesitated. Out of the buried past he had, during his hurried passage from his friend's to this house of death, irresistibly drawn the one tender romance of his young manhood. Not even Bruce knew that.

Daily In His Word
"And He will wipe away every tear from their eyes; and there will no longer be any death; there will no longer be any mourning, or crying, or pain."
REVELATION 21:4 NASB

But there had been a time when the Bishop had offered the incense of a singularly undivided affection upon the altar of his youth to the beautiful Camilla Rolfe, and she had chosen between him and the millionaire. The Bishop carried no bitterness with his memory; but it was still a memory.

For answer to the Bishop's unfinished query, Felicia turned and went back into her mother's room. She had not said a word yet, but both men were struck with her wonderful calm. She returned to the hall door and beckoned to them, and the two ministers, with a feeling that they were about to behold something very unusual, entered.

Rose lay with her arms outstretched upon the bed. Clara, the nurse, sat with her head covered, sobbing in spasms of terror. And Mrs. Sterling with "the light that never was on sea or land" luminous on her face, lay there so still that even the Bishop was deceived at first. Then, as the great truth broke upon him and Dr. Bruce, he staggered, and the sharp agony of the old wound shot through him. It passed, and left him standing there in that chamber of death with the eternal calmness and strength that the children of God have a right to possess. And right well he used that calmness and strength in the days that followed.

Daily In His Word

These things I have spoken unto you, that in me ye might have peace. In the world ye shall have tribulation: but be of good cheer; I have overcome the world.

John 16:33 kjv

The next moment the house below was in a tumult. Almost at the same time the doctor who had been sent for at once, but lived some distance away, came in, together with police officers, who had been summoned by frightened servants. With them were four or five newspaper correspondents and several neighbors. Dr. Bruce and the Bishop met this miscellaneous crowd at the head of the stairs and succeeded in excluding all except those whose presence was necessary. With these the two friends learned all the facts ever known about the "Sterling tragedy," as the papers in their sensational accounts next day called it.

Mr. Sterling had gone into his room that evening about nine o'clock and that was the last seen of him until, in half an hour, a shot was heard in the room, and a servant who was in the hall ran into the room and found him dead on the floor, killed by his own hand. Felicia at the time was sitting by her mother. Rose was reading in the library. She ran upstairs, saw her father as he was being lifted upon the couch by the servants, and then ran screaming into her mother's room, where she flung herself down at the foot of the bed in a swoon. Mrs. Sterling had at first fainted at the shock, then rallied with a wonderful swiftness and sent for Dr. Bruce. She had then insisted on seeing her husband.

Daily In His Word

Just as Christ was raised from the dead through the glory of the Father, we too may live a new life.

Romans 6:4 niv

In spite of Felicia's efforts, she had compelled Clara to support her while she crossed the hall and entered the room where her husband lay. She had looked upon him with a tearless face, had gone back to her own room, was laid on her bed, and as Dr. Bruce and the Bishop entered the house she, with a prayer of forgiveness for herself and for her husband on her quivering lips, had died, with Felicia bending over her and Rose still lying senseless at her feet.

So great and swift had been the entrance of grim Death into that palace of luxury that Sunday night! But the full cause of his coming was not learned until the facts in regard to Mr. Sterling's business affairs were finally disclosed.

Then it was learned that for some time he had been facing financial ruin owing to certain speculations that had in a month's time swept his supposed wealth into complete destruction. With the cunning and desperation of a man who battles for his very life when he saw his money, which was all the life he ever valued, slipping from him, he had put off the evil day to the last moment. Sunday afternoon, however, he had received news that proved to him beyond a doubt the fact of his utter ruin.

Daily In His Word

He that trusteth in his riches shall fall;
but the righteous shall flourish as a branch.

PROVERBS 11:28 KJV

T he very house that he called his, the chairs in which he sat, his carriage, the dishes from which he ate, had all been bought with money for which he himself had never really done an honest stroke of pure labor.

It had all rested on a tissue of deceit and speculation that had no foundation in real values. He knew that fact better than any one else, but he had hoped, with the hope such men always have, that the same methods that brought him the money would also prevent the loss. He had been deceived in this as many others have been. As soon as the truth that he was practically a beggar had dawned upon him, he saw no escape from suicide. It was the irresistible result of such a life as he had lived. He had made money his god. As soon as that god was gone out of his little world there was nothing more to worship; and when a man's object of worship is gone he has no more to live for. Thus died the great millionaire, Charles R. Sterling. And, verily, he died as the fool dieth, for what is the gain or the loss of money compared with the unsearchable riches of eternal life which are beyond the reach of speculation, loss or change?

Daily In His Word

Charge them that are rich in this world, that they be not highminded, nor trust in uncertain riches, but in the living God, who giveth us richly all things to enjoy.

1 TIMOTHY 6:17 KJV

Mrs. Sterling's death was the result of the shock. She had not been taken into her husband's confidence for years, but she knew that the source of his wealth was precarious. Her life for several years had been a death in life. The Rolfes always gave an impression that they could endure more disaster unmoved than any one else. Mrs. Sterling illustrated the old family tradition when she was carried into the room where her husband lay. But the feeble tenement could not hold the spirit and it gave up the ghost, torn and weakened by long years of suffering and disappointment.

The effect of this triple blow, the death of father and mother, and the loss of property, was instantly apparent in the sisters. The horror of events stupefied Rose for weeks. She lay unmoved by sympathy or any effort to rally. She did not seem yet to realize that the money which had been so large a part of her very existence was gone. Even when she was told that she and Felicia must leave the house and be dependent on relatives and friends, she did not seem to understand what it meant.

Felicia, however, was fully conscious of the facts. She knew just what had happened and why.

Daily In His Word

Surely they busy themselves in vain; he heaps up riches,
and does not know who will gather them.

Psalm 39:6 NKJV

She was talking over her future plans with her cousin Rachel a few days after the funerals. Mrs. Winslow and Rachel had left Raymond and come to Chicago at once as soon as the terrible news had reached them, and with other friends of the family were planning for the future of Rose and Felicia.

"Felicia, you and Rose must come to Raymond with us. That is settled. Mother will not hear to any other plan at present," Rachel had said, while her beautiful face glowed with love for her cousin, a love that had deepened day by day, and was intensified by the knowledge that they both belonged to the new discipleship.

"Unless I can find something to do here," answered Felicia. She looked wistfully at Rachel, and Rachel said gently:

"What could you do, dear?"

"Nothing. I was never taught to do anything except a little music, and I do not know enough about it to teach it or earn my living at it. I have learned to cook a little," Felicia added with a slight smile.

"Then you can cook for us. Mother is always having trouble with her kitchen," said Rachel, understanding well enough she was now dependent for her very food and shelter upon the kindness of family friends. It is true the girls received a little something out of the wreck of their father's fortune, but with a speculator's mad folly he had managed to involve both his wife's and his children's portion in the common ruin.

Daily In His Word

As we talk to our God and Father about you, we think of your faithful work, your loving deeds, and your continual anticipation of the return of our Lord Jesus Christ.

1 Thessalonians 1:3 NLT

Can I? Can I?" Felicia responded to Rachel's proposition as if it were to be considered seriously. "I am ready to do anything honorable to make my living and that of Rose. Poor Rose! She will never be able to get over the shock of our trouble."

"We will arrange the details when we get to Raymond," Rachel said, smiling through her tears at Felicia's eager willingness to care for herself.

So in a few weeks Rose and Felicia found themselves a part of the Winslow family in Raymond. It was a bitter experience for Rose, but there was nothing else for her to do and she accepted the inevitable, brooding over the great change in her life and in many ways adding to the burden of Felicia and her cousin Rachel.

Felicia at once found herself in an atmosphere of discipleship that was like heaven to her in its revelation of companionship. It is true that Mrs. Winslow was not in sympathy with the course that Rachel was taking, but the remarkable events in Raymond since the pledge was taken were too powerful in their results not to impress even such a woman as Mrs. Winslow. With Rachel, Felicia found a perfect fellowship. She at once found a part to take in the new work at the Rectangle. In the spirit of her new life she insisted upon helping in the housework at her aunt's, and in a short time demonstrated her ability as a cook so clearly that Virginia suggested that she take charge of the cooking at the Rectangle.

Daily In His Word
But if we walk in the light as He is in the light, we have fellowship with one another, and the blood of Jesus Christ His Son cleanses us from all sin.

1 JOHN 1:7 NKJV

Felicia entered upon this work with the keenest pleasure. For the first time in her life she had the delight of doing something of value for the happiness of others. Her resolve to do everything after asking, "What would Jesus do?" touched her deepest nature. She began to develop and strengthen wonderfully. Even Mrs. Winslow was obliged to acknowledge the great usefulness and beauty of Felicia's character. The aunt looked with astonishment upon her niece, this city-bred girl, reared in the greatest luxury, the daughter of a millionaire, now walking around in her kitchen, her arms covered with flour and occasionally a streak of it on her nose, for Felicia at first had a habit of rubbing her nose forgetfully when she was trying to remember some recipe, mixing various dishes with the greatest interest in their results, washing up pans and kettles and doing the ordinary work of a servant in the Winslow kitchen and at the rooms at the Rectangle Settlement. At first Mrs. Winslow remonstrated.

"Felicia, it is not your place to be out here doing this common work. I cannot allow it."

Daily In His Word

"For the poor will never cease from the land; therefore I command you, saying, 'You shall open your hand wide to your brother, to your poor and your needy, in your land.'"

DEUTERONOMY 15:11 NKJV

Why, Aunt? Don't you like the muffins I made this morning?" Felicia would ask meekly, but with a hidden smile, knowing her aunt's weakness for that kind of muffin.

"They were beautiful, Felicia. But it does not seem right for you to be doing such work for us."

"Why not? What else can I do?"

Her aunt looked at her thoughtfully, noting her remarkable beauty of face and expression.

"You do not always intend to do this kind of work, Felicia?"

"Maybe I shall. I have had a dream of opening an ideal cook shop in Chicago or some large city and going around to the poor families in some slum district like the Rectangle, teaching the mothers how to prepare food properly. I remember hearing Dr. Bruce say once that he believed one of the great miseries of comparative poverty consisted in poor food. He even went so far as to say that he thought some kinds of crime could be traced to soggy biscuit and tough beefsteak. I'm sure I would be able to make a living for Rose and myself and at the same time help others."

Daily In His Word

This should be your ambition: to live a quiet life, minding your own business and working with your hands, just as we commanded you before.

1 Thessalonians 4:11 nlt

Chapter Twenty-five

T hree months had gone by since the Sunday morning when Dr. Bruce came into his pulpit with the message of the new discipleship. They were three months of great excitement in Nazareth Avenue Church. Never before had Rev. Calvin Bruce realized how deep the feeling of his members flowed. He humbly confessed that the appeal he had made met with an unexpected response from men and women who, like Felicia, were hungry for something in their lives that the conventional type of church membership and fellowship had failed to give them.

But Dr. Bruce was not yet satisfied for himself. He cannot tell what his feeling was or what led to the movement he finally made, to the great astonishment of all who knew him, better than by relating a conversation between him and the Bishop at this time in the history of the pledge in Nazareth Avenue Church. The two friends were as before in Dr. Bruce's house, seated in his study.

"You know what I have come in this evening for?" the Bishop was saying after the friends had been talking some time about the results of the pledge with the Nazareth Avenue people.

Dr. Bruce looked over at the Bishop and shook his head.

Daily In His Word
Show me the path where I should walk, O Lord; point out the right road for me to follow.

Psalm 25:4 NLT

I have come to confess that I have not yet kept my promise to walk in His steps in the way that I believe I shall be obliged to if I satisfy my thought of what it means to walk in His steps."

Dr. Bruce had risen and was pacing his study. The Bishop remained in the deep easy chair with his hands clasped, but his eye burned with the glow that belonged to him before he made some great resolve.

"Edward," Dr. Bruce spoke abruptly, "I have not yet been able to satisfy myself, either, in obeying my promise. But I have at last decided on my course. In order to follow it I shall be obliged to resign from Nazareth Avenue Church."

"I knew you would," replied the Bishop quietly. "And I came in this evening to say that I shall be obliged to do the same thing with my charge."

Dr. Bruce turned and walked up to his friend. They were both laboring under a repressed excitement.

"Is it necessary in your case?" asked Bruce.

"Yes. Let me state my reasons. Probably they are the same as yours. In fact, I am sure they are." The Bishop paused a moment, then went on with increasing feeling.

Daily In His Word

Lead me by your truth and teach me, for you are the God who saves me. All day long I put my hope in you.

Psalm 25:5 NLT

Calvin, you know how many years I have been doing the work of my position, and you know something of the responsibility and care of it. I do not mean to say that my life has been free from burden-bearing or sorrow. But I have certainly led what the poor and desperate of this sinful city would call a very comfortable, yes, a very luxurious life. I have had a beautiful house to live in, the most expensive food, clothing and physical pleasures. I have been able to go abroad at least a dozen times, and have enjoyed for years the beautiful companionship of art and letters and music and all the rest, of the very best. I have never known what it meant to be without money or its equivalent. And I have been unable to silence the question of late: 'What have I suffered for the sake of Christ?' Paul was told what great things he must suffer for the sake of his Lord. Maxwell's position at Raymond is well taken when he insists that to walk in the steps of Christ means to suffer. Where has my suffering come in? The petty trials and annoyances of my clerical life are not worth mentioning as sorrows or sufferings. Compared with Paul or any of the Christian martyrs or early disciples I have lived a luxurious, sinful life, full of ease and pleasure. I cannot endure this any longer. I have that within me which of late rises in overwhelming condemnation of such a following of Jesus. I have not been walking in His steps."

Daily In His Word

We live close to death, but here we are, still alive. We have been beaten within an inch of our lives. Our hearts ache, but we always have joy. We are poor, but we give spiritual riches to others. We own nothing, and yet we have everything.

2 Corinthians 6:9–10 nlt

Under the present system of church and social life I see no escape from this condemnation except to give the most of my life personally to the actual physical and soul needs of the wretched people in the worst part of this city."

The Bishop had risen now and walked over to the window. The street in front of the house was as light as day, and he looked out at the crowds passing, then turned and with a passionate utterance that showed how deep the volcanic fire in him burned, he exclaimed:

"Calvin, this is a terrible city in which we live! Its misery, its sin, its selfishness, appall my heart. And I have struggled for years with the sickening dread of the time when I should be forced to leave the pleasant luxury of my official position to put my life into contact with the modern paganism of this century. The awful condition of the girls in some great business places, the brutal selfishness of the insolent society fashion and wealth that ignores all the sorrow of the city, the fearful curse of the drink and gambling hell, the wail of the unemployed, the hatred of the church by countless men who see in it only great piles of costly stone and upholstered furniture and the minister as a luxurious idler, all the vast tumult of this vast torrent of humanity with its false and its true ideas, its exaggeration of evils in the church and its bitterness and shame that are the result of many complex causes, all this as a total fact in its contrast with the easy, comfortable life I have lived, fills me more and more with a sense of mingled terror and self accusation."

Daily In His Word

Arise, O LORD; let not man prevail: let the heathen be judged in thy sight. Put them in fear, O LORD: that the nations may know themselves to be but men.

PSALM 9:19–20 KJV

I have heard the words of Jesus many times lately: 'Inasmuch as ye did it not unto one of these least My brethren, ye did it not unto Me.' And when have I personally visited the prisoner or the desperate or the sinful in any way that has actually caused me suffering? Rather, I have followed the conventional soft habits of my position and have lived in the society of the rich, refined, aristocratic members of my congregations. Where has the suffering come in? What have I suffered for Jesus' sake? Do you know, Calvin," he turned abruptly toward his friend, "I have been tempted of late to lash myself with a scourge. If I had lived in Martin Luther's time I should have bared my back to a self-inflicted torture."

Dr. Bruce was very pale. Never had he seen the Bishop or heard him when under the influence of such a passion. There was a sudden silence in the room. The Bishop sat down again and bowed his head.

Dr. Bruce spoke at last: "Edward, I do not need to say that you have expressed my feelings also. I have been in a similar position for years. My life has been one of comparative luxury. I do not, of course, mean to say that I have not had trials and discouragements and burdens in my church ministry. But I cannot say that I have suffered any for Jesus. That verse in Peter constantly haunts me: 'Christ also suffered for you, leaving you an example that ye should follow His steps.'"

Daily In His Word

Let no one look down on your youthfulness, but rather in speech, conduct, love, faith and purity, show yourself an example of those who believe.

1 TIMOTHY 4:12 NASB

I have lived in luxury. I do not know what it means to want. I also have had my leisure for travel and beautiful companionship. I have been surrounded by the soft, easy comforts of civilization. The sin and misery of this great city have beaten like waves against the stone walls of my church and of this house in which I live, and I have hardly heeded them, the walls have been so thick. I have reached a point where I cannot endure this any longer. I am not condemning the Church. I love her. I am not forsaking the Church. I believe in her mission and have no desire to destroy. Least of all, in the step I am about to take do I desire to be charged with abandoning the Christian fellowship. But I feel that I must resign my place as pastor of Nazareth Church in order to satisfy myself that I am walking as I ought to walk in His steps. In this action I judge no other minister and pass no criticism on others' discipleship. But I feel as you do. Into a close contact with the sin and shame and degradation of this great city I must come personally. And I know that to do that I must sever my immediate connection with Nazareth Avenue Church. I do not see any other way for myself to suffer for His sake as I feel that I ought to suffer."

Daily In His Word

Everything God gives to his Son, Christ, is ours, too. But if we are to share his glory, we must also share his suffering.

Romans 8:17 NLT

Again that sudden silence fell over those two men. It was no ordinary action they were deciding. They had both reached the same conclusion by the same reasoning, and they were too thoughtful, too well accustomed to the measuring of conduct, to underestimate the seriousness of their position.

"What is your plan?" The Bishop at last spoke gently, looking with the smile that always beautified his face. The Bishop's face grew in glory now every day.

"My plan," replied Dr. Bruce slowly, "is, in brief, the putting of myself into the center of the greatest human need I can find in this city and living there. My wife is fully in accord with me. We have already decided to find a residence in that part of the city where we can make our personal lives count for the most."

"Let me suggest a place." The Bishop was on fire now. His fine face actually glowed with the enthusiasm of the movement in which he and his friend were inevitably embarked. He went on and unfolded a plan of such far-reaching power and possibility that Dr. Bruce, capable and experienced as he was, felt amazed at the vision of a greater soul than his own.

Daily In His Word

I have learned the secret of being content in any and every situation, whether well fed or hungry, whether living in plenty or in want.

PHILIPPIANS 4:12 NIV

They sat up late, and were as eager and even glad as if they were planning for a trip together to some rare land of unexplored travel. Indeed, the Bishop said many times afterward that the moment his decision was reached to live the life of personal sacrifice he had chosen he suddenly felt an uplifting as if a great burden were taken from him. He was exultant. So was Dr. Bruce from the same cause.

Their plan as it finally grew into a workable fact was in reality nothing more than the renting of a large building formerly used as a warehouse for a brewery, reconstructing it and living in it themselves in the very heart of a territory where the saloon ruled with power, where the tenement was its filthiest, where vice and ignorance and shame and poverty were congested into hideous forms. It was not a new idea. It was an idea started by Jesus Christ when He left His Father's House and forsook the riches that were His in order to get nearer humanity and, by becoming a part of its sin, helping to draw humanity apart from its sin. The University Settlement idea is not modern. It is as old as Bethlehem and Nazareth. And in this particular case it was the nearest approach to anything that would satisfy the hunger of these two men to suffer for Christ.

Daily In His Word

Everyone who sins breaks the law; in fact, sin is lawlessness.

1 JOHN 3:4 NIV

There had sprung up in them at the same time a longing that amounted to a passion, to get nearer the great physical poverty and spiritual destitution of the mighty city that throbbed around them. How could they do this except as they became a part of it as nearly as one man can become a part of another's misery? Where was the suffering to come in unless there was an actual self-denial of some sort? And what was to make that self-denial apparent to themselves or any one else, unless it took this concrete, actual, personal form of trying to share the deepest suffering and sin of the city?

So they reasoned for themselves, not judging others. They were simply keeping their own pledge to do as Jesus would do, as they honestly judged He would do. That was what they had promised. How could they quarrel with the result if they were irresistibly compelled to do what they were planning to do?

Daily In His Word

Watch your life and doctrine closely. Persevere in them, because if you do, you will save both yourself and your hearers.

1 TIMOTHY 4:16 NIV

CHAPTER TWENTY-SIX

Meanwhile, Nazareth Avenue Church was experiencing something never known before in all its history. The simple appeal on the part of its pastor to his members to do as Jesus would do had created a sensation that still continued. The result of that appeal was very much the same as in Henry Maxwell's church in Raymond, only this church was far more aristocratic, wealthy and conventional. Nevertheless when, one Sunday morning in early summer, Dr. Bruce came into his pulpit and announced his resignation, the sensation deepened all over the city, although he had advised with his board of trustees, and the movement he intended was not a matter of surprise to them. But when it become publicly known that the Bishop had also announced his resignation and retirement from the position he had held so long, in order to go and live himself in the center of the worst part of Chicago, the public astonishment reached its height.

"But why?" the Bishop replied to one valued friend who had almost with tears tried to dissuade him from his purpose. "Why should what Dr. Bruce and I propose to do seem so remarkable a thing, as if it were unheard of that a Doctor of Divinity and a Bishop should want to save lost souls in this particular manner?"

Daily In His Word

"We must work the works of him who sent me while it is day; night is coming when no one can work."

JOHN 9:4 NRSV

If we were to resign our charge for the purpose of going to Bombay or Hong Kong or any place in Africa, the churches and the people would exclaim at the heroism of missions. Why should it seem so great a thing if we have been led to give our lives to help rescue the heathen and the lost of our own city in the way we are going to try it? Is it then such a tremendous event that two Christian ministers should be not only willing but eager to live close to the misery of the world in order to know it and realize it? Is it such a rare thing that love of humanity should find this particular form of expression in the rescue of souls?"

And however the Bishop may have satisfied himself that there ought to be nothing so remarkable about it at all, the public continued to talk and the churches to record their astonishment that two such men, so prominent in the ministry, should leave their comfortable homes, voluntarily resign their pleasant social positions and enter upon a life of hardship, of self-denial and actual suffering. Christian America! Is it a reproach on the form of our discipleship that the exhibition of actual suffering for Jesus on the part of those who walk in His steps always provokes astonishment as at the sight of something very unusual?

Daily In His Word

That I may know Him and the power of His resurrection, and the fellowship of His sufferings.

PHILIPPIANS 3:10 NKJV

Nazareth Avenue Church parted from its pastor with regret for the most part, although the regret was modified with a feeling of relief on the part of those who had refused to take the pledge. Dr. Bruce carried with him the respect of men who, entangled in business in such a way that obedience to the pledge would have ruined them, still held in their deeper, better natures a genuine admiration for courage and consistency. They had known Dr. Bruce many years as a kindly, conservative, safe man, but the thought of him in the light of sacrifice of this sort was not familiar to them. As fast as they understood it, they gave their pastor the credit of being absolutely true to his recent convictions as to what following Jesus meant. Nazareth Avenue Church never lost the impulse of that movement started by Dr. Bruce. Those who went with him in making the promise breathed into the church the very breath of divine life, and are continuing that life-giving work at this present time.

Daily In His Word

"For I have given you an example, that you should do as I have done to you."

JOHN 13:15 NKJV

It was fall again, and the city faced another hard winter. The Bishop one afternoon came out of the Settlement and walked around the block, intending to go on a visit to one of his new friends in the district. He had walked about four blocks when he was attracted by a shop that looked different from the others. The neighborhood was still quite new to him, and every day he discovered some strange spot or stumbled upon some unexpected humanity.

The place that attracted his notice was a small house close by a Chinese laundry. There were two windows in the front, very clean, and that was remarkable to begin with. Then, inside the window, was a tempting display of cookery, with prices attached to the various articles that made him wonder somewhat, for he was familiar by this time with many facts in the life of the people once unknown to him. As he stood looking at the windows, the door between them opened and Felicia Sterling came out.

"Felicia!" exclaimed the Bishop. "When did you move into my parish without my knowledge?"

"How did you find me so soon?" inquired Felicia.

"Why, don't you know? These are the only clean windows in the block."

"I believe they are," replied Felicia with a laugh that did the Bishop good to hear.

Daily In His Word

"This is My commandment, that you love one another as I have loved you."

JOHN 15:12 NKJV

But why have you dared to come to Chicago without telling me, and how have you entered my diocese without my knowledge?" asked the Bishop. And Felicia looked so like that beautiful, clean, educated, refined world he once knew, that he might be pardoned for seeing in her something of the old Paradise. Although, to speak truth for him, he had no desire to go back to it.

"Well, dear Bishop," said Felicia, who had always called him so, "I knew how overwhelmed you were with your work. I did not want to burden you with my plans. And besides, I am going to offer you my services. Indeed, I was just on my way to see you and ask your advice. I am settled here for the present with Mrs. Bascom, a saleswoman who rents our three rooms, and with one of Rachel's music pupils who is being helped to a course in violin by Virginia Page. She is from the people," continued Felicia, using the words "from the people" so gravely and unconsciously that her hearer smiled, "and I am keeping house for her and at the same time beginning an experiment in pure food for the masses. I am an expert and I have a plan I want you to admire and develop. Will you, dear Bishop?"

"Indeed I will," he replied. The sight of Felicia and her remarkable vitality, enthusiasm and evident purpose almost bewildered him.

Daily In His Word

Though one may be overpowered, two can defend themselves. A cord of three strands is not quickly broken.

ECCLESIASTES 4:12 NIV

Martha can help at the Settlement with her violin and I will help with my messes. You see, I thought I would get settled first and work out something, and then come with some real thing to offer. I'm able to earn my own living now."

"You are?" the Bishop said a little incredulously. "How? Making those things?"

"Those things!" said Felicia with a show of indignation. "I would have you know, sir, that 'those things' are the best-cooked, purest food products in this whole city."

"I don't doubt it," he replied hastily, while his eyes twinkled. "Still, 'the proof of the pudding'—you know the rest."

"Come in and try some!" she exclaimed. "You poor Bishop! You look as if you hadn't had a good meal for a month."

She insisted on his entering the little front room where Martha, a wide-awake girl with short, curly hair, and an unmistakable air of music about her, was busy with practice.

"Go right on, Martha. This is the Bishop. You have heard me speak of him so often. Sit down there and let me give you a taste of the fleshpots of Egypt, for I believe you have been actually fasting."

So they had an improvised lunch, and the Bishop who, to tell the truth, had not taken time for weeks to enjoy his meals, feasted on the delight of his unexpected discovery and was able to express his astonishment and gratification at the quality of the cookery.

Daily In His Word
She gets up while it is still dark; she provides food for her family and portions for her servant girls.

Proverbs 31:15 niv

I thought you would at least say it is as good as the meals you used to get at the Auditorium at the big banquets," said Felicia slyly.

"As good as! The Auditorium banquets were simply husks compared with this one, Felicia. But you must come to the Settlement. I want you to see what we are doing. And I am simply astonished to find you here earning your living this way. I begin to see what your plan is. You can be of infinite help to us. You don't really mean that you will live here and help these people to know the value of good food?"

"Indeed I do," she answered gravely. "That is my gospel. Shall I not follow it?"

"Aye, Aye! You're right. Bless God for sense like yours! When I left the world," the Bishop smiled at the phrase, "they were talking a good deal about the 'new woman.' If you are one of them, I am a convert right now and here."

"Flattery! Still is there no escape from it, even in the slums of Chicago?" Felicia laughed again. And the man's heart, heavy though it had grown during several months of vast sin-bearing, rejoiced to hear it! It sounded good. It was good. It belonged to God.

Daily In His Word

True religion with contentment is great wealth. . . .
So if we have enough food and clothing, let us be content.

1 TIMOTHY 6:6, 8 NLT

Felicia wanted to visit the Settlement, and went back with him. She was amazed at the results of what considerable money and a good deal of consecrated brains had done. As they walked through the building they talked incessantly. She was the incarnation of vital enthusiasm, and he wondered at the exhibition of it as it bubbled up and sparkled over.

They went down into the basement and the Bishop pushed open a door from behind which came the sound of a carpenter's plane. It was a small but well equipped carpenter's shop. A young man with a paper cap on his head and clad in blouse and overalls was whistling and driving the plane as he whistled. He looked up as the two entered, and took off his cap. As he did so, his little finger carried a small curling shaving up to his hair and it caught there.

"Miss Sterling, Mr. Stephen Clyde," said the Bishop. "Clyde is one of our helpers here two afternoons in the week."

Just then the bishop was called upstairs and he excused himself a moment, leaving Felicia and the young carpenter together.

"We have met before," said Felicia looking at Clyde frankly.

"Yes, 'back in the world,' as the Bishop says," replied the young man, and his fingers trembled a little as they lay on the board he had been planing.

"Yes." Felicia hesitated. "I am very glad to see you."

Daily In His Word

There are "friends" who destroy each other, but a real friend sticks closer than a brother.

Proverbs 18:24 NLT

Are you?" The flush of pleasure mounted to the young carpenter's forehead. "You have had a great deal of trouble since—since—then," he said, and then he was afraid he had wounded her, or called up painful memories. But she had lived over all that.

"Yes, and you also. How is it that you're working here?"

"It is a long story, Miss Sterling. My father lost his money and I was obliged to go to work. A very good thing for me. The Bishop says I ought to be very grateful. I am. I am very happy now. I learned the trade, hoping some time to be of use, I am night clerk at one of the hotels. That Sunday morning when you took the pledge at Nazareth Avenue Church, I took it with the others."

"Did you?" said Felicia slowly. "I am glad."

Just then the Bishop came back, and very soon he and Felicia went away leaving the young carpenter at his work. Some one noticed that he whistled louder than ever as he planed.

"Felicia," said the Bishop, "did you know Stephen Clyde before?"

"Yes, 'back in the world,' dear Bishop. He was one of my acquaintances in Nazareth Avenue Church."

"Ah!" said the Bishop.

"We were very good friends," added Felicia.

Daily In His Word

Happy are the people to whom such blessings fall; happy are the people whose God is the LORD.

Psalm 144:15 nrsv

Bᵁᵗ nothing more?" the Bishop ventured to ask.

Felicia's face glowed for an instant. Then she looked her companion in the eyes frankly and answered: "Truly and truly, nothing more."

"It would be just the way of the world for these two people to come to like each other, though," thought the man to himself, and somehow the thought made him grave. It was almost like the old pang over Camilla. But it passed, leaving him afterwards, when Felicia had gone back, with tears in his eyes and a feeling that was almost hope that Felicia and Stephen would like each other. "After all," he said, like the sensible, good man that he was, "is not romance a part of humanity? Love is older than I am, and wiser."

The week following, the Bishop had an experience that belongs to this part of the Settlement history. He was coming back to the Settlement very late from some gathering of the striking tailors, and was walking along with his hands behind him, when two men jumped out from behind an old fence that shut off an abandoned factory from the street, and faced him. One of the men thrust a pistol in his face, and the other threatened him with a ragged stake that had evidently been torn from the fence.

"Hold up your hands, and be quick about it!" said the man with the pistol.

Daily In His Word
But if we love each other, God lives in us, and his love has been brought to full expression through us.

1 JOHN 4:12 NLT

Chapter Twenty-seven

*"Righteousness shall go before him
and shall set us in the way of his steps."*

The Bishop was not in the habit of carrying much money with him, and the man with the stake who was searching him uttered an oath at the small amount of change he found. As he uttered it, the man with the pistol savagely said, "Jerk out his watch! We might as well get all we can out of the job!"

The man with the stake was on the point of laying hold of the chain where there was a sound of footsteps coming towards him.

"Get behind the fence! We haven't half searched him yet! Mind you keep shut now, if you don't want—"

The man with the pistol made a significant gesture with it and, with his companion, pulled and pushed the Bishop down the alley and through a ragged, broken opening in the fence. The three stood still there in the shadow until the footsteps passed.

"Now, then, have you got the watch?" asked the man with the pistol.

"No, the chain is caught somewhere!" and the other man swore again.

"Break it then!"

"No, don't break it," the Bishop said, and it was the first time he had spoken. "The chain is the gift of a very dear friend. I should be sorry to have it broken."

Daily In His Word

Let him that stole steal no more: but rather let him labour, work-ing with his hands the thing which is good, that he may have to give to him that needeth.

Ephesians 4:28 kjv

At the sound of the Bishop's voice the man with the pistol started as if he had been suddenly shot by his own weapon. With a quick movement of his other hand he turned the Bishop's head towards what little light was shining from the alleyway, at the same time taking a step nearer. Then, to the amazement of his companion, he said roughly: "Leave the watch alone! We've got the money. That's enough!"

"Enough! Fifty cents! You don't reckon—"

Before the man with the stake could say another word he was confronted with the muzzle of the pistol turned from the Bishop's head towards his own.

"Leave that watch be! And put back the money too. This is the Bishop we've held up—the Bishop—do you hear?"

"And what of it! The President of the United States wouldn't be too good to hold up, if—"

"I say, you put the money back, or in five seconds I'll blow a hole through your head that'll let in more sense than you have to spare now!" said the other.

For a second the man with the stake seemed to hesitate at this strange turn in events, as if measuring his companion's intention. Then he hastily dropped the money back into the rifled pocket.

Daily In His Word

Paul replied, "Brothers, I did not realize that he was the high priest; for it is written: 'Do not speak evil about the ruler of your people.'"

Acts 23:5 niv

Y ou can take your hands down, sir." The man lowered his weapon slowly, still keeping an eye on the other man, and speaking with rough respect. The Bishop slowly brought his arms to his side, and looked earnestly at the two men. In the dim light it was difficult to distinguish features. He was evidently free to go his way now, but he stood there making no movement.

"You can go on. You needn't stay any longer on our account." The man who had acted as spokesman turned and sat down on a stone. The other man stood viciously digging his stake into the ground.

"That's just what I am staying for," replied the Bishop. He sat down on a board that projected from the broken fence.

"You must like our company. It is hard sometimes for people to tear themselves away from us," and the man standing up laughed coarsely.

"Shut up!" exclaimed the other. "We're on the road to hell, though, that's sure enough. We need better company than ourselves and the devil."

"If you would only allow me to be of any help," the Bishop spoke gently, even lovingly. The man on the stone stared at the Bishop through the darkness. After a moment of silence he spoke slowly like one who had finally decided upon a course he had at first rejected.

"Do you remember ever seeing me before?"

Daily In His Word

The Lord preserveth the simple:
I was brought low, and he helped me.

Psalm 116:6 kjv

N o," said the Bishop. "The light is not very good and I have really not had a good look at you."

"Do you know me now?" The man suddenly took off his hat and getting up from the stone walked over to the Bishop until they were near enough to touch each other.

The man's hair was coal black except one spot on the top of his head about as large as the palm of the hand, which was white.

The minute the Bishop saw that, he started. The memory of fifteen years ago began to stir in him. The man helped him.

"Don't you remember one day back in '81 or '82 a man came to your house and told a story about his wife and child having been burned to death in a tenement fire in New York?"

"Yes, I begin to remember now." The other man seemed to be interested. He ceased digging his stake in the ground and stood still listening.

"Do you remember how you took me into your own house that night and spent all next day trying to find me a job? And how when you succeeded in getting me a place in a warehouse as foreman, I promised to quit drinking because you asked me to?"

"I remember it now. I hope you have kept your promise."

Daily In His Word
We are to God the fragrance of Christ among those who are being saved and among those who are perishing.

2 CORINTHIANS 2:15 NKJV

The man laughed savagely. Then he struck his hand against the fence with such sudden passion that he drew blood.

"Kept it! I was drunk inside of a week! I've been drinking ever since. But I've never forgotten you nor your prayer. Do you remember the morning after I came to your house, after breakfast you had prayers and asked me to come in and sit with the rest? That got me! But my mother used to pray! I can see her now kneeling down by my bed when I was a lad. Father came in one night and kicked her while she was kneeling there by me. But I never forgot that prayer of yours that morning. You prayed for me just as mother used to, and you didn't seem to take 'count of the fact that I was ragged and tough-looking and more than half drunk when I rang your door bell. Oh, what a life I've lived! The saloon has housed me and homed me and made hell on earth for me. But that prayer stuck to me all the time. My promise not to drink was broken into a thousand pieces inside of two Sundays, and I lost the job you found for me and landed in a police station two days later, but I never forgot you nor your prayer. I don't know what good it has done me, but I never forgot it. And I won't do any harm to you nor let any one else. So you're free to go. That's why."

Daily In His Word

Therefore I want the men in every place to pray, lifting up holy hands, without wrath and dissension.

1 TIMOTHY 2:8 NASB

The Bishop did not stir. Somewhere a church clock struck one. The man had put on his hat and gone back to his seat on the stone. The Bishop was thinking hard.

"How long is it since you had work?" he asked, and the man standing up answered for the other.

"More'in six months since either of us did anything to tell of; unless you count 'holding up' work. I call it pretty wearing kind of a job myself, especially when we put in a night like this and don't make nothin'."

"Suppose I found good jobs for both of you? Would you quit this and begin all over?"

"What's the use?" the man on the stone spoke sullenly. "I've reformed a hundred times. Every time I go down deeper. The devil's begun to foreclose on me already. It's too late."

"No!" said the Bishop. And never before the most entranced audience had he felt the desire for souls burn up in him so strongly. All the time he sat there during the remarkable scene he prayed, "O Lord Jesus, give me the souls of these two for Thee! I am hungry for them. Give them to me!"

Daily In His Word
The fruit of the righteous is a tree of life;
and he that winneth souls is wise.

PROVERBS 11:30 KJV

N o!" the Bishop repeated. "What does God want of you two men? It doesn't so much matter what I want. But He wants just what I do in this case. You two men are of infinite value to Him." And then his wonderful memory came to his aid in an appeal such as no one on earth among men could make under such circumstances. He had remembered the man's name in spite of the wonderfully busy years that lay between his coming to the house and the present moment.

"Burns," he said, and he yearned over the men with an unspeakable longing for them both, "if you and your friend here will go home with me tonight I will find you both places of honorable employment. I will believe in you and trust you. You are both comparatively young men. Why should God lose you? It is a great thing to win the love of the Great Father. It is a small thing that I should love you. But if you need to feel again that there is love in the world, you will believe me when I say, my brothers, that I love you, and in the name of Him who was crucified for our sins I cannot bear to see you miss the glory of the human life. Come, be men! Make another try for it, God helping you. No one but God and you and myself need ever know anything of this tonight. He has forgiven it the minute you ask Him to. You will find that true."

Daily In His Word

Be kind and compassionate to one another, forgiving each other, just as in Christ God forgave you.

Ephesians 4:32 niv

Come! We'll fight it out together, you two and I. It's worth fighting for, everlasting life is. It was the sinner that Christ came to help. I'll do what I can for you. O God, give me the souls of these two men!" and he broke into a prayer to God that was a continuation of his appeal to the men. His pent-up feeling had no other outlet. Before he had prayed many moments Burns was sitting with his face buried in his hands, sobbing. Where were his mother's prayers now? They were adding to the power of the Bishop's. And the other man, harder, less moved, without a previous knowledge of the Bishop, leaned back against the fence, stolid at first. But as the prayer went on, he was moved by it. What force of the Holy Spirit swept over his dulled, brutal, coarsened life, nothing but the eternal records of the recording angel can ever disclose. But the same supernatural Presence that smote Paul on the road to Damascus, and poured through Henry Maxwell's church the morning he asked disciples to follow in Jesus' steps, and had again broken irresistibly over the Nazareth Avenue congregation, now manifested Himself in this foul corner of the mighty city and over the natures of these two sinful sunken men, apparently lost to all the pleadings of conscience and memory and God. The prayer seemed to break open the crust that for years had surrounded them and shut them off from divine communication. And they themselves were thoroughly startled by it.

Daily In His Word

Then Peter said to them, "Repent, and let every one of you be baptized in the name of Jesus Christ for the remission of sins; and you shall receive the gift of the Holy Spirit."

ACTS 2:38 NKJV

The Bishop ceased, and at first he himself did not realize what had happened. Neither did they. Burns still sat with his head bowed between his knees. The man leaning against the fence looked at the Bishop with a face in which new emotions of awe, repentance, astonishment and a broken gleam of joy struggled for expression. The Bishop rose.

"Come, my brothers. God is good. You shall stay at the Settlement tonight, and I will make good my promise as to the work."

The two men followed him in silence. When they reached the Settlement it was after two o'clock. He let them in and led them to a room. At the door he paused a moment. His tall, commanding figure stood in the doorway and his pale face was illuminated with the divine glory.

"God bless you, my brothers!" he said, and leaving them his benediction he went away.

Daily In His Word

Love your enemies, bless them that curse you, do good to them that hate you, and pray for them which despitefully use you, and persecute you.

MATTHEW 5:44 KJV

Chapter Twenty-eight

It was the afternoon of that morning when Burns was installed in his new position as assistant janitor that he was cleaning off the front steps of the Settlement, when he paused a moment and stood up to look about him. The first thing he noticed was a beer sign just across the alley. He could almost touch it with his broom from where he stood. Over the street immediately opposite were two large saloons, and a little farther down were three more.

Suddenly the door of the nearest saloon opened and a man came out. At the same time two more went in. A strong odor of beer floated up to Burns as he stood on the steps. He clutched his broom handle tightly and began to sweep again. He had one foot on the porch and another on the steps just below. He took another step down, still sweeping. The sweat stood on his forehead although the day was frosty and the air chill. The saloon door opened again and three or four men came out. A child went in with a pail, and came out a moment later with a quart of beer. The child went by on the sidewalk just below him, and the odor of the beer came up to him. He took another step down, still sweeping desperately. His fingers were purple as he clutched the handle of the broom.

Daily In His Word

No one who wants to do wrong should ever say,
"God is tempting me." God is never tempted to
do wrong, and he never tempts anyone else either.
James 1:13 nlt

The suddenly he pulled himself up one step and swept over the spot he had just cleaned. He then dragged himself by a tremendous effort back to the floor of the porch and went over into the corner of it farthest from the saloon and began to sweep there. "O God!" he cried, "if the Bishop would only come back!" The Bishop had gone out with Dr. Bruce somewhere, and there was no one about that he knew. He swept in the corner for two or three minutes. His face was drawn with the agony of his conflict. Gradually he edged out again towards the steps and began to go down them. He looked towards the sidewalk and saw that he had left one step unswept. The sight seemed to give him a reasonable excuse for going down there to finish his sweeping.

He was on the sidewalk now, sweeping the last step, with his face towards the Settlement and his back turned partly on the saloon across the alley. He swept the step a dozen times. The sweat rolled over his face and dropped down at his feet. By degrees he felt that he was drawn over towards that end of the step nearest the saloon. He could smell the beer and rum now as the fumes rose around him. It was like the infernal sulphur of the lowest hell, and yet it dragged him as by a giant's hand nearer its source.

Daily In His Word

Awake to righteousness, and sin not; for some have not the knowledge of God: I speak this to your shame.

1 CORINTHIANS 15:34 KJV

He was down in the middle of the sidewalk now, still sweeping. He cleared the space in front of the Settlement and even went out into the gutter and swept that. He took off his hat and rubbed his sleeve over his face. His lips were pallid and his teeth chattered. He trembled all over like a palsied man and staggered back and forth as if he was already drunk. His soul shook within him.

He had crossed over the little piece of stone flagging that measured the width of the alley, and now he stood in front of the saloon, looking at the sign, and staring into the window at the pile of whiskey and beer bottles arranged in a great pyramid inside. He moistened his lips with his tongue and took a step forward, looking around him stealthily. The door suddenly opened again and someone came out. Again the hot, penetrating smell of liquor swept out into the cold air, and he took another step towards the saloon door which had shut behind the customer. As he laid his fingers on the door handle, a tall figure came around the corner. It was the Bishop.

Daily In His Word
Putting aside all filthiness and all that remains
of wickedness, in humility receive the word implanted,
which is able to save your souls.

JAMES 1:21 NASB

He seized Burns by the arm and dragged him back upon the sidewalk. The frenzied man, now mad for a drink, shrieked out a curse and struck at his friend savagely. It is doubtful if he really knew at first who was snatching him away from his ruin. The blow fell upon the Bishop's face and cut a gash in his cheek. He never uttered a word. But over his face a look of majestic sorrow swept. He picked Burns up as if he had been a child and actually carried him up the steps and into the house. He put him down in the hall and then shut the door and put his back against it.

Burns fell on his knees sobbing and praying. The Bishop stood there panting with his exertion, although Burns was a slightly-built man and had not been a great weight for a man of his strength to carry. He was moved with unspeakable pity.

"Pray, Burns—pray as you never prayed before! Nothing else will save you!"

"O God! Pray with me. Save me! Oh, save me from my hell!" cried Burns. And, the Bishop knelt by him in the hall and prayed as only he could pray.

Daily In His Word

But I am poor and needy; please hurry to my aid, O God. You are my helper and my savior; O LORD, do not delay!

PSALM 70:5 NLT

After that they rose and Burns went to his room. He came out of it that evening like a humble child. And the Bishop went his way older from that experience, bearing on his body the marks of the Lord Jesus. Truly he was learning something of what it means to walk in His steps.

But the saloon! It stood there, and all the others lined the street like so many traps set for Burns. How long would the man be able to resist the smell of the damnable stuff? The Bishop went out on the porch. The air of the whole city seemed to be impregnated with the odor of beer. "How long, O Lord, how long?" he prayed. Dr. Bruce came out, and the two friends talked about Burns and his temptation.

"Did you ever make any inquiries about the ownership of this property adjoining us?" the Bishop asked.

"No, I haven't taken time for it. I will now if you think it would be worthwhile. But what can we do, Edward, against the saloon in this great city? It is as firmly established as the churches or politics. What power can ever remove it?"

"God will do it in time, as He has removed slavery," was the grave reply. "Meanwhile I think we have a right to know who controls this saloon so near the Settlement."

"I'll find out," said Dr. Bruce.

Daily In His Word

Deliver me, oh my God, out of the hand of the wicked, out of the hand of the unrighteous and cruel man.

Psalm 71:4 KJV

T wo days later he walked into the business office of one of the members of Nazareth Avenue Church and asked to see him a few moments. He was cordially received by his old parishioner, who welcomed him into his room and urged him to take all the time he wanted.

"I called to see you about that property next the Settlement where the Bishop and myself now are, you know. I am going to speak plainly, because life is too short and too serious for us both to have any foolish hesitation about this matter. Clayton, do you think it is right to rent that property for a saloon?"

Dr. Bruce's question was as direct and uncompromising as he had meant it to be. The effect of it on his old parishioner was instantaneous.

The hot blood mounted to the face of the man who sat there beneath a picture of business activity in a great city. Then he grew pale, dropped his head on his hands, and when he raised it again Dr. Bruce was amazed to see a tear roll over his face.

"Doctor, did you know that I took the pledge that morning with the others?"

"Yes, I remember."

"But you never knew how I have been tormented over my failure to keep it in this instance. That saloon property has been the temptation of the devil to me."

Daily In His Word

Therefore submit to God. Resist the devil and he will flee from you. Draw near to God and He will draw near to you.

JAMES 4:7–8 NKJV

It is the best paying investment at present that I have. And yet it was only a minute before you came in here that I was in an agony of remorse to think how I was letting a little earthly gain tempt me into a denial of the very Christ I had promised to follow. I knew well enough that He would never rent property for such a purpose. There is no need, Dr. Bruce, for you to say a word more."

Clayton held out his hand and Dr. Bruce grasped it and shook it hard. After a little he went away. But it was a long time afterwards that he learned all the truth about the struggle that Clayton had known. It was only a part of the history that belonged to Nazareth Avenue Church since that memorable morning when the Holy Spirit sanctioned the Christlike pledge. Not even the Bishop and Dr. Bruce, moving as they now did in the very presence itself of divine impulses, knew yet that over the whole sinful city the Spirit was brooding with mighty eagerness, waiting for the disciples to arise to the call of sacrifice and suffering, touching hearts long dull and cold, making businessmen and money-makers uneasy in their absorption by the one great struggle for more wealth, and stirring through the church as never in all the city's history the church had been moved. The Bishop and Dr. Bruce had already seen some wonderful things in their brief life at the Settlement. They were to see far greater soon, more astonishing revelations of the divine power than they had supposed possible in this age of the world.

Daily In His Word

I am not ashamed of the gospel, because it is the power of God for the salvation of everyone who believes.

ROMANS 1:16 NIV

Within a month the saloon next the Settlement was closed. The saloon-keeper's lease had expired, and Clayton not only closed the property to the whiskey men, but offered the building to the Bishop and Dr. Bruce to use for the Settlement work, which had now grown so large that the building they had first rented was not sufficient for the different industries that were planned.

One of the most important of these was the pure-food department suggested by Felicia. It was not a month after Clayton turned the saloon property over to the Settlement that Felicia found herself installed in the very room where souls had been lost, as head of the department not only of cooking but of a course of housekeeping for girls who wished to go out to service. She was now a resident of the Settlement, and found a home with Mrs. Bruce and the other young women from the city who were residents. Martha, the violinist, remained at the place where the Bishop had first discovered the two girls, and came over to the Settlement certain evenings to give lessons in music.

Daily In His Word

"But you, be strong and do not let your hands be weak, for your work shall be rewarded!"

2 Chronicles 15:7 nkjv

F elicia, tell us your plan in full now," said the Bishop one evening when, in a rare interval of rest from the great pressure of work, he was with Dr. Bruce, and Felicia had come in from the other building.

"Well, I have long thought of the hired girl problem," said Felicia with an air of wisdom that made Mrs. Bruce smile as she looked at the enthusiastic, vital beauty of this young girl, transformed into a new creature by the promise she had made to live the Christlike life. "And I have reached certain conclusions in regard to it that you men are not yet able to fathom, but Mrs. Bruce will understand me."

"We acknowledge our infancy, Felicia. Go on," said the Bishop humbly.

"Then this is what I propose to do. The old saloon building is large enough to arrange into a suite of rooms that will represent an ordinary house. My plan is to have it so arranged, and then teach housekeeping and cooking to girls who will afterwards go out to service. The course will be six months' long; in that time I will teach plain cooking, neatness, quickness, and a love of good work."

"Hold on, Felicia!" the Bishop interrupted. "This is not an age of miracles!"

"Then we will make it one," replied Felicia.

Daily In His Word

Jesus looked at them and said, "With man this is impossible, but with God all things are possible."

Matthew 19:26 niv

I know this seems like an impossibility, but I want to try it. I know a score of girls already who will take the course, and if we can once establish something like an esprit de corps among the girls themselves, I am sure it will be of great value to them. I know already that the pure food is working a revolution in many families."

"Felicia, if you can accomplish half what you propose it will bless this community," said Mrs. Bruce. "I don't see how you can do it, but I say, God bless you, as you try."

"So say we all!" cried Dr. Bruce and the Bishop, and Felicia plunged into the working out of her plan with the enthusiasm of her discipleship which every day grew more and more practical and serviceable.

It must be said here that Felicia's plan succeeded beyond all expectations. She developed wonderful powers of persuasion, and taught her girls with astonishing rapidity to do all sorts of housework. In time, the graduates of Felicia's cooking school came to be prized by housekeepers all over the city. But that is anticipating our story. The history of the Settlement has never yet been written. When it is, Felicia's part will be found of very great importance.

Daily In His Word

Make it your ambition to lead a quiet life and attend to your own business and work with your hands, just as we commanded you.

1 THESSALONIANS 4:11 NASB

T he depth of winter found Chicago presenting, as every great city of the world presents to the eyes of Christendom the marked contrast between riches and poverty, between culture, refinement, luxury, ease, and ignorance, depravity, destitution and the bitter struggle for bread. It was a hard winter but a gay winter. Never had there been such a succession of parties, receptions, balls, dinners, banquets, fetes, gayeties. Never had the opera and the theatre been so crowded with fashionable audiences. Never had there been such a lavish display of jewels and fine dresses and equipages. And on the other hand, never had the deep want and suffering been so cruel, so sharp, so murderous. Never had the winds blown so chilling over the lake and through the thin shells of tenements in the neighborhood of the Settlement. Never had the pressure for food and fuel and clothes been so urgently thrust up against the people of the city in their most importunate and ghastly form. Night after night the Bishop and Dr. Bruce with their helpers went out and helped save men and women and children from the torture of physical privation. Vast quantities of food and clothing and large sums of money were donated by the churches, the charitable societies, the civic authorities and the benevolent associations. But the personal touch of the Christian disciple was very hard to secure for personal work. Where was the discipleship that was obeying the Master's command to go itself to the suffering and give itself with its gift in order to make the gift of value in time to come?

Daily In His Word
"Go and make disciples of all the nations, baptizing them in the name of the Father and the Son and the Holy Spirit."
MATTHEW 28:19 NLT

T he Bishop found his heart sink within him as he faced this fact more than any other. Men would give money who would not think of giving themselves. And the money they gave did not represent any real sacrifice because they did not miss it. They gave what was the easiest to give, what hurt them the least. Where did the sacrifice come in? Was this following Jesus? Was this going with Him all the way? He had been to members of his own aristocratic, splendidly wealthy congregations, and was appalled to find how few men and women of that luxurious class in the churches would really suffer any genuine inconvenience for the sake of suffering humanity. Is charity the giving of worn-out garments? Is it a ten-dollar bill given to a paid visitor or secretary of some benevolent organization in the church? Shall the man never go and give his gift himself? Shall the woman never deny herself her reception or her party or her musicale, and go and actually touch, herself, the foul, sinful sore of diseased humanity as it festers in the great metropolis? Shall charity be conveniently and easily done through some organization? Is it possible to organize the affections so that love shall work disagreeable things by proxy?

All this the Bishop asked as he plunged deeper into the sin and sorrow of that bitter winter. He was bearing his cross with joy. But he burned and fought within over the shifting of personal love by the many upon the hearts of the few. And still, silently, powerfully, resistlessly, the Holy Spirit was moving through the churches, even the aristocratic, wealthy, ease-loving members who shunned the terrors of the social problem as they would shun a contagious disease.

Daily In His Word
There is no fear in love; but perfect love casts out fear.
1 JOHN 4:18 NASB

Chapter Twenty-nine

The breakfast hour at the settlement was the one hour in the day when the whole family found a little breathing space to fellowship together. It was an hour of relaxation. There was a great deal of good-natured repartee and much real wit and enjoyable fun at this hour. The Bishop told his best stories. Dr. Bruce was at his best in anecdote. This company of disciples was healthily humorous in spite of the atmosphere of sorrow that constantly surrounded them. In fact, the Bishop often said the faculty of humor was as God-given as any other and in his own case it was the only safety valve he had for the tremendous pressure put upon him.

This particular morning he was reading extracts from a morning paper for the benefit of the others. Suddenly he paused and his face instantly grew stern and sad. The rest looked up and a hush fell over the table.

"Shot and killed while taking a lump of coal from a car! His family was freezing and he had no work for six months. Six children and a wife all packed into a cabin with three rooms, on the West Side. One child wrapped in rags in a closet!"

These were headlines that he read slowly. He then went on and read the detailed account of the shooting and the visit of the reporter to the tenement where the family lived. He finished, and there was silence around the table. The humor of the hour was swept out of existence by this bit of human tragedy.

Daily In His Word

"For the waves of death encompassed me. . . . The snares of death confronted me. In my distress I called upon the LORD."

2 Samuel 22:5–7 NASB

T he great city roared about the Settlement. The awful current of human life was flowing in a great stream past the Settlement House, and those who had work were hurrying to it in a vast throng. But thousands were going down in the midst of that current, clutching at last hopes, dying literally in a land of plenty because the boon of physical toil was denied them.

There were various comments on the part of the residents. One of the newcomers, a young man preparing for the ministry, said: "Why don't the man apply to one of the charity organizations for help? Or to the city? It certainly is not true that even at its worst this city full of Christian people would knowingly allow any one to go without food or fuel."

"No, I don't believe it would," replied Dr. Bruce. "But we don't know the history of this man's case. He may have asked for help so often before that, finally, in a moment of desperation he determined to help himself. I have known such cases this winter."

"That is not the terrible fact in this case," said the Bishop. "The awful thing about it is the fact that the man had not had any work for six months."

Daily In His Word

Then the LORD God took the man and put him into the garden of Eden to cultivate it and keep it.

GENESIS 2:15 NASB

Why don't such people go out into the country?" asked the divinity student.

Someone at the table who had made a special study of the opportunities for work in the country answered the question. According to the investigator the places that were possible for work in the country were exceedingly few for steady employment, and in almost every case they were offered only to men without families. Suppose a man's wife or children were ill. How would he move or get into the country? How could he pay even the meager sum necessary to move his few goods? There were a thousand reasons probably why this particular man did not go elsewhere.

"Meanwhile there are the wife and children," said Mrs. Bruce. "How awful! Where is the place, did you say?"

"Why, it is only three blocks from here. This is the 'Penrose district.' I believe Penrose himself owns half of the houses in that block. They are among the worst houses in this part of the city. And Penrose is a church member."

"Yes, he belongs to the Nazareth Avenue Church," replied Dr. Bruce in a low voice.

The Bishop rose from the table the very figure of divine wrath. He had opened his lips to say what seldom came from him in the way of denunciation, when the bell rang and one of the residents went to the door.

Daily In His Word

"If you sell land to one of your countrymen or buy any from him, do not take advantage of each other.'"

Leviticus 25:14 niv

Tell Dr. Bruce and the Bishop I want to see them. Penrose is the name—Clarence Penrose. Dr. Bruce knows me."

The family at the breakfast table heard every word. The Bishop exchanged a significant look with Dr. Bruce and the two men instantly left the table and went out into the hall.

"Come in here, Penrose," said Dr. Bruce, and they ushered the visitor into the reception room, closed the door and were alone.

Clarence Penrose was one of the most elegant looking men in Chicago. He came from an aristocratic family of great wealth and social distinction. He was exceedingly wealthy and had large property holdings in different parts of the city. He had been a member of Dr. Bruce's church many years. He faced the two ministers with a look of agitation on his face that showed plainly the mark of some unusual experience. He was very pale and his lips trembled as he spoke. When had Clarence Penrose ever before yielded to such a strange emotion?

"This affair of the shooting! You understand? You have read it? The family lived in one of my houses. It is a terrible event. But that is not the primary cause of my visit." He stammered and looked anxiously into the faces of the two men. The Bishop still looked stern. He could not help feeling that this elegant man of leisure could have done a great deal to alleviate the horrors in his tenements, possibly have prevented this tragedy if he had sacrificed some of his personal ease and luxury to better the conditions of the people in his district.

Daily In His Word

The eyes of the LORD are on the righteous and his ears are attentive to their cry.

Psalm 34:15 NIV

P enrose turned toward Dr. Bruce. "Doctor!" he exclaimed, and there was almost a child's terror in his voice. "I came to say that I have had an experience so unusual that nothing but the supernatural can explain it. You remember I was one of those who took the pledge to do as Jesus would do. I thought at the time, poor fool that I was, that I had all along been doing the Christian thing. I gave liberally out of my abundance to the church and charity. I never gave myself to cost me any suffering. I have been living in a perfect hell of contradictions ever since I took that pledge. My little girl, Diana, you remember, also took the pledge with me. She has been asking me a great many questions lately about the poor people and where they live. I was obliged to answer her. One of her questions last night touched my sore: 'Do you own any houses where these poor people live? Are they nice and warm like ours?' You know how a child will ask questions like these. I went to bed tormented with what I now know to be the divine arrows of conscience. I could not sleep. I seemed to see the judgment day. I was placed before the Judge. I was asked to give an account of my deeds done in the body."

Daily In His Word

Pray for us, for our conscience is clear and we want to live honorably in everything we do.

HEBREWS 13:18 NLT

How many sinful souls had I visited in prison? What had I done with my stewardship? How about those tenements where people froze in winter and stifled in summer? Did I give any thought to them except to receive the rentals from them? Where did my suffering come in? Would Jesus have done as I had done and was doing? Had I broken my pledge? How had I used the money and the culture and the social influence I possessed? Had I used it to bless humanity, to relieve the suffering, to bring joy to the distressed and hope to the desponding? I had received much. How much had I given?'

"All this came to me in a waking vision as distinctly as I see you two men and myself now. I was unable to see the end of the vision. I had a confused picture in my mind of the suffering Christ pointing a condemning finger at me, and the rest was shut out by mist and darkness. I have not slept for twenty-four hours. The first thing I saw this morning was the account of the shooting at the coal yards. I read the account with a feeling of horror I have not been able to shake off. I am a guilty creature before God."

Penrose paused suddenly. The two men looked at him solemnly. What power of the Holy Spirit moved the soul of this hitherto self-satisfied, elegant, cultured man who belonged to the social life that was accustomed to go its way placidly, unmindful of the great sorrows of a great city and practically ignorant of what it means to suffer for Jesus' sake?

Daily In His Word

Yet what we suffer now is nothing compared
to the glory he will give us later.

Romans 8:18 NLT

Into that room came a breath such as before swept over Henry Maxwell's church and through Nazareth Avenue. The Bishop laid his hand on the shoulder of Penrose and said: "My brother, God has been very near to you. Let us thank Him."

"Yes! Yes!" sobbed Penrose. He sat down on a chair and covered his face. The Bishop prayed. Then Penrose quietly said: "Will you go with me to that house?"

For answer the two men put on their overcoats and went with him to the home of the dead man's family.

That was the beginning of a new and strange life for Clarence Penrose. From the moment he stepped into that wretched hovel of a home and faced for the first time in his life a despair and suffering such as he had read of but did not know by personal contact, he dated a new life. It would be another long story to tell how, in obedience to his pledge he began to do with his tenement property as he knew Jesus would do. What would Jesus do with tenement property if He owned it in Chicago or any other great city of the world? Any man who can imagine any true answers to this question can easily tell what Clarence Penrose began to do.

Daily In His Word

For as the sufferings of Christ abound in us, so our consolation also abounds through Christ.

2 Corinthians 1:5 nkjv

Now before that winter reached its bitter climax many things occurred in the city which concerned the lives of all the characters in this history of the disciples who promised to walk in His steps.

It chanced by one of those coincidences that seem to occur preternaturally that one afternoon just as Felicia came out of the Settlement with a basket of food which she was going to leave as a sample with a baker in the Penrose district, Stephen Clyde opened the door of the carpenter shop in the basement and came out in time to meet her as she reached the sidewalk.

"Let me carry your basket, please," he said.

"Why do you say 'please'?" asked Felicia, handing over the basket while they walked along.

"I would like to say something else," replied Stephen, glancing at her shyly and yet with a boldness that frightened him, for he had been loving Felicia more every day since he first saw her and especially since she stepped into the shop that day with the Bishop, and for weeks now they had been thrown in each other's company.

"What else?" asked Felicia, innocently falling into the trap.

"Why—" said Stephen, turning his fair, noble face full toward her and eyeing her with the look of one who would have the best of all things in the universe, "I would like to say: 'Let me carry your basket, dear Felicia.'"

Daily In His Word

. . .with all lowliness and gentleness, with longsuffering, bearing with one another in love.

Ephesians 4:2 nkjv

Felicia never looked so beautiful in her life. She walked on a little way without even turning her face toward him. It was no secret with her own heart that she had given it to Stephen some time ago. Finally she turned and said shyly, while her face grew rosy and her eyes tender: "Why don't you say it, then?"

"May I?" cried Stephen, and he was so careless for a minute of the way he held the basket, that Felicia exclaimed:

"Yes! But oh, don't drop my goodies!"

"Why, I wouldn't drop anything so precious for all the world, dear Felicia," said Stephen, who now walked on air for several blocks, and what was said during that walk is private correspondence that we have no right to read. Only it is a matter of history that day that the basket never reached its destination, and that over in the other direction, late in the afternoon, the Bishop, walking along quietly from the Penrose district, in rather a secluded spot near the outlying part of the Settlement district, heard a familiar voice say:

"But tell me, Felicia, when did you begin to love me?"

"I fell in love with a little pine shaving just above your ear that day when I saw you in the shop!" said the other voice with a laugh so clear, so pure, so sweet that it did one good to hear it.

Daily In His Word
Love never fails.

1 CORINTHIANS 13:8 NKJV

W here are you going with that basket?" he tried to say sternly. "We are taking it to—where are we taking it, Felicia?"

"Dear Bishop, we are taking it home to begin—"

"To begin housekeeping with," finished Stephen, coming to the rescue.

"Are you?" said the Bishop. "I hope you will invite me to share. I know what Felicia's cooking is."

"Bishop, dear Bishop!" said Felicia, and she did not pretend to hide her happiness; "indeed, you shall be the most honored guest. Are you glad?"

"Yes, I am," he replied, interpreting Felicia's words as she wished. Then he paused a moment and said gently: "God bless you both!" and went his way with a tear in his eye and a prayer in his heart, and left them to their joy.

Yes. Shall not the same divine power of love that belongs to earth be lived and sung by the disciples of the Man of Sorrows and the Burden-bearer of sins? Yea, verily! And this man and woman shall walk hand in hand through this great desert of human woe in this city, strengthening each other, growing more loving with the experience of the world's sorrows, walking in His steps even closer yet because of their love for each other, bringing added blessing to thousands of wretched creatures because they are to have a home of their own to share with the homeless. "For this cause," said our Lord Jesus Christ, "shall a man leave his father and mother and cleave unto his wife." And Felicia and Stephen, following the Master, love him with a deeper, truer service and devotion because of the earthly affection which Heaven itself sanctions with its solemn blessing.

Daily In His Word

Therefore shall a man leave his father and his mother,
and shall cleave unto his wife: and they shall be one flesh.

Genesis 2:24 kjv

But it was a little after the love story of the Settlement became a part of its glory that Henry Maxwell of Raymond came to Chicago with Rachel Winslow and Virginia Page and Rollin and Alexander Powers and President Marsh, and the occasion was a remarkable gathering at the hall of the Settlement arranged by the Bishop and Dr. Bruce, who had finally persuaded Mr. Maxwell and his fellow disciples in Raymond to come on to be present at this meeting.

There were invited into the Settlement Hall, meeting for that night men out of work, wretched creatures who had lost faith in God and man, anarchists and infidels, free-thinkers and no-thinkers. The representation of all the city's worst, most hopeless, most dangerous, depraved elements faced Henry Maxwell and the other disciples when the meeting began. And still the Holy Spirit moved over the great, selfish, pleasure-loving, sin-stained city, and it lay in God's hand, not knowing all that awaited it. Every man and woman at the meeting that night had seen the Settlement motto over the door blazing through the transparency set up by the divinity student: "What would Jesus do?"

And Henry Maxwell, as for the first time he stepped under the doorway, was touched with a deeper emotion than he had felt in a long time as he thought of the first time that question had come to him in the piteous appeal of the shabby young man who had appeared in the First Church of Raymond at the morning service.

Daily In His Word

Remember, it is better to suffer for doing good, if that is what God wants, than to suffer for doing wrong!

1 PETER 3:17 NLT

Chapter Thirty

"Now, when Jesus heard these things, He said unto him,
Yet lackest thou one thing: sell all that thou hast,
and distribute unto the poor, and thou shalt have
treasure in heaven: and come, follow Me."

When Henry Maxwell began to speak to the souls crowded into the Settlement Hall that night it is doubtful if he ever faced such an audience in his life. It is quite certain that the city of Raymond did not contain such a variety of humanity. Not even the Rectangle at its worst could furnish so many men and women who had fallen entirely out of the reach of the church and of all religious and even Christian influences.

What did he talk about? He had already decided that point. He told in the simplest language he could command some of the results of obedience to the pledge as it had been taken in Raymond. Every man and woman in that audience knew something about Jesus Christ. They all had some idea of His character, and however much they had grown bitter toward the forms of Christian ecclesiasticism or the social system, they preserved some standard of right and truth, and what little some of them still retained was taken from the person of the Peasant of Galilee.

So they were interested in what Maxwell said. "What would Jesus do?"

Daily In His Word
Thou shalt call his name JESUS: for he
shall save his people from their sins.
Matthew 1:21 KJV

He began to apply the question to the social problem in general, after finishing the story of Raymond. The audience was respectfully attentive. It was more than that. It was genuinely interested. As Mr. Maxwell went on, faces all over the hall leaned forward in a way seldom seen in church audiences or anywhere except among workingmen or the people of the street when once they are thoroughly aroused. "What would Jesus do?" Suppose that were the motto not only of the churches but of the businessmen, the politicians, the newspapers, the workingmen, the society people—how long would it take under such a standard of conduct to revolutionize the world? What was the trouble with the world? It was suffering from selfishness. No one ever lived who had succeeded in overcoming selfishness like Jesus. If men followed Him regardless of results the world would at once begin to enjoy a new life.

Maxwell never knew how much it meant to hold the respectful attention of that hall full of diseased and sinful humanity. The Bishop and Dr. Bruce, sitting there, looking on, seeing many faces that represented scorn of creeds, hatred of the social order, desperate narrowness and selfishness, marveled that even so soon under the influence of the Settlement life, the softening process had begun already to lessen the bitterness of hearts, many of which had grown bitter from neglect and indifference.

Daily In His Word

In all things show yourself to be an example of good deeds, with purity in doctrine, dignified, sound in speech which is beyond reproach, that the opponent will be put to shame, having nothing bad to say.

TITUS 2:7–8 NASB

And still, in spite of the outward show of respect to the speaker, no one, not even the Bishop, had any true conception of the feeling pent up in that room that night. Among those who had heard of the meeting and had responded to the invitation were twenty or thirty men out of work who had strolled past the Settlement that afternoon, read the notice of the meeting, and had come in out of curiosity and to escape the chill east wind. It was a bitter night and the saloons were full. But in that whole district of over thirty thousand souls, with the exception of the saloons, there was not a door open except the clean, pure Christian door of the Settlement. Where would a man without a home or without work or without friends naturally go unless to the saloon?

It had been the custom at the Settlement for a free discussion to follow any open meeting of this kind, and when Mr. Maxwell finished and sat down, the Bishop, who presided that night, rose and made the announcement that any man in the hall was at liberty to ask questions, to speak out his feelings or declare his convictions, always with the understanding that whoever took part was to observe the simple rules that governed parliamentary bodies and obey the three-minute rule which, by common consent, would be enforced on account of the numbers present.

Daily In His Word

For a whole year they assembled with the church and taught a great many people.

Acts 11:26 nkjv

Instantly a number of voices from men who had been at previous meetings of this kind exclaimed, "Consent! Consent!"

The Bishop sat down, and immediately a man near the middle of the hall rose and began to speak.

"I want to say that what Mr. Maxwell has said tonight comes pretty close to me. I knew Jack Manning, the fellow he told about who died at his house. I worked on the next case to his in a printer's shop in Philadelphia for two years. Jack was a good fellow. He loaned me five dollars once when I was in a hole and I never got a chance to pay him back. He moved to New York, owing to a change in the management of the office that threw him out, and I never saw him again. When the linotype machines came in I was one of the men to go out, just as he did. I have been out most of the time since. They say inventions are a good thing. I don't always see it myself; but I suppose I'm prejudiced. A man naturally is when he loses a steady job because a machine takes his place. About this Christianity he tells about, it's all right. But I never expect to see any such sacrifices on the part of the church people. So far as my observation goes they're just as selfish and as greedy for money and worldly success as anybody. I except the Bishop and Dr. Bruce and a few others."

Daily In His Word

"Since I, the Lord and Teacher, have washed your feet, you ought to wash each other's feet. I have given you an example to follow. Do as I have done to you."

JOHN 13:14–15 NLT

But I never found much difference between men of the world, as they are called, and church members when it came to business and money making. One class is just as bad as another there."

Cries of "That's so!" "You're right!" "Of course!" interrupted the speaker, and the minute he sat down two men who were on the floor for several seconds before the first speaker was through began to talk at once.

The Bishop called them to order and indicated which was entitled to the floor. The man who remained standing began eagerly:

"This is the first time I was ever in here, and may be it'll be the last. Fact is, I am about at the end of my string. I've tramped this city for work till I'm sick. I'm in plenty of company. Say! I'd like to ask a question of the minister, if it's fair. May I?"

"That's for Mr. Maxwell to say," said the Bishop.

"By all means," replied Mr. Maxwell quickly. "Of course, I will not promise to answer it to the gentleman's satisfaction."

"This is my question." The man leaned forward and stretched out a long arm with a certain dramatic force that grew naturally enough out of his condition as a human being. "I want to know what Jesus would do in my case. I haven't had a stroke of work for two months."

Daily In His Word

If one of you says to him, "Go, I wish you well; keep warm and well fed," but does nothing about his physical needs, what good is it?

James 2:16 NIV

Iʹve got a wife and three children, and I love them as much as if I was worth a million dollars. Iʹve been living off a little earnings I saved up during the Worldʹs Fair jobs I got. Iʹm a carpenter by trade, and Iʹve tried every way I know to get a job. You say we ought to take for our motto, ʹWhat would Jesus do?ʹ What would He do if He was out of work like me? I canʹt be somebody else and ask the question. I want to work. Iʹd give anything to grow tired of working ten hours a day the way I used to. Am I to blame because I canʹt manufacture a job for myself? Iʹve got to live, and my wife and my children have got to live. But how? What would Jesus do? You say thatʹs the question we ought to ask.ʺ

Mr. Maxwell sat there staring at the great sea of faces all intent on his, and no answer to this manʹs question seemed for the time being to be possible. ʺO God!ʺ his heart prayed; ʺthis is a question that brings up the entire social problem in all its perplexing entanglement of human wrongs and its present condition contrary to every desire of God for a human beingʹs welfare.ʺ

Daily In His Word

He is the one who keeps every promise forever, who gives justice to the oppressed and food to the hungry.

PSALM 146:6–7 NLT

Is there any condition more awful than for a man in good health, able and eager to work, with no means of honest livelihood unless he does work, actually unable to get anything to do, and driven to one of three things: begging or charity at the hands of friends or strangers, suicide or starvation? "What would Jesus do?" It was a fair question for the man to ask. It was the only question he could ask, supposing him to be a disciple of Jesus. But what a question for any man to be obliged to answer under such conditions?

All this and more did Henry Maxwell ponder. All the others were thinking in the same way. The Bishop sat there with a look so stern and sad that it was not hard to tell how the question moved him. Dr. Bruce had his head bowed. The human problem had never seemed to him so tragical as since he had taken the pledge and left his church to enter the Settlement. What would Jesus do? It was a terrible question. And still the man stood there, tall and gaunt and almost terrible, with his arm stretched out in an appeal which grew every second in meaning. At length Mr. Maxwell spoke.

"Is there any man in the room, who is a Christian disciple, who has been in this condition and has tried to do as Jesus would do? If so, such a man can answer this question better than I can."

Daily In His Word
"Stop oppressing the helpless and stop making false accusations and spreading vicious rumors. Feed the hungry and help those in trouble."
ISAIAH 58:9–10 NLT

There was a moment's hush over the room and then a man near the front of the hall slowly rose. He was an old man, and the hand he laid on the back of the bench in front of him trembled as he spoke.

"I think I can safely say that I have many times been in just such a condition, and I have always tried to be a Christian under all conditions. I don't know as I have always asked this question, 'What would Jesus do?' when I have been out of work, but I do know I have tried to be His disciple at all times. Yes," the man went on, with a sad smile that was more pathetic to the Bishop and Mr. Maxwell than the younger man's grim despair; "yes, I have begged, and I have been to charity institutions, and I have done everything when out of a job except steal and lie in order to get food and fuel. I don't know as Jesus would have done some of the things I have been obliged to do for a living, but I know I have never knowingly done wrong when out of work. Sometimes I think maybe He would have starved sooner than beg. I don't know."

Daily In His Word

Men do not despise a thief if he steals to satisfy himself when he is hungry.

Proverbs 6:30 nasb

The old man's voice trembled and he looked around the room timidly. A silence followed, broken by a fierce voice from a large, black-haired, heavily-bearded man who sat three seats from the Bishop. The minute he spoke nearly every man in the hall leaned forward eagerly. The man who had asked the question, "What would Jesus do in my case?" slowly sat down and whispered to the man next to him: "Who's that?"

"That's Carlsen, the Socialist leader. Now you'll hear something."

"This is all bosh, to my mind," began Carlsen, while his great bristling beard shook with the deep inward anger of the man. "The whole of our system is at fault. What we call civilization is rotten to the core. There is no use trying to hide it or cover it up. We live in an age of trusts and combines and capitalistic greed that means simply death to thousands of innocent men, women and children. I thank God, if there is a God—which I very much doubt—that I, for one, have never dared to marry and make a home. Home! Talk of hell! Is there any bigger one than this man and his three children has on his hands right this minute? And he's only one out of thousands. And yet this city, and every other big city in this country, has its thousands of professed Christians who have all the luxuries and comforts, and who go to church Sundays and sing their hymns about giving all to Jesus and bearing the cross and following Him all the way and being saved!"

Daily In His Word
Do what is just and right. Rescue from the hand of his oppressor the one who has been robbed.

Jeremiah 22:3 niv

I don't say that there aren't good men and women among them, but let the minister who has spoken to us here tonight go into any one of a dozen aristocratic churches I could name and propose to the members to take any such pledge as the one he's mentioned here tonight, and see how quick the people would laugh at him for a fool or a crank or a fanatic. Oh, no! That's not the remedy. That can't ever amount to anything. We've got to have a new start in the way of government. The whole thing needs reconstructing. I don't look for any reform worth anything to come out of the churches. They are not with the people. They are with the aristocrats, with the men of money. The trusts and monopolies have their greatest men in the churches. The ministers as a class are their slaves. What we need is a system that shall start from the common basis of socialism, founded on the rights of the common people—"

Carlsen had evidently forgotten all about the three-minutes rule and was launching himself into a regular oration that meant, in his usual surroundings before his usual audience, an hour at least, when the man just behind him pulled him down unceremoniously and arose.

Daily In His Word

When words are many, sin is not absent, but he who holds his tongue is wise.

PROVERBS 10:19 NIV

Carlsen was angry at first and threatened a little disturbance, but the Bishop reminded him of the rule, and he subsided with several mutterings in his beard, while the next speaker began with a very strong eulogy on the value of the single tax as a genuine remedy for all the social ills. He was followed by a man who made a bitter attack on the churches and ministers, and declared that the two great obstacles in the way of all true reform were the courts and the ecclesiastical machines.

When he sat down a man who bore every mark of being a street laborer sprang to his feet and poured a perfect torrent of abuse against the corporations, especially the railroads. The minute his time was up a big, brawny fellow, who said he was a metal worker by trade, claimed the floor and declared that the remedy for the social wrongs was Trades Unionism. This, he said, would bring on the millennium for labor more surely than anything else. The next man endeavored to give some reasons why so many persons were out of employment, and condemned inventions as works of the devil. He was loudly applauded by the rest.

Finally the Bishop called time on the "free for all," and asked Rachel to sing.

Daily In His Word

Why do the heathen rage, and the people imagine a vain thing?
Psalm 2:1 kjv

Rachel Winslow had grown into a very strong, healthful, humble Christian during that wonderful year in Raymond dating from the Sunday when she first took the pledge to do as Jesus would do, and her great talent for song had been fully consecrated to the service of the Master. When she began to sing tonight at this Settlement meeting, she had never prayed more deeply for results to come from her voice, the voice which she now regarded as the Master's, to be used for Him.

Certainly her prayer was being answered as she sang. She had chosen the words, "Hark! The voice of Jesus calling, Follow me, follow me!"

Again Henry Maxwell, sitting there, was reminded of his first night at the Rectangle in the tent when Rachel sang the people into quiet. The effect was the same here. What wonderful power a good voice consecrated to the Master's service always is! Rachel's great natural ability would have made her one of the foremost opera singers of the age. Surely this audience had never heard such a melody. How could it? The men who had drifted in from the street sat entranced by a voice which "back in the world," as the Bishop said, never could be heard by the common people because the owner of it would charge two or three dollars for the privilege.

Daily In His Word

He put a new song in my mouth, a song of praise to our God; Many will see and fear and will trust in the LORD.

PSALM 40:3 NASB

The song poured out through the hall as free and glad as if it were a foretaste of salvation itself. Carlsen, with his great, black-bearded face uplifted, absorbed the music with the deep love of it peculiar to his nationality, and a tear ran over his cheek and glistened in his beard as his face softened and became almost noble in its aspect. The man out of work who had wanted to know what Jesus would do in his place sat with one grimy hand on the back of the bench in front of him, with his mouth partly open, his great tragedy for the moment forgotten. The song, while it lasted, was food and work and warmth and union with his wife and babies once more. The man who had spoken so fiercely against the churches and ministers sat with his head erect, at first with a look of stolid resistance, as if he stubbornly resisted the introduction into the exercises of anything that was even remotely connected with the church or its forms of worship. But gradually he yielded to the power that was swaying the hearts of all the persons in that room, and a look of sad thoughtfulness crept over his face.

Daily In His Word

My heart trusts in him, and I am helped. My heart leaps for joy and I will give thanks to him in song.

Psalm 28:7 niv

The Bishop said that night while Rachel was singing that if the world of sinful, diseased, depraved, lost humanity could only have the gospel preached to it by consecrated prima donnas and professional tenors and altos and bassos, he believed it would hasten the coming of the Kingdom quicker than any other one force. "Why, oh why," he cried in his heart as he listened, "has the world's great treasure of song been so often held far from the poor because the personal possessor of voice or fingers, capable of stirring divinest melody, has so often regarded the gift as something with which to make money? Shall there be no martyrs among the gifted ones of the earth? Shall there be no giving of this great gift as well as of others?"

And Henry Maxwell, again as before, called up that other audience at the Rectangle with increasing longing for a larger spread of the new discipleship. What he had seen and heard at the Settlement burned into him deeper the belief that the problem of the city would be solved if the Christians in it should once follow Jesus as He gave commandment. But what of this great mass of humanity, neglected and sinful, the very kind of humanity the Savior came to save, with all its mistakes and narrowness, its wretchedness and loss of hope, above all its unqualified bitterness towards the church? That was what smote him deepest.

Daily In His Word

Do not neglect the gift that is in you,
which was given to you by prophecy.

1 TIMOTHY 4:14 NKJV

Was the church then so far from the Master that the people no longer found Him in the church? Was it true that the church had lost its power over the very kind of humanity which in the early ages of Christianity it reached in the greatest numbers? How much was true in what the Socialist leader said about the uselessness of looking to the church for reform or redemption, because of the selfishness and seclusion and aristocracy of its members?

He was more and more impressed with the appalling fact that the comparatively few men in that hall, now being held quiet for a while by Rachel's voice, represented thousands of others just like them, to whom a church and a minister stood for less than a saloon or a beer garden as a source of comfort or happiness. Ought it to be so? If the church members were all doing as Jesus would do, could it remain true that armies of men would walk the streets for jobs and hundreds of them curse the church and thousands of them find in the saloon their best friend? How far were the Christians responsible for this human problem that was personally illustrated right in this hall tonight? Was it true that the great city churches would as a rule refuse to walk in Jesus' steps so closely as to suffer—actually suffer—for His sake?

Daily In His Word

Is anyone among you suffering? . . . Let him sing psalms. Is anyone among you sick? Let him call for the elders of the church.
JAMES 5:13–14 NKJV

CHAPTER THIRTY-ONE

He had planned when he came to the city to return to Raymond and be in his own pulpit on Sunday. But Friday morning he had received at the Settlement a call from the pastor of one of the largest churches in Chicago, and had been invited to fill the pulpit for both morning and evening service.

At first he hesitated, but finally accepted, seeing in it the hand of the Spirit's guiding power. He would test his own question. He would prove the truth or falsity of the charge made against the church at the Settlement meeting. How far would it go in its self-denial for Jesus' sake? How closely would it walk in His steps? Was the church willing to suffer for its Master?

Saturday night he spent in prayer, nearly the whole night. There had never been so great a wrestling in his soul, not even during his strongest experiences in Raymond. He had in fact entered upon another new experience. The definition of his own discipleship was receiving an added test at this time, and he was being led into a larger truth of the Lord.

Daily In His Word

"A son honors his father, and a servant his master. If I am a father, where is the honor due me? If I am a master, where is the respect due me?" says the LORD Almighty.

MALACHI 1:6 NIV

Sunday morning the great church was filled to its utmost. Henry Maxwell, coming into the pulpit from that all-night vigil, felt the pressure of a great curiosity on the part of the people. They had heard of the Raymond movement, as all the churches had, and the recent action of Dr. Bruce had added to the general interest in the pledge. With this curiosity was something deeper, more serious. Mr. Maxwell felt that also. And in the knowledge that the Spirit's presence was his living strength, he brought his message and gave it to that church that day.

He had never been what would be called a great preacher. He had not the force nor the quality that makes remarkable preachers. But ever since he had promised to do as Jesus would do, he had grown in a certain quality of persuasiveness that had all the essentials of true eloquence. This morning the people felt the complete sincerity and humility of a man who had gone deep into the heart of a great truth.

After telling briefly of some results in his own church in Raymond since the pledge was taken, he went on to ask the question he had been asking since the Settlement meeting.

Daily In His Word

Does it mean he no longer loves us if we have trouble or calamity, or are persecuted, or are hungry or cold or in danger or threatened with death? . . . No, despite all these things, overwhelming victory is ours through Christ, who loved us.

ROMANS 8:35, 37 NLT

He had taken for his theme the story of the young man who came to Jesus asking what he must do to obtain eternal life. Jesus had tested him. "Sell all that thou hast and give to the poor, and thou shalt have treasure in heaven; and come follow me." But the young man was not willing to suffer to that extent. If following Jesus meant suffering in that way, he was not willing. He would like to follow Jesus, but not if he had to give so much.

"Is it true," continued Henry Maxwell, and his fine, thoughtful face glowed with a passion of appeal that stirred the people as they had seldom been stirred, "is it true that the church of today, the church that is called after Christ's own name, would refuse to follow Him at the expense of suffering, of physical loss, of temporary gain? The statement was made at a large gathering in the Settlement last week by a leader of workingmen that it was hopeless to look to the church for any reform or redemption of society. On what was that statement based? Plainly on the assumption that the church contains for the most part men and women who think more 'of their own ease and luxury' than of the sufferings and needs and sins of humanity. How far is that true?"

Daily In His Word

And He put all things in subjection under His feet, and gave Him as head over all things to the church.

Ephesians 1:22 NASB

Are the Christians of America ready to have their discipleship tested? How about the men who possess large wealth? Are they ready to take that wealth and use it as Jesus would? How about the men and women of great talent? Are they ready to consecrate that talent to humanity as Jesus undoubtedly would do?

"Is it not true that the call has come in this age for a new exhibition of Christian discipleship? You who live in this great sinful city must know that better than I do. Is it possible you can go your ways careless or thoughtless of the awful condition of men and women and children who are dying, body and soul, for need of Christian help? Is it not a matter of concern to you personally that the saloon kills its thousands more surely than war? Is it not a matter of personal suffering in some form for you that thousands of able-bodied, willing men tramp the streets of this city and all cities, crying for work and drifting into crime and suicide because they cannot find it? Can you say that this is none of your business? Let each man look after himself?"

Daily In His Word

"The greatest love is shown when people lay down their lives for their friends. . . . You didn't choose me. I chose you. I appointed your to go and produce fruit that will last, so that the Father will give you whatever you ask for, using my name. I command you to love each other."

JOHN 15:13, 16–17 NLT

Would it not be true, think you, that if every Christian in America did as Jesus would do, society itself, the business world, yes, the very political system under which our commercial and governmental activity is carried on, would be so changed that human suffering would be reduced to a minimum?

"What would be the result if all the church members of this city tried to do as Jesus would do? It is not possible to say in detail what the effect would be. But it is easy to say, and it is true, that instantly the human problem would begin to find an adequate answer.

"What is the test of Christian discipleship? Is it not the same as in Christ's own time? Have our surroundings modified or changed the test? If Jesus were here today would He not call some of the members of this very church to do just what He commanded the young man, and ask them to give up their wealth and literally follow Him? I believe He would do that if He felt certain that any church member thought more of his possessions than of the Savior. The test would be the same today as then."

Daily In His Word

So let us come boldly to the throne of our gracious God. There we will receive his mercy, and we will find grace to help us when we need it.

Hebrews 4:16 nlt

I believe Jesus would demand—He does demand now—as close a following, as much suffering, as great self-denial as when He lived in person on the earth and said, 'Except a man renounce all that he hath he cannot be my disciple.' That is, unless he is willing to do it for my sake, he cannot be my disciple.

"What would be the result if in this city every church member should begin to do as Jesus would do? It is not easy to go into details of the result. But we all know that certain things would be impossible that are now practiced by church members.

"What would Jesus do in the matter of wealth? How would He spend it?

"What principle would regulate His use of money? Would He be likely to live in great luxury and spend ten times as much on personal adornment and entertainment as He spent to relieve the needs of suffering humanity? How would Jesus be governed in the making of money? Would He take rentals from saloons and other disreputable property, or even from tenement property that was so constructed that the inmates had no such things as a home and no such possibility as privacy or cleanliness?"

Daily In His Word

For Christ died for sins once for all, the righteous for the unrighteous, to bring you to God.

1 Peter 3:18 niv

What would Jesus do about the great army of unemployed and desperate who tramp the streets and curse the church, or are indifferent to it, lost in the bitter struggle for the bread that tastes bitter when it is earned on account of the desperate conflict to get it? Would Jesus care nothing for them? Would He go His way in comparative ease and comfort? Would He say that it was none of His business? Would He excuse Himself from all responsibility to remove the causes of such a condition?

"What would Jesus do in the center of a civilization that hurries so fast after money that the very girls employed in great business houses are not paid enough to keep soul and body together without fearful temptations so great that scores of them fall and are swept over the great boiling abyss; where the demands of trade sacrifice hundreds of lads in a business that ignores all Christian duties toward them in the way of education and moral training and personal affection? Would Jesus, if He were here today as a part of our age and commercial industry, feel nothing, do nothing, say nothing, in the face of these facts which every businessman knows?

"What would Jesus do? Is not that what the disciple ought to do? Is he not commanded to follow in His steps?"

Daily In His Word

So he made a whip out of cords, and drove all from the temple area, both sheep and cattle; he scattered the coins of the money changers and overturned their tables.

JOHN 2:15 NIV

How much is the Christianity of the age suffering for Him? Is it denying itself at the cost of ease, comfort, luxury, elegance of living? What does the age need more than personal sacrifice? Does the church do its duty in following Jesus when it gives a little money to establish missions or relieve extreme cases of want? Is it any sacrifice for a man who is worth ten million dollars simply to give ten thousand dollars for some benevolent work? Is he not giving something that cost him practically nothing so far as any personal suffering goes? Is it true that the Christian disciples today in most of our churches are living soft, easy, selfish lives, very far from any sacrifice that can be called sacrifice? What would Jesus do?

"It is the personal element that Christian discipleship needs to emphasize. 'The gift without the giver is bare.' The Christianity that attempts to suffer by proxy is not the Christianity of Christ. Each individual Christian business-man, citizen, needs to follow in His steps along the path of personal sacrifice to Him. There is not a different path today from that of Jesus' own times. It is the same path. The call of this dying century and of the new one soon to be, is a call for a new discipleship, a new following of Jesus, more like the early, simple, apostolic Christianity, when the disciples left all and literally followed the Master. Nothing but a disciple-ship of this kind can face the destructive selfishness of the age with any hope of overcoming it."

Daily In His Word

Now the multitude of those who believed were of one heart and one soul; neither did anyone say that any of the things he possessed was his own, but they had all things in common.

ACTS 4:32–33 NKJV

Thereisagreat quantity of nominal Christianity today. There is need of more of the real kind. We need revival of the Christianity of Christ. We have, unconsciously, lazily, selfishly, formally grown into a discipleship that Jesus himself would not acknowledge. He would say to many of us when we cry, 'Lord, Lord,' 'I never knew you!' Are we ready to take up the cross? Is it possible for this church to sing with exact truth,

> *Jesus, I my cross have taken,*
> *All to leave and follow Thee?'*

"If we can sing that truly, then we may claim discipleship. But if our definition of being a Christian is simply to enjoy the privileges of worship, be generous at no expense to ourselves, have a good, easy time surrounded by pleasant friends and by comfortable things, live respectably and at the same time avoid the world's great stress of sin and trouble because it is too much pain to bear it—if this is our definition of Christianity, surely we are a long way from following the steps of Him who trod the way with groans and tears and sobs of anguish for a lost humanity; who sweat, as it were, great drops of blood, who cried out on the unprepared cross, 'My God, my God, why hast thou forsaken me?'"

Daily In His Word

So they took Jesus and led him away Carrying the cross
by himself, Jesus went to the place called Skull Hill. . .
there they crucified him.

JOHN 19:16–18 NLT

Are we ready to make and live a new discipleship? Are we ready to reconsider our definition of a Christian? What is it to be a Christian? It is to imitate Jesus. It is to do as He would do. It is to walk in His steps."

When Henry Maxwell finished his sermon, he paused and looked at the people with a look they never forgot and, at the moment, did not understand. Crowded into that fashionable church that day were hundreds of men and women who had for years lived the easy, satisfied life of a nominal Christianity. A great silence fell over the congregation. Through the silence there came to the consciousness of all the souls there present a knowledge, stranger to them now for years, of a Divine Power. Every one expected the preacher to call for volunteers who would do as Jesus would do. But Maxwell had been led by the Spirit to deliver his message this time and wait for results to come.

He closed the service with a tender prayer that kept the Divine Presence lingering very near every hearer, and the people slowly rose to go out. Then followed a scene that would have been impossible if any mere man had been alone in his striving for results.

Daily In His Word

As we know Jesus better, his divine power gives us everything we need for living a godly life. He has called us to receive his own glory and goodness!

2 PETER 1:3 NLT

Men and women in great numbers crowded around the platform to see Mr. Maxwell and to bring him the promise of their consecration to the pledge to do as Jesus would do. It was a voluntary, spontaneous movement that broke upon his soul with a result he could not measure. But had he not been praying for is very thing? It was an answer that more than met his desires.

There followed this movement a prayer service that in its impressions repeated the Raymond experience. In the evening, to Mr. Maxwell's joy, the Endeavor Society almost to a member came forward, as so many of the church members had done in the morning, and seriously, solemnly, tenderly, took the pledge to do as Jesus would do. A deep wave of spiritual baptism broke over the meeting near its close that was indescribable in its tender, joyful, sympathetic results.

That was a remarkable day in the history of that church, but even more so in the history of Henry Maxwell. He left the meeting very late. He went to his room at the Settlement where he was still stopping, and after an hour with the Bishop and Dr. Bruce, spent in a joyful rehearsal of the wonderful events of the day, he sat down to think over again by himself all the experience he was having as a Christian disciple.

Daily In His Word
He has promised that you will escape the decadence
all around you caused by evil desires and that you
will share in his divine nature.

2 Peter 1:4 NLT

He had kneeled to pray, as he always did before going to sleep, and it was while he was on his knees that he had a waking vision of what might be in the world when once the new discipleship had made its way into the conscience and conscientiousness of Christendom. He was fully conscious of being awake, but no less certainly did it seem to him that he saw certain results with great distinctiveness, partly as realities of the future, partly great longings that they might be realities. And this is what Henry Maxwell saw in this waking vision:

He saw himself, first, going back to the First Church in Raymond, living there in a simpler, more self-denying fashion than he had yet been willing to live, because he saw ways in which he could help others who were really dependent on him for help. He also saw, more dimly, that the time would come when his position as pastor of the church would cause him to suffer more on account of growing opposition to his interpretation of Jesus and His conduct. But this was vaguely outlined. Through it all he heard the words "My grace is sufficient for thee."

He saw Rachel Winslow and Virginia Page going on with their work of service at the Rectangle, and reaching out loving hands of helpfulness far beyond the limits of Raymond. Rachel he saw married to Rollin Page, both fully consecrated to the Master's use, both following His steps with an eagerness intensified and purified by their love for each other. And Rachel's voice sang on, in slums and dark places of despair and sin, and drew lost souls back to God and heaven once more.

Daily In His Word

All the paths of the LORD are mercy and truth,
to such as keep His covenant and His testimonies.

PSALM 25:10 NKJV

He saw President Marsh of the college using his great learning and his great influence to purify the city, to ennoble its patriotism, to inspire the young men and women who loved as well as admired him to lives of Christian service, always teaching them that education means great responsibility for the weak and the ignorant.

He saw Alexander Powers meeting with sore trials in his family life, with a constant sorrow in the estrangement of wife and friends, but still going his way in all honor, serving in all his strength the Master whom he had obeyed, even unto the loss of social distinction and wealth.

He saw Milton Wright, the merchant, meeting with great reverses. Thrown upon the future by a combination of circumstances, with vast business interests involved in ruin through no fault of his own, but coming out of his reverses with clean Christian honor, to begin again and work up to a position where he could again be to hundreds of young men an example of what Jesus would do in business.

He saw Edward Norman, editor of the *News*, by means of the money given by Virginia, creating a force in journalism that in time came to be recognized as one of the real factors of the nation to mold its principles and actually shape its policy, a daily illustration of the might of a Christian press, and the first of a series of such papers begun and carried on by other disciples who had also taken the pledge.

Daily In His Word

He who pursues righteousness and love finds life,
prosperity and honor.

Proverbs 21:21 NIV

He saw Jasper Chase, who had denied his Master, growing into a cold, cynical, formal life, writing novels that were social successes, but each one with a sting in it, the reminder of his denial, the bitter remorse that, do what he would, no social success could remove.

He saw Rose Sterling, dependent for some years upon her aunt and Felicia, finally married to a man far older than herself, accepting the burden of a relation that had no love in it on her part, because of her desire to be the wife of a rich man and enjoy the physical luxuries that were all of life to her. Over this life also the vision cast certain dark and awful shadows but they were not shown in detail.

He saw Felicia and Stephen Clyde happily married, living a beautiful life together, enthusiastic, joyful in suffering, pouring out their great, strong, fragrant service into the dull, dark, terrible places of the great city, and redeeming souls through the personal touch of their home, dedicated to the Human Homesickness all about them.

He saw Dr. Bruce and the Bishop going on with the Settlement work. He seemed to see the great blazing motto over the door enlarged, "What would Jesus do?" and by this motto every one who entered the Settlement walked in the steps of the Master.

Daily In His Word

"Come, follow me," Jesus said.

Mark 1:17 niv

He saw Burns and his companion and a great company of men like them, redeemed and giving in turn to others, conquering their passions by the divine grace, and proving by their daily lives the reality of the new birth even in the lowest and most abandoned.

And now the vision was troubled. It seemed to him that as he kneeled he began to pray, and the vision was more of a longing for a future than a reality in the future. The church of Jesus in the city and throughout the country! Would it follow Jesus? Was the movement begun in Raymond to spend itself in a few churches like Nazareth Avenue and the one where he had preached today, and then die away as a local movement, a stirring on the surface but not to extend deep and far? He felt with agony after the vision again. He thought he saw the church of Jesus in America open its heart to the moving of the Spirit and rise to the sacrifice of its ease and self-satisfaction in the name of Jesus. He thought he saw the motto, "What would Jesus do?" inscribed over every church door, and written on every church member's heart.

Daily In His Word
Wilt thou not revive us again: that thy people may rejoice in thee?
Psalm 85:6 kjv

The vision vanished. It came back clearer than before, and he saw the Endeavor Societies all over the world carrying in their great processions at some mighty convention a banner on which was written, "What would Jesus do?" And he thought in the faces of the young men and women he saw future joy of suffering, loss, self-denial, martyrdom. And when this part of the vision slowly faded, he saw the figure of the Son of God beckoning to him and to all the other actors in his life history. An angel choir somewhere was singing. There was a sound as of many voices and a shout as of a great victory. And the figure of Jesus grew more and more splendid. He stood at the end of a long flight of steps. "Yes! Yes! O my Master, has not the time come for this dawn of the millennium of Christian history? Oh, break upon the Christendom of this age with the light and the truth! Help us to follow Thee all the way!"

He rose at last with the awe of one who has looked at heavenly things. He felt the human forces and the human sins of the world as never before. And with a hope that walks hand in hand with faith and love Henry Maxwell, disciple of Jesus, laid him down to sleep and dreamed of the regeneration of Christendom, and saw in his dream a church of Jesus without spot or wrinkle or any such thing, following him all the way, walking obediently in His steps.

Daily In His Word

To this you were called, because Christ suffered for you, leaving you an example, that you should follow in his steps.

1 PETER 2:21 NIV

Scripture Index

Genesis
1:27   Day 258
2:15   Day 326
2:24   Day 334

Exodus
23:2   Day 63
23:9   Day 4
33:13   Day 78

Leviticus
19:16   Day 73
25:14   Day 327

Deuteronomy
6:4–5   Day 268
8:18   Day 70
15:7–8   Day 16
15:11   Day 283
33:27   Day 158

Joshua
24:15   Day 67

1 Samuel
2:3   Day 49

2 Samuel
22:5, 7   Day 325

2 Chronicles
15:7   Day 320

Job
11:14–15   Day 37
31:6   Day 40

Psalms
2:1   Day 346
7:11   Day 183
9:9   Day 194
9:19–20   Day 288
15:5   Day 169
17:8–9   Day 185
21:13   Day 120
25:4   Day 285
25:5   Day 286
25:10   Day 362
25:12   Day 102
27:14   Day 89
28:7   Day 348
30:5   Day 191
31:23   Day 224
34:15   Day 328
37:9   Day 270
37:16–17   Day 105
39:6   Day 280
40:3   Day 347
41:1   Day 251
51:7   Day 129
51:10–11   Day 117
56:4   Day 177
59:16   Day 189
62:12   Day 227
70:5   Day 316

SCRIPTURE INDEX

71:4	Day 317	14:7	Day 151
72:13–14	Day 260	14:8	Day 152
82:1–3	Day 144	14:34	Day 103
85:6	Day 365	16:18	Day 8
90:12	Day 214	17:17	Day 272
94:3	Day 195	18:24	Day 301
95:1–2	Day 90	19:1	Day 270
105:2–3	Day 91	19:22	Day 211
111:10	Day 52	20:7	Day 46
116:6	Day 306	21:21	Day 363
119:57	Day 236	22:29	Day 72
133:1	Day 55	28:27	Day 212
138:2–3	Day 263	31:10–11	Day 71
143:10	Day 240	31:15	Day 299
144:15	Day 302	31:20	Day 249
145:10–11	Day 118		
146:6–7	Day 341	**Ecclesiastes**	
		3:1, 6–7	Day 50
Proverbs		4:12	Day 298
2:6	Day 210		
3:13–14	Day 218	**Isaiah**	
4:7	Day 35	11:2	Day 213
6:30	Day 343	32:17	Day 108
8:14	Day 84	33:15–16	Day 43
10:2	Day 47	42:16	Day 22
10:3	Day 48	45:23–24	Day 139
10:19	Day 345	55:1	Day 61
11:4	Day 104	55:8	Day 32
11:10	Day 222	56:1	Day 111
11:25	Day 157	58:9–10	Day 342
11:28	Day 278	58:11	Day 27
11:30	Day 309	66:13	Day 173
12:26	Day 235		

Scripture Index

Jeremiah
22:3   Day 344

Daniel
9:9   Day 156

Joel
1:5   Day 153

Micah
4:12   Day 256
6:8   Day 106

Malachi
1:6   Day 351

Matthew
1:21   Day 336
4:10   Day 82
4:19–20   Day 13
5:4   Day 20
5:7   Day 154
5:16   Day 115
5:41   Day 274
5:44   Day 312
6:1   Day 187
6:33   Day 204
7:1–2   Day 162
9:13   Day 99
9:35–36   Day 100
10:8   Day 98
10:16   Day 179
10:24–25   Day 25

10:28   Day 176
10:29   Day 60
10:39   Day 219
10:41   Day 45
10:42   Day 3
11:19   Day 160
18:3   Day 201
19:21   Day 56
19:26   Day 321
19:29   Day 243
25:29   Day 69
25:34–36, 40   Day 14
28:19   Day 323

Mark
1:15   Day 205
1:17   Day 364
2:15   Day 137
11:23–24   Day 262
12:43–44   Day 68

Luke
5:11   Day 232
8:1   Day 207
9:23   Day 6
9:58   Day 12
10:27   Day 250
10:36–37   Day 17,
            Day 161
11:13   Day 26
12:12   Day 54,
            Day 239
12:51–52   Day 266

Scripture Index

14:33	Day 246
14:26	Day 24
14:27	Day 21
15:7	Day 221
17:9–10	Day 136
20:46	Day 215
24:32	Day 273

John

2:15	Day 357
3:3	Day 146
3:11	Day 220
3:19, 21	Day 226
6:39	Day 44
7:16–17	Day 57
7:17–18	Day 245
8:10–11	Day 101
8:31–32	Day 229, Day 242
9:4	Day 237, Day 294
11:33	Day 257
12:26	Day 51
13:14–15	Day 339
13:15	Day 296
15:3–4	Day 247
15:9	Day 198
15:12	Day 297
15:13, 16–17	Day 354
16:33	Day 276
19:16–18	Day 359
19:26–27	Day 159

Acts

2:38	Day 311
2:42	Day 231
2:44–45	Day 234
4:31	Day 175
4:32–33	Day 358
11:26	Day 338
20:29	Day 149
20:35	Day 208
23:5	Day 305

Romans

1:16	Day 319
3:3–4	Day 36
3:22	Day 223
5:1–2	Day 96
6:4	Day 277
8:6	Day 190
8:12–13	Day 92
8:17	Day 290
8:18	Day 330
8:26	Day 261
8:35, 37	Day 352
10:14	Day 7, Day 53
12:2	Day 259
12:9	Day 200
12:10–11	Day 112
12:17	Day 39
12:17–18	Day 114
13:10	Day 123
13:13	Day 180

Scripture Index

1 Corinthians

1:9	Day 172
1:18	Day 107
1:25	Day 110
1:27	Day 10
2:4–5	Day 95
2:14	Day 38
3:13	Day 206
4:2	Day 170
4:5	Day 116
5:12	Day 74
6:9–10	Day 143
6:11	Day 230
13:5–6	Day 65
13:8	Day 333
14:25	Day 113
15:26	Day 19
15:33–34	Day 225
15:34	Day 314
15:54–55	Day 181
16:9	Day 228
16:13	Day 202

2 Corinthians

1:5	Day 331
1:8–9	Day 186
1:20	Day 83
2:15	Day 307
5:15	Day 15
6:9–10	Day 287
6:14	Day 81
8:9	Day 248
8:13–14	Day 241

9:11	Day 174
13:8	Day 244

Galatians

5:1	Day 252
6:1	Day 150
6:2	Day 238
6:14–15	Day 164

Ephesians

1:13	Day 171
1:14	Day 119
1:22	Day 353
2:17	Day 188
2:19	Day 132
4:2	Day 79, Day 332
4:15	Day 80
4:28	Day 304
4:32	Day 310
5:1	Day 33
5:1–2	Day 93
5:19	Day 253
5:25	Day 199
6:5–7	Day 58
6:7–8	Day 59
6:10–11	Day 138
6:19–20	Day 264
6:24	Day 126

Philippians

2:8	Day 135
2:15	Day 267

Scripture Index

3:7	Day 168
3:8	Day 42,
	Day 167
3:10	Day 295
4:12	Day 291

Colossians

1:9	Day 94,
	Day 209
3:2–3	Day 18
3:17	Day 28

1 Thessalonians

1:3	Day 281
1:5	Day 66
4:11	Day 284,
	Day 322

2 Thessalonians

3:4	Day 62

1 Timothy

2:8	Day 308
4:12	Day 203,
	Day 289
4:14	Day 349
4:16	Day 293
5:17	Day 142
6:6, 8	Day 300
6:10	Day 193,
	Day 269
6:17	Day 279

2 Timothy

1:7	Day 134
2:2	Day 34
2:26	Day 155
4:2	Day 130

Titus

2:7–8	Day 337
2:12	Day 197
3:1	Day 141
3:5	Day 127

Hebrews

4:16	Day 355
6:10	Day 217
10:24	Day 122
10:25	Day 5
13:2	Day 2
13:16	Day 163,
	Day 265
13:18	Day 329
13:20	Day 192

James

1:13	Day 313
1:17	Day 85
1:21	Day 315
1:22	Day 29
2:2–4	Day 11
2:5	Day 97
2:16	Day 340
4:4	Day 41
4:7–8	Day 147,

Scripture Index

	Day 318
4:17	Day 64
5:10–11	Day 133
5:13–14	Day 350
5:16	Day 131

1 Peter
1:18–19	Day 216
2:5	Day 87
2:16	Day 140
2:19	Day 86
2:21	Day 1,
	Day 145,
	Day 365
2:25	Day 178
3:12	Day 182
3:13	Day 166
3:17	Day 335
3:18	Day 356
4:1	Day 233
5:8	Day 148
5:10	Day 76

2 Peter
1:3	Day 360
1:4	Day 254,
	Day 361
3:9	Day 109

1 John
| 1:3 | Day 165 |
| 1:7 | Day 282 |

2:6	Day 30
2:15	Day 75
2:17	Day 31
2:24	Day 255
3:4	Day 292
4:6	Day 77
4:7	Day 124
4:8	Day 125
4:12	Day 303
4:18	Day 324
5:4–5	Day 184

2 John
| 6 | Day 128 |

Revelation
2:19	Day 196
3:1–2	Day 9
3:17	Day 88
5:12	Day 121
14:4	Day 23
21:4	Day 275

ALSO AVAILABLE FROM
BARBOUR PUBLISHING

God Is in the Small Stuff. . .
and it all matters
ISBN 1-57748-448-7
Bruce & Stan remind us
that God is personal and
intimate, involved in
every detail of our lives—
however minute.

God Is in the Hard Stuff
ISBN 1-59310-924-5
Life is hard—but God is
good. Bruce & Stan show
you where to turn when
the going gets rough.

Available wherever Christian books are sold.